INTRODUCTION TO
MATHEMATICAL ANALYSIS

This book is in the
ADDISON-WESLEY SERIES IN MATHEMATICS

INTRODUCTION TO MATHEMATICAL ANALYSIS

With Applications To Problems of Economics

by

PAUL H. DAUS

Department of Mathematics
University of California at Los Angeles

and

WILLIAM M. WHYBURN

Department of Mathematics
University of North Carolina

ADDISON-WESLEY PUBLISHING COMPANY

READING, MASSACHUSETTS · MENLO PARK, CALIFORNIA
LONDON · AMSTERDAM · DON MILLS, ONTARIO · SYDNEY

PREFACE

There is increased recognition of the need for students of business to know about mathematical topics and procedures which ordinarily fall outside the scope of the standard courses in college algebra, trigonometry, and mathematics of finance. Some knowledge of analytic geometry and calculus, and of their applications in various fields of economics, is essential for adequate understanding of the business-administration curricula. The present book is designed as a text for a one-semester course to meet this need. Demand for such a course developed in the School of Business Administration of the University of California at Los Angeles, and such a demand reflects a definite trend in forward-looking schools of business administration throughout the country.

A second course in algebra, preferably taken in college, is presupposed for this text. These courses are given in most colleges under such titles as College Algebra, Intermediate Algebra, Algebra for College Students, Commercial Algebra, Mathematics of Finance, and Business Mathematics. Among other topics, the course should have included the fundamental operations of algebra, simultaneous linear equations, quadratic equations, exponents, logarithms, and the elementary curve plotting related to these topics. Students should have readily available reference texts to review these areas as needed. Topics in business mathematics, although important in themselves, are seldom used in this text. It is recognized, of course, that the more mathematics in a student's background the better his capacity for mastery of a course based on this book.

This text is designed to complement a study of elementary courses in economics. The language of economics is used, and a mathematical approach should increase the student's understanding of economic concepts. This is perhaps best achieved when courses in economics are taken simultaneously with a course using the present text. The book was planned with these ideas in mind.

The book, however, makes no attempt to present a complete course in economics, statistics, or pure mathematics. Its aim is to develop mathematical tools and techniques of analytic geometry and calculus needed in economics, business statistics, and related fields. It introduces students to problems in business fields that can be solved by elementary mathematical methods. Obviously, not all the important mathematical ideas could be included in a one-semester text, and it was with some regret that the topics of linear programming and vector algebra were excluded. However, the authors felt that a proper treatment of these topics not only

v

would require considerable time and space but also would not be sufficiently well related to the other ideas being developed. Section 7–8 makes
a number of suggestions for future study by the interested student.

Since the book contains many more problems than can ordinarily be
completed in a one-semester course, there is opportunity for selection.
Exercise Groups 2–3, 2–6, 3–4, 3–5, 6–2, and 7–3 require two full assignments each, even with such selection. Exercise Groups 1–3, 6–1, 6–4,
and 6–5 each require one assignment and part of another unless special
care is taken in the selection of the problems assigned. The other Exercises ordinarily require one assignment only.

Some of the topics discussed can be omitted without loss of continuity
in the treatment. Although the final choice must lie with the instructor,
and depend upon the ability and interests of the class, several suggestions
are made (without implying that the topics listed are unimportant):
Section 1–5 (Linear Equations in Several Variables) and Exercise Group
1–3, Section 1–11 (Taxation for Two Commodities) and Exercise Group
1–8, Section 3–8 (Effect of Taxation on Monopoly) and Exercise Group 3–5,
Section 5–4 (Demand Surfaces) and Exercise Group 5–3, Section 6–4
(Production under Pure Competition with Two Inputs) and Exercise
Group 6–3, Section 7–5 (Fitting a Parabola to Given Data), Section 7–7
(Linear Regression and Correlation) and Exercise Group 7–4. As an
alternative, Chapter 7 might be omitted entirely.

It is expected that the need which stimulated the writing of the present
book will continue to increase and expand with respect to the degree of
mathematical background required. Already, high-speed computers are
playing an important role in business and industry. Full development of
this role is limited primarily by the supply of people who have sufficient
training in the two fields of mathematics and business to direct the program
of activities centering around the machines. To fully meet this particular
need, mathematical training beyond the scope of the present text is required. However, courses of the type for which this book is written can
do much to introduce mathematical thinking and techniques into the
training of business students. With this beginning it is felt that further
mathematical training can be accomplished through standard mathematics courses.

The authors express their appreciation to members of the staff of the
Addison-Wesley Publishing Company for the care used in the preparation
of this book. It is our hope that its contents, which are the authors'
responsibility, will in some measure justify the effort expended in bringing
the book to publication.

P. H. D.

W. M. W.

September 1958

CONTENTS

CHAPTER 1. APPLICATIONS OF GRAPHICAL ANALYSIS 1

1–1 Laws of economics and mathematical simplifications 1
1–2 Demand and supply curves. 2
1–3 Linear laws of demand and supply 5
1–4 Market equilibrium for linear demand and supply functions . . 7
1–5 Linear equations in several variables 8
1–6 Parabolic laws 12
1–7 Market equilibrium and quadratic equations 16
1–8 Hyperbolic laws 19
1–9 Applications of hyperbolic laws 21
1–10 Effect of taxation on market equilibrium 26
1–11 Taxation for two commodities 31

CHAPTER 2. INTRODUCTION TO DIFFERENTIAL CALCULUS . . . 35

2–1 The real number system 35
2–2 Limits and continuity 37
2–3 Difference quotient and derivative 40
2–4 General laws of differentiation 44
2–5 Differentiation of special functions 46
2–6 Chain rule of differentiation 50
2–7 Techniques of differentiation 53
2–8 Implicit differentiation 56
2–9 Derivatives of higher order 57
2–10 Curve tracing 59
2–11 Maximum and minimum points 63
2–12 Points of inflection 65
2–13 Exponents and logarithms 67
2–14 Derivatives of exponential and logarithmic functions 73

CHAPTER 3. APPLICATIONS OF DIFFERENTIAL CALCULUS 79

3–1 Elasticity of demand 79
3–2 Constant elasticity of demand 82
3–3 Cost, average cost, and marginal cost 83
3–4 Revenue and marginal revenue 89
3–5 Maximum revenue from taxation 92
3–6 Profit under monopoly 95
3–7 Geometric interpretation of maximum profit 96
3–8 Effect of taxation on monopoly 101

CHAPTER 4. INTRODUCTION TO INTEGRATION 106

4–1 Differentials 106
4–2 Inverse of differentiation. Indefinite integral 107

4–3   Marginal revenue and marginal cost 110
4–4   The definite integral 113
4–5   Consumers' surplus and producers' surplus 118

CHAPTER 5.   INTRODUCTION TO PARTIAL DIFFERENTIATION 124

5–1   Functions of two independent variables 124
5–2   Rectangular coordinates and surfaces 124
5–3   Indifference maps 127
5–4   Demand surfaces 130
5–5   Production functions 134
5–6   Partial derivatives 137
5–7   Partial derivatives of higher order 142
5–8   Implicit differentiation 143

CHAPTER 6.   MAXIMA AND MINIMA PROBLEMS 148

6–1   Maxima and minima of a function of two variables . . . 148
6–2   Necessary and sufficient conditions for an extremum . . . 149
6–3   Monopoly and the production of two commodities 154
6–4   Production under pure competition with two inputs . . . 159
6–5   Maxima and minima under constraint 164
6–6   Utility index and the budget equation 170
6–7   Maximum utility index subject to the budget equation . . . 172

CHAPTER 7.   INTRODUCTION TO CURVE FITTING 178

7–1   Curves through given points 178
7–2   Method of average points 179
7–3   Method of least squares 182
7–4   Fitting a line to given data 184
7–5   Fitting a parabola to given data 189
7–6   Fitting exponential and power curves 191
7–7   Linear regression and correlation 194
7–8   Prospect and references 200

ANSWERS TO PROBLEMS 203

APPENDIX 219

Table   I.   Powers and Roots 223
Table   II.   Squares 226
Table   III. Common Logarithms 230
Table   IV.   Natural Logarithms 234
Table   V.   Exponentials 238

INDEX 239

CHAPTER 1

APPLICATIONS OF GRAPHICAL ANALYSIS

1–1 Laws of economics and mathematical simplifications. The laws of economics depend upon many variables: the number of consumers, their tastes, preferences, and incomes, the prices of various commodities and the supply available, time, and many other factors. Some of the variables are measurable in the sense that they obey the usual axioms or laws of algebra. Others, like satisfaction or preference, are not measurable. Even if it is assumed that the individual consumer's preferences are consistent, these variables, being qualitative, differ from such variables as quantity or price. For the latter variables there are natural units of measure; for the former, there are none. However, the *axioms of order** may apply to these qualitative variables, and one might seek some artificial unit of measure based upon statistical data. This proposed method should indicate to the reader the complexity involved in economic problems.

In order to simplify treatment of these problems, the time variable is not taken into account. That is, this text is concerned with what may be called *statics* rather than *dynamics*. Furthermore, the number of variables is restricted and it is assumed, for some problems whose variables are specified, "that all other things are equal." To apply the tools of mathematics to the variables which *are* considered, the ultimate divisibility and continuity of the variables is assumed even though these concepts are not yet made precise. Further limitations on, and discussions of, these concepts will be made as the subject is developed.

In the field of economics we utilize both theory and observation, and hence mathematics is a useful tool for such a study. The use of mathematics in economics has developed along two lines, mathematical analysis (that is, analytic geometry and the calculus) and statistics. Although this text is primarily concerned with mathematical analysis, it should be recognized that the tools of analysis help in the study of statistics and that many of the laws studied by use of analysis are based upon statistical information. If the mathematical simplifications seem to be unrealistic, it should be realized that the study of complicated problems is preceded by a study of simpler ones.

---

* The axioms of order are concerned with the concepts of "less than" and "greater than" as applied to real numbers. For a brief discussion of these axioms, see Whyburn and Daus, *Algebra for College Students*, pp. 32–35.

1–2 Demand and supply curves. * *Demand curves.* In economics a demand function for a specified commodity indicates the relationship between the quantity of the commodity demanded and such other variables as the price of this commodity, the prices of other commodities, or the time. Consider an ideal situation where the demand and the price are the only variables, thus assuming that "all other things are equal." There are actual economic situations where this is a reasonable assumption, based on statistical verification.

Let x units be the quantity demanded and p the price in monetary units for each unit of x. The relationship between x and p may be expressed in three ways: the price p may be given directly in terms of the quantity x, x may be given directly in terms of p, or a relationship between p and x may be given.

EXAMPLE 1–1. Any one of the forms

$$p = \sqrt{9 - x}, \qquad x = 9 - p^2, \qquad x + p^2 - 9 = 0$$

could be used for the same demand law. More generally, in functional notation, we would have

$$p = f(x), \qquad x = g(p), \qquad \phi(x, p) = 0. \tag{1–1}$$

Since the time of the economist Alfred Marshall it has become customary to represent these relationships geometrically by measuring x along a horizontal axis and p along a vertical axis, thus considering x as the independent variable and writing the relationship as $p = f(x)$. The form $x = g(p)$, which is due to the mathematical economist A. A. Cournot, can often be found by solving the equation $p = f(x)$ for x; the functions f and g are known as *inverse* functions of each other. The form $\phi(x, p) = 0$ gives either variable *implicitly* in terms of the other. Any one of the above three forms is known as a *demand law*. In some cases the symbol x_D is used to emphasize that the quantity *demanded* is involved.

Demand laws arrived at statistically are based upon the assumption that there is "pure competition" among consumers. Thus, each consumer determines the quantity he will purchase, depending upon the price, independently of all other consumers. There are, however, definite and reasonable restrictions which must be imposed on the variables x and p and on the function f or g if the demand law is to represent a "normal" economic situation:

---

* For a further discussion of this topic see Henry Schultz, *The Theory and Measurement of Demand*, University of Chicago Press, 1938.

(1) *The variables x and p must be zero or positive.* Since the particular law under consideration may not apply for all values of the variables, it may be necessary to restrict them to certain intervals of the form

$$0 \leq x \leq A \qquad \text{or} \qquad 0 \leq p \leq B$$

("zero is less than or equal to x, and x is less than or equal to A"). It is assumed that the variables may take on any values in the permissible range, and that they are continuous. At first sight these assumptions may seem unrealistic, since actual quantities and prices jump by definite units. From a statistical point of view, however, these assumptions are reasonable and indeed are not as strong as other assumptions which have been made in this field.

(2) *The demand law is bi-unique,* that is, for each value of x there is one and only one value of p, and for each value of p there is one and only one value of x.

(3) Except for the trivial case where the price is a constant, and independent of the demand, *the demand is a monotonically decreasing function of the price**, that is, the higher the price, the lower the corresponding demand. If x_1 and x_2 represent two demands and p_1 and p_2 represent the corresponding prices, then $x_2 > x_1$ if and only if $p_2 < p_1$. In the example $p = \sqrt{9 - x}$ or $x = 9 - p^2$, we would have the limitations $0 \leq x \leq 9$ in order to keep p positive and real, and $0 \leq p \leq 3$ in order to keep x positive. For each value of x in this range there is one value of p, and for each p there is one value of x. It is easily observed that as p increases, x decreases; and as x increases, p decreases.

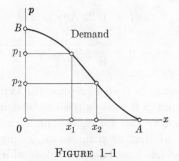

FIGURE 1–1

If a commodity is *free*, that is, if $p = 0$, the demand x_D, although necessarily finite, may be large. If the price becomes sufficiently large, the demand tends to zero ($x \to 0$) and the corresponding price p_0 represents the maximum price that any consumer would pay for the commodity. The geometric representation of the demand curve is shown in Fig. 1–1.

Supply curves. Consider a supply function for a specified commodity in an ideal situation. Here the quantity offered on the market by the

---

* Although "abnormal" demand functions are discussed in research journals, this text will consider only the "normal" cases, not only for demand functions but also for the other economic functions considered.

producers and the price of the commodity are the only variables. Let x be the quantity supplied and p the price of one unit of x. Then the relationship between x and p can be expressed as

$$p = F(x), \qquad x = G(p), \qquad \Phi(x, p) = 0, \qquad (1\text{-}2)$$

where F and G are inverse functions.

Supply laws arrived at statistically are based upon the assumption that there is "pure competition" among the producers. Based upon the price, each producer determines the quantity he will offer on the market independently of the actions of other producers. The following reasonable restrictions on the variables x and p and on the functions F or G are imposed for the "normal" case:

(1) *The variables x and p are restricted to positive values for some specified intervals and are considered continuous.*

(2) *The supply law is bi-unique.*

(3) Except for the trivial case where the price is a constant, *the price is a monotonically increasing function of the quantity supplied*, that is, the higher the price, the greater the amount offered on the market. If x_1 and x_2 represent two quantities supplied, and p_1 and p_2 represent the corresponding prices, then

$$x_2 > x_1 \qquad \text{if and only if} \quad p_2 > p_1.$$

EXAMPLE 1–2. Any one of the three forms

$$p = 2 + \frac{x^2}{8}, \quad x = \sqrt{8p - 16}, \quad x^2 - 8p + 16 = 0, \qquad (x \geqq 0)$$

could be used to represent a typical supply function. The first form shows that p is always positive and increases as x increases. The second form shows that for each value of $p \geq 2$ there is one and only one value of x, and that as p increases, x increases. If $x = 0$ there is some price p_0, which may be zero, below which none of the commodity will be offered.

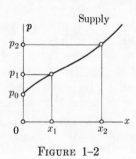

FIGURE 1–2

It represents the smallest price that would induce the producers to sell. If the price is large, the producers would offer large amounts of the commodity on the market. Natural limits exist above which the assumption "all other things being equal" would no longer apply. The geometric representation of the supply curve is shown in Fig. 1–2.

1–3 Linear laws of demand and supply. The simplest demand curve is the straight line* whose equation can be written in the form

$$p = p_0 + mx, \tag{1-3}$$

where p_0 corresponds to $x = 0$ and $p_0 > 0$ is the highest price anyone would pay under the given demand law. The slope m of the line is *negative* (or zero). A straight line can be drawn if two points on it are located. One convenient point is $(0, p_0)$, and another can be found by changing the values of p and x in such a way that the ratio of these changes is m. Another convenient point is found by setting $p = 0$ and solving for x to obtain x_0, where x_0 is the demand for a "free" commodity. (The size of the units used in a given diagram is arbitrarily chosen so as to make the diagram fit the paper.) The x-unit and p-unit are, in general, different; the values of x_0 and p_0 suggest convenient units for use. The units are taken into account when the slope is used to draw the line.

If Eq. (1–3) is solved for x, the demand law takes the form

$$x = x_0 - kp, \tag{1-4}$$

where k is a positive constant (the negative reciprocal of the slope of the line) and x_0 is positive. A third form is obtained by writing the general equation of the first degree, $ax + bp = c$, in intercept form:

$$\frac{x}{x_0} + \frac{p}{p_0} = 1, \tag{1-5}$$

where x_0 and p_0 have the meanings previously given.†

The simplest supply curve is a straight line whose equation can be written in the form

$$p = P_0 + Mx, \tag{1-6}$$

where P_0 is the lowest price at which the producers will offer the commodity under the assumed supply law and M is the slope of the line, now *positive* (or zero).‡ If Eq. (1–6) is solved for x, the supply law takes the form

$$x = Kp - X_0, \tag{1-7}$$

---

* For further study of the analytic geometry of the straight line, the reader should consult any standard text in analytic geometry. (See references listed in Section 7–8 of this book.)

† It often happens that a given demand law fits an economic situation over a wide range of the variables but fails for very small values of x or p.

‡ If the slope of a demand or supply line is zero, the corresponding line is horizontal and has the simple equation $p = $ constant. No other form is available.

where K and X_0 are positive constants and $-X_0$ is the x-intercept of the line (corresponding to $p = 0$). This gives a convenient point for drawing the line, but that part of the line where x is negative has no significance in the application.

EXAMPLE 1–3. (a) A demand law is given in the form $3p + 2x = 27$. Determine the permissible ranges of x and p and draw the corresponding line segment. (b) A supply law is given in the form $6p - 2x = 9$. Show the corresponding line in the same diagram.

(a) If $x = 0$, $p = 9$; if $p = 0$, $x = 13.5$. This shows that $0 \leq x \leq 13.5$ and $0 \leq p \leq 9$, and suggests the size of units for use in the diagram.

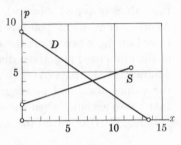

FIGURE 1–3

(b) The supply law can be written $p = \frac{1}{3}x + \frac{3}{2}$. One point is $(0, 3/2)$, and another can be found by changing x by 12 units and changing p by 4 units to make the slope $1/3$, thus obtaining the second point $(12, 11/2)$ (Fig. 1–3).

EXERCISE GROUP 1–1

1. If the demand law is $p = 36 - 4x$, (a) what is the highest price anyone would pay for the commodity, and (b) what is the demand if the commodity is free? Draw the demand curve. (c) If the given demand law were restricted to the range $0 \leq x \leq 8$ and the price remained constant for the range $8 \leq x \leq 10$, what is the nature of the demand curve?

2. The demand law for a commodity is $p = 12 - 5x$. Draw the corresponding demand curve from the intercepts, selecting appropriate size units. Verify the result by finding a third point, using the slope of the line.

3. The demand law is $x = 100 - 5p$. (a) What is the highest price anyone would pay for the commodity? (b) What is the amount of the demand if the commodity is free? Draw the demand curve. (c) If the given demand law were valid until the price fell to $p = 2$, and thereafter remained fixed until $x = 120$, what is the nature of the demand curve? Write the corresponding equations for p as a function of x, and indicate the appropriate limitations on x.

4. The demand for sugar in the United States for the years 1915–1929 can be given approximately by $x = 135 - 8p$, where x and p are expressed in convenient units. Draw the demand curve, using three points on it to ensure accuracy.

5. Draw the demand curve $x = 12.5 - 2.25p$, using the values $p = 0, 2, 4$.

6. The demand law is $2p + 3x = 24$. Solve this equation for x, then for p. Draw the demand curve. In the same diagram show the supply curve $x = p - 5$.

7. The supply function is $x = \frac{5}{2}p - 5$. Solve this equation for p. Draw the corresponding supply curve from the two intercepts. As a check, find a third point.

8. The supply function is $p = 2 + \frac{3}{2}x$, $(0 \leq x \leq 7)$. Draw the supply curve. Compare this supply curve with that whose equations are $p = 2 + \frac{3}{2}x$, $(0 \leq x \leq 5)$, and $p(x) = p(5)$, $(5 \leq x \leq 7)$.

9. The estimated wholesale price of imported sugar is related to the supply by the equation $x = 1.1p - 0.1$, where x and p are measured in convenient units. Draw the supply curve for $0 \leq p \leq 1$. What part of the curve is significant?

10. Can each of the following equations represent either a demand function or a supply function? Explain.

(a) $p = -3 - \frac{3}{2}x$,   (b) $p = 3 + \frac{3}{2}x$,

(c) $p = -3 + \frac{3}{2}x$,   (d) $p = 3 - \frac{3}{2}x$.

1–4 Market equilibrium for linear demand and supply functions. By definition of pure competition, no individual consumer and no individual producer can, by themselves, influence the market price. *Market equilibrium* is said to occur under pure competition if the quantity of a commodity demanded is equal to the quantity supplied. The use of the same variables x and p to express both the demand and supply laws indicates that the equilibrium amount and the equilibrium price correspond to the coordinates of the point of intersection of the demand and supply curves when these are drawn in the same diagram. The equilibrium amount and price can be found algebraically by solving the two equations simultaneously.

The following economic considerations indicate how such a situation may arise. If the actual price were higher than the equilibrium price, then the quantity demanded (represented by OA in Fig. 1–4) would be less than the quantity supplied (OB). Some producers could not sell their products at these higher prices, and would lower their prices rather than fail to sell. Competition among the producers would lower the average price until an equilibrium price was reached. Here the quantity demanded just equals the quantity supplied.

On the other hand, if the actual price were below the equilibrium price, the amount supplied would be insufficient to meet the demand, and rather than go without a given commodity some consumers would be willing to pay a higher price for it. Competition among the consumers would raise the average price until equilibrium was reached.

In the foregoing discussion the effect of other commodities, such as substitutes, has been neglected, in line with the assumption that the

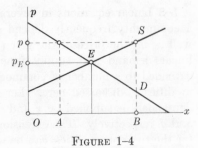

FIGURE 1–4

demand and supply laws depend only on the quantity of the commodity and the price of that commodity. More general problems are considered in later sections.

EXAMPLE 1–4. Find the market equilibrium quantity and price if the demand and supply laws are $3p + 2x = 27$ and $6p - 2x = 9$, respectively. (See Section 1–3.)

From Fig. 1–3 we see that the equilibrium quantity is about $7\frac{1}{2}$ and the equilibrium price is about 4. To solve the equations algebraically, we add the two equations, with the result that $9p = 36$, or $p = 4$. Then $24 - 2x = 9$, which yields $x = 15/2$ and verifies the geometric solution.

EXERCISE GROUP 1–2

For each of the following problems, first draw the demand and supply curves and estimate the market equilibrium quantity and price. Then solve the equations algebraically and verify the results.

1. The demand and supply curves are given by the equations $p = 10 - 2x$ and $p = \frac{3}{2}x + 1$, respectively.

2. The demand function is $p = 12 - 5x$ and the supply function is $p = 4 + 4x$.

3. The quantities demanded and supplied are $x_D = 10 - p$ and $x_S = 2p - 5$, respectively.

4. The demand function is $p = 6$ and the supply function is $x = 3p - 3$.

5. The demand curve is given by $8p + 5x = 40$ and the supply curve by $p = 2$.

6. The demand function is $x = 15 - 2p$ and the supply function is $x = 3p - 3$.

7. The demand curve is given by $8p + 12x = 40$ and the supply curve by $x = 4p - 6$.

8. The demand and supply laws are $10p + 6x = 80$ and $x = 4p - 8$, respectively.

9. The demand and supply laws are $x = 1.8 - 0.4p$ and $x = -0.3 + 0.8p$, respectively.

10. The demand and supply laws are $p = 1.5 - 0.6x$ and $p = 0.6 + 0.5x$, respectively.

1–5 Linear equations in several variables. The demand and supply of a commodity frequently depend on the prices of related commodities as well as on the price of the given commodity. Although the concepts of linear demand and supply functions and market equilibrium can be extended to a number of commodities, the case of only two related commodities is discussed here. Let the quantities of the two commodities demanded or supplied be x and y and let the corresponding prices be p and q, respectively. The extension of Eq. (1–4), that is, the demand laws for the two commodities, can be written

$$x = x_0 - kp + cq, \qquad (1\text{--}8)$$

$$y = y_0 + dp - nq, \qquad (1\text{--}9)$$

where x_0, y_0, k, and n are *positive* constants, and c and d are constants whose signs depend upon the nature of the commodities (see Section 5–4). If these laws are to correspond to a "normal" economic situation, the constants are subject to certain restrictions. An obvious restriction is that $x_0 + cq$ and $y_0 + dp$ must be positive; this may impose restrictions on p and q. There is, however, a restriction which is not so obvious. If Eqs. (1–8) and (1–9) are solved for p and q in terms of x and y, the result must be consistent with the form of the demand law $p = p_0 + mx$ (Eq. 1–3), where p_0 is positive and m is negative. If these conditions are satisfied, Eqs. (1–8) and (1–9) are said to be "normal" demand equations.

EXAMPLE 1–5. It might appear that the equations $x = 10 - p - 2q$, $(q \leqq 5)$, and $y = 6 - p - q$, $(p \leqq 6)$, could be considered demand equations. If, however, they are solved for p, we find that $p = 2 + x - 2y$, which violates the condition that the coefficient of x must be negative.

The linear supply functions for two commodities can be written

$$x = -X_0 + Kp + Cq, \qquad (1\text{--}10)$$

$$y = -Y_0 + Dp + Nq, \qquad (1\text{--}11)$$

where X_0, Y_0, K, and N are *positive*, and C and D are constants whose signs depend upon the nature of the commodities. If these equations are solved for p and q in terms of x and y, the result must be consistent with the supply law $p = P_0 + Mx$ (Eq. 1–6), where P_0 and M are both positive. If these conditions are satisfied, then Eqs. (1–10) and (1–11) are said to be "normal" supply equations.

Market equilibrium, under pure competition, occurs when the quantities demanded equal the quantities supplied. Hence the equilibrium prices and quantities are found by solving the system of equations (1–8), (1–9), (1–10), and (1–11) for p, q, x, y. In general, these four linear equations have one and only one solution for the four unknowns. To correspond to a possible economic situation, the values of p, q, x, and y in the solution must all be positive and satisfy any restrictions on the variables. In that case the solution is said to be *significant*. The solution can be found by eliminating x between Eqs. (1–8) and (1–10) and by eliminating y between Eqs. (1–9) and (1–11). The resulting two equations are linear in p and q and can be solved by various methods. The values of x and y are then obtained by substitution. There are too many variables (four) to have a

simple geometric interpretation of the complete situation. However, when x and y are eliminated, the resulting equations represent lines in a pq-plane.

EXAMPLE 1–6. The demand laws for two commodities are

$$x = 5 - p + q, \qquad y = 10 - p - q,$$

and the supply laws are

$$x = -5 + p + q, \qquad y = -2 - p + 2q.$$

(a) Show that the demand and supply laws are "normal" under appropriate restrictions. (b) Find the market equilibrium prices and quantities.

(a) For the demand laws, the first restriction is $p \leqq 10$ in order that y be positive. If the demand laws are solved for p and q, it is readily found that

$$p = \tfrac{1}{2}(15 - x - y), \qquad q = \tfrac{1}{2}(5 + x - y).$$

The coefficient of x in the value of p is negative, as it should be, since p must be a decreasing function of x; but a second restriction, $y \leqq 15$, is required so that p is always positive. The coefficient of y in the value of q is negative, as required; no restriction need be placed on x, since the coefficient of x is positive. The given equations are normal under these restrictions.

If the supply laws are solved, then

$$p = \tfrac{1}{3}(8 + 2x - y), \qquad q = \tfrac{1}{3}(7 + x + y).$$

The coefficient of x in the expression for p and the coefficient of y in the expression for q are both positive, as required. The equations are normal for a supply law under the restrictions $q \leqq 5$, since x must be negative when $p = 0$, and $y \leqq 8$ in order that p be positive for $x = 0$. No restrictions are needed for p or x, since y is negative when $q = 0$ and q is positive for $y = 0$.

(b) Market equilibrium implies that

$$x = 5 - p + q = -5 + p + q, \qquad \text{or} \qquad 2p = 10,$$
$$y = 10 - p - q = -2 - p + 2q, \qquad \text{or} \qquad 3q = 12.$$

The values $p = 5$, $q = 4$ yield $x = 4$, $y = 1$, and since these values satisfy all restrictions the solution is significant.

Exercise Group 1–3*

1. The demand laws

$$x = 10 - 3p + q \quad \text{and} \quad y = 20 + 4p - 5q$$

can be used for all p and q. (a) Solve these equations for p and q, and determine the values of x and y for which they can be used. (b) The supply laws have the special forms $x = 9$, $y = 14$. Find the market equilibrium prices.

2. (a) Determine the restrictions on x and y so that $x = 4 - 2p + q$ and $y = 20 + p - 5q$ may be normal demand laws. (b) If the supply laws are $x = 4p$, $y = -1 + 6q$, find the market equilibrium prices and quantities.

3. If the demand laws are

$$p = 24 - x - 2y, \quad q = 27 - x - 3y,$$

and the supply laws are

$$x = -6 + 2p - q, \quad y = -3 - p + 8q,$$

find the equilibrium prices and quantities. Show that the results are significant.

4. Determine the restrictions on p, q, x, and y so that the demand and supply equations may have the forms

$$x_D = 5 - 2p + q, \quad x_S = -5 + 4p - q,$$
$$y_D = 6 + p - q, \quad y_S = -4 - p + 3q.$$

Find the equilibrium values of p and q.

5. If the demand equations are

$$p = 4 - x + y, \quad q = 4 + x - 2y,$$

and the supply equations are

$$4p = 7 + 2x - y, \quad 2q = y + 1,$$

find the equilibrium prices and quantities. Prove that the result is significant.

6. Determine the restrictions on p, q, x, and y so that

$$x = 17 - 2p - q, \quad y = 14 - p - 2q$$

are normal demand equations, and so that

$$x = -10 + 4p + q, \quad y = -7 + p + 2q$$

are normal supply equations. Find the equilibrium values of p, q, x, and y.

---

* The solution of each problem in this set is fairly long and even the selection of alternate problems will make a long assignment.

7. Proceed as in problem 6 for the following equations (D = Demand, S = Supply):

D: $2p = 14 - x - y,$ $2q = 4 + x - y,$

S: $p = 3 + x - y,$ $q = 2 + y.$

8. Proceed as in problem 6 for

D: $x = 3 - p + 2q,$ $y = 14 - 2p - q,$

S: $x = -4 + 2p + q,$ $y = -p + 2q.$

1–6 Parabolic* laws. The graph of the curve $y = ax^2 + bx + c$ is a parabola whose axis of symmetry is vertical. In sketching the curve, important points to find are the intercepts $x = 0$, $y = c$, and $y = 0$, $x = x_1$ and x_2, where x_1 and x_2 are the roots of $ax^2 + bx + c = 0$, provided these roots are real. Another important point is the highest or lowest point on the curve. This point can be located by the method of "completing the square" (or, more simply, by the method of the calculus to be considered in the next chapter). At least three points should be located, and such other points as are needed to furnish a good sketch.

EXAMPLE 1–7.   Sketch the parabola $y = 8 - 2x - x^2$.
By factoring,

$$y = (2 - x)(4 + x).$$

By completing the square,

$$y = 8 - (x^2 + 2x\quad) = 8 + 1 - (x^2 + 2x + 1)$$
$$= 9 - (x + 1)^2.$$

The largest value of y, which occurs when $x = -1$, is $y = 9$.

The first four points in the following table are sufficient to make a sketch (others are added for illustration).

The point $x = 1$, $y = 5$ is especially useful if only that part of the curve for which x and y are positive is wanted (Fig. 1–5).

x	0	2	-4	-1	1	3
y	8	0	0	9	5	-7

The graph of the curve $x = Ay^2 + By + C$ is a parabola whose axis of symmetry is horizontal. The curve is sketched from the intercepts, the largest or smallest value of x, and from such other points as are needed.

If the parabola with a vertical or horizontal axis is to be used as a demand function $p = f(x)$, a part of it must be selected on which p and

---

* For more detailed study of the analytic geometry of the parabola, circle, ellipse, and hyperbola (called *conic sections*), the reader should consult any standard text in analytic geometry. (See references in Section 7–8.)

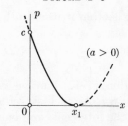

FIGURE 1–6

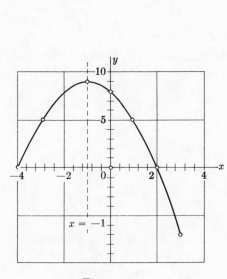

FIGURE 1–5   FIGURE 1–7

x are both positive, the function $f(x)$ and its inverse are single-valued, and the function is monotonically decreasing. The function

$$p = 8 - 2x - x^2, \qquad (0 \leq x \leq 2),$$

is such a demand function (Fig. 1–5).

If the demand law is

$$p = ax^2 + bx + c, \qquad (0 \leq x \leq x_1), \qquad (1\text{–}12)$$

then c must be positive, representing the highest price a consumer would pay for the commodity. If a is negative, b must also be negative so that the highest point will occur for some negative value of x; otherwise the function could not be considered as monotonically decreasing. (For further details see Section 2–11.) The positive root x_1 of $ax^2 + bx + c = 0$ determines the interval for which this law represents a normal demand function. If a is positive, then b is again negative (or zero) and x_1 is the smaller root of $ax^2 + bx + c = 0$. The special cases

$$p = k(d - x^2), \qquad (0 \leq x \leq \sqrt{d}), \qquad (1\text{–}13)$$

and

$$p = k(x - x_1)^2, \qquad (0 \leq x \leq x_1), \qquad (1\text{–}14)$$

shown in Figs. 1–6 and 1–7, respectively, are useful forms of Eq. (1–12) which illustrate the two possibilities.

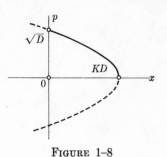

FIGURE 1–8

A demand law may be written

$$x = C + Bp + Ap^2, \qquad (1\text{--}15)$$

whose graph is a parabola with horizontal axis. An important special case is

$$x = K(D - p^2), \qquad (0 \leq p \leq \sqrt{D}), \qquad (1\text{--}16)$$

which is often written in the equivalent form

$$p = \sqrt{D - kx}, \qquad (0 \leq x \leq D/k). \qquad (1\text{--}17)$$

Equation (1–17) can be verified by solving Eq. (1–16) for p, setting $1/K = k$. A quick sketch of such a demand curve is easily obtained by using the intercepts and one intermediate point (Fig. 1–8).

The parabola can also be used for supply curves, where p must be a positive, single-valued, and monotonically increasing function of x. Three useful types of supply curves are given below, and each is illustrated numerically.

EXAMPLE 1–8.

Type 1: $p = ax^2 + bx + c,$ (a, b, c all positive).   (1–18)

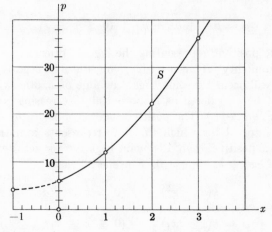

FIGURE 1–9

Type 1 is illustrated by $p = 2x^2 + 4x + 6$. This equation can be written

$$p = 2(x^2 + 2x + 1) + 4 = 2(x + 1)^2 + 4,$$

showing that the smallest value of p (that is, $p = 4$) occurs for $x = -1$. For $x \geqq 0$, p is monotonically increasing. The x unit should be selected considerably larger than the p unit. Without further instructions, the range of x is arbitrary (Fig. 1–9).

EXAMPLE 1–9.

$$\textit{Type 2:} \quad x = Ap^2 + Bp + C, \tag{1–19}$$

where A is positive and the coefficients are selected so that the equation $Ap^2 + Bp + C = 0$ has at least one positive (or zero) real root.

Type 2 is illustrated by

$$x = 2p^2 - 4p = 2p(p - 2), \quad (0 \leqq p \leqq 4),$$

$$x = 2(p^2 - 2p + 1) - 2.$$

The intercepts are $x = 0$, $p = 0$ and $p = 2$. The least value of x is -2, corresponding to $p = +1$. By using the points corresponding to $p = 3$ and $p = 4$, a good sketch can be made (Fig. 1–10). Only that part of the curve where $x \geqq 0$ and $p \geqq 2$ is the supply curve. If the given equation $2p^2 - 4p - x = 0$ is solved for p, then $p = 1 + \sqrt{1 + (x/2)}$, where the plus sign is chosen so that p is a monotonically increasing function of x. From this form, additional points on the curve could be found by assigning values to x. (A table of square roots is useful.)

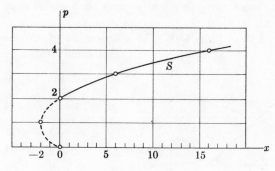

FIGURE 1–10

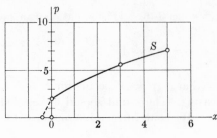

FIGURE 1-11

EXAMPLE 1-10.   Example 1-9 suggests

$$Type\ 3: \quad p = \sqrt{mx + n},$$
$$(m \text{ and } n \text{ positive}) \quad (1\text{-}20)$$

as a monotonically increasing function which corresponds to the special case of Eq. (1-19), where $B = 0$.

Type 3 is illustrated by

$$p = \sqrt{9x + 4}, \quad (0 \le x \le 5).$$

The three points $(0, 2)$, $(3, 5.6)$, $(5, 7)$ are sufficient to obtain a good sketch (Fig. 1-11).

1-7 Market equilibrium and quadratic equations. The market equilibrium price and quantity can be found geometrically by drawing the demand and supply curves in the same diagram. In certain cases they can also be found algebraically by solving quadratic equations. These cases occur (1) when one law is linear and the other is parabolic, (2) when the demand and supply laws are both given with the price expressed as a quadratic function of the quantity, and (3) when the demand and supply laws are both given with the quantity expressed as a quadratic function of the price. These three cases are illustrated below. In other cases of parabolic demand and supply laws, it may be necessary to solve an equation of the fourth degree, techniques for which are not discussed in this text.

EXAMPLE 1-11. Find the equilibrium price and quantity for the following laws:

$$D: \quad 9x + 4p = 40; \qquad S: \quad 9x = p^2 - 4.$$

Figure 1-12 shows that x is slightly more than 2 and that p is near 5. If the results are read as accurately as possible from the diagram, they might be recorded as $(2.3, 4.9)$. The elimination of x between the two equations yields

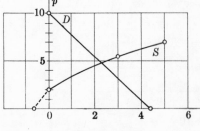

FIGURE 1-12

$$9x = 40 - 4p = p^2 - 4,$$
$$p^2 + 4p + 4 = 44 + 4 = 48,$$
$$p = -2 + \sqrt{48}$$
$$= -2 + 6.93 = 4.93,$$
$$x = \frac{40 - 4(4.93)}{9} = 2.25.$$

EXAMPLE 1–12. Find the equilibrium price and quantity for the following laws:

$$D: \quad p = 30 - 6x^2; \qquad S: \quad p = 2x^2 + 4x + 6.$$

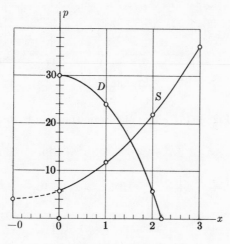

FIGURE 1–13

The supply curve was discussed in Section 1–6; the demand curve is drawn from the intercepts and by assigning x the values of 1 and 2. The point of intersection appears to be $(1.5, 16)$ (see Fig. 1–13). Eliminating p between the two equations yields

$$30 - 6x^2 = 2x^2 + 4x + 6,$$

$$8x^2 + 4x - 24 = 0,$$

$$2x^2 + x - 6 = 0,$$

$$x = \frac{-1 + \sqrt{1 + 48}}{4} = \frac{-1 + 7}{4} = \frac{3}{2} = 1.5,$$

$$p = 30 - 6 \cdot \frac{9}{4} = \frac{33}{2} = 16.5.$$

EXAMPLE 1–13. Find the equilibrium price and quantity for the following laws:

$$D: \quad x = 16 - p^2; \qquad S: \quad x = 2p^2 - 4p.$$

The supply curve was discussed in Section 1–6; the demand curve is drawn from the intercepts and the point $p = 2$, $x = 12$. The geometric solution

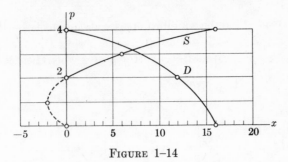

FIGURE 1–14

is (6.5, 3.2) (see Fig. 1–14). The algebraic solution is then given by

$$16 - p^2 = 2p^2 - 4p, \qquad 3p^2 - 4p - 16 = 0,$$

$$p = \frac{4 + \sqrt{16 + 192}}{6} = 3.1, \qquad x = 16 - 9.6 = 6.4.$$

Exercise Group 1–4

For each of the following problems, determine the market equilibrium price and quantity, both geometrically and algebraically. Record the geometric solution before the algebraic solution is found.

	Demand	*Supply*
1.	$x = 16 - 2p$	$4x = 4p + p^2$
2.	$x = 130 - 4p$	$p = 10 + \dfrac{x}{5} + \dfrac{x^2}{100}$
3.	$p = \dfrac{30 - x}{4}$	$p = 2 + \dfrac{x}{5} + \dfrac{x^2}{20}$
4.	$p = 16 - x^2$	$p = 4 + x$
5.	$x = 32 - 4p - p^2$	$p = \dfrac{x}{20} + 1$
6.	$p = 39 - 3x^2$	$p = 9x + 12$
7.	$x = \sqrt{36 - p}$	$p = 6 + \dfrac{x^2}{4}$
8.	$p = 39 - 3x^2$	$p = (x + 2)^2$
9.	$p = 48 - 3x^2$	$p = x^2 + 4x + 16$
10.	$x = 84 - p^2$	$x = p + 4p^2$
11.	$x = 64 - 8p - 2p^2$	$x = 10p + 5p^2$
12.	$x = 96 - 8p - 2p^2$	$x = 10p + 4p^2$

1–8 Hyperbolic laws. Many natural phenomena which relate two variables can be expressed in terms of inverse proportion. If the variables are x and y, then y is inversely proportional to x when there is a constant c such that

$$y = \frac{c}{x} \quad \text{or} \quad xy = c.$$

If the constant c is positive, it is often written as a^2. Also, y is inversely proportional to a positive power of x provided that

$$y = \frac{c}{x^n} \quad \text{or} \quad yx^n = c.$$

The case $n = 1$ is discussed in this chapter. Other important cases are discussed in a later chapter after the topic of logarithms has been introduced.

The curve corresponding to $xy = a^2$ is called an *equilateral hyperbola*, and the curve corresponding to $xy^n = c$, $(n > 0)$, is a *generalized equilateral hyperbola*. Since these curves have many essential properties in common, a discussion of the case $n = 1$ will essentially suffice for all n, especially when x and y are both positive. The curve $xy = a^2$ can be sketched by assigning values to x and by computing y. Important points, namely, the point (a, a) in the first quadrant and $(-a, -a)$ in the third quadrant, have $x = y$. The curve has two branches and is symmetrical with respect to the origin. If one branch is drawn, the other can be drawn as needed. It should be noted that the curve has no intercepts, for if $x = 0$, y is not defined, and if $y = 0$, x is not defined. However, if x is very small, y is very large, and if x is very large, y is very small. These statements are often expressed in the following way: "If x tends to zero, y tends to infinity; and if y tends to zero, x tends to infinity." The line $x = 0$ is called a *vertical asymptote* and the line $y = 0$ a *horizontal asymptote*. If these lines are used as guides, a few points yield a good sketch of the curve. The absence of intercepts shows that such laws would not fit a true economic situation for very small quantities or for very small prices. This kind of difficulty can be avoided by specifying the interval for one of the variables, excluding very small values, or by using a generalization of the equation for an equilateral hyperbola in the form

$$(x - h)(y - k) = a^2.$$

Translation of axes. Let the coordinates of a point P be (x, y) and consider a new set of axes $O'x'$, $O'y'$, which are parallel to the original axes. Let the original coordinates of O' be $x = h$, $y = k$. The point P also has coordinates (x', y') referred to the new axes, and the two systems of

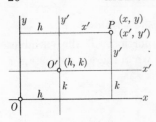

FIGURE 1-15

coordinates (Fig. 1-15) are related by the equations

$$x = x' + h, \qquad y = y' + k, \qquad (1\text{-}21)$$

or

$$x' = x - h, \qquad y' = y - k. \qquad (1\text{-}22)$$

Since one set of axes can be obtained from the other by a translation, Eqs. (1-21) and (1-22) are called the equations of *translation of axes*. By using these equations, the equation of a curve can be changed from one system of coordinates to the other. By Eqs. (1-22),

$$(x - h)(y - k) = a^2 \qquad (1\text{-}23)$$

becomes $x'y' = a^2$, and the curve is an equilateral hyperbola with asymptotes $x' = 0$, $y' = 0$, or $x = h$, $y = k$. The points corresponding to $x = 0$ and to $y = 0$, together with symmetry considerations, are usually sufficient to obtain a satisfactory graph.

EXAMPLE 1-14. Determine the asymptotes of the equilateral hyperbola

$$y = \frac{4}{x + 2} + 3$$

and the points corresponding to $x = 0$ and to $y = 0$. Draw the curve.

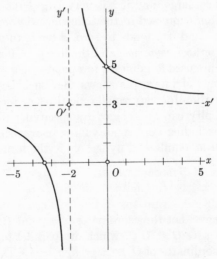

FIGURE 1-16

The given equation can be written in the alternative forms

$$y = \frac{3x + 10}{x + 2} = \frac{3 + 10/x}{1 + 2/x}, \qquad (x + 2)(y - 3) = 4.$$

From any of these forms it can be seen that $x = -2$ is the vertical asymptote. Also, if x is extremely large in absolute value, y is very near 3; that is, $y = 3$ is the horizontal asymptote. If $x = 0$, $2(y - 3) = 4$, so that $y = 5$; if $y = 0$, the third form shows that $x = -10/3$. This is sufficient data for a rough sketch (Fig. 1–16). If more detail is desired, the given equation can be written in the symmetric form $x'y' = 4$, where $x' = x + 2$ and $y' = y - 3$, and additional points (x', y') are then readily computed.

EXERCISE GROUP 1–5

1. Sketch the hyperbola $(x + 2)(y + 3) = 12$. Show the asymptotes and parts of both branches.

2. Sketch the part of the hyperbola $(x + 5)(y - 7) = 15$ which corresponds to $x \geqq 0$.

3. Sketch the hyperbola $(x - 2)(y - 3) = 2$. Show the asymptotes and parts of both branches.

4. Sketch the part of the hyperbola $(x - 40)(y - 30) = 300$ which corresponds to $0 \leqq x \leqq 40$, $y \geqq 0$.

5. Find the asymptotes of the equilateral hyperbola $y = [8/(x - 2)] + 2$, and the points corresponding to $x = 0$ and to $y = 0$. Draw the curve.

6. Find the asymptotes of the equilateral hyperbola $y = [8/(x - 2)] - 4$ and the points corresponding to $x = 0$ and to $y = 0$. Draw the curve.

7. Sketch the hyperbola $y = 4x/(x - 2)$. Show the asymptotes and parts of both branches.

8. Sketch the hyperbola $y = (2x - 4)/(x + 2)$. Show the asymptotes and parts of both branches.

9. Solve the equation $xy + 6x + 3y - 18 = 0$ for x and for y. Draw that branch of this hyperbola which passes through the first quadrant.

10. Solve the equation $xy - 30y - 40x + 900 = 0$ for x and for y. Draw that part of the hyperbola in the first quadrant which is concave to the origin.

1–9 Applications of hyperbolic laws. *Market equilibrium.* A demand law may be given in the simple form $p = c/x$, $(a \leqq x \leqq b)$, and used in equilibrium problems. More generally, the demand law is given in one of the following equivalent forms:

$$(x + b)(p + c) = a, \qquad p = \frac{a}{x + b} - c, \qquad p = \frac{c(A - x)}{x + b},$$

where a, b, c, and A are positive. From any of these forms it is possible to recognize that the asymptotes are $x = -b$, $p = -c$, and to compute the intercepts. If the supply law is linear, no difficulty arises; if the supply law is parabolic, a graphical solution can be found, but the algebraic solution may involve a cubic equation.

EXAMPLE 1–15. Find the market equilibrium price and quantity if the demand law is $px = 25$, $(2 \leq x \leq 10)$, and the supply law is $p = 2 + (x/2)$.

The demand curve is drawn (Fig. 1–17) from the points $(2, 12.5)$, $(5, 5)$, $(10, 2.5)$, and the supply line from the points $(0, 2)$, $(10, 7)$. Thus,

$$px = 25 = 2x + \frac{x^2}{2},$$

$$x^2 + 4x + (4) = 50 + (4),$$

$$x = -2 + \sqrt{54} = 5.35,$$

$$p = 2 + \frac{5.35}{2} = 4.68.$$

These results appear reasonable on the diagram of Fig. 1–17.

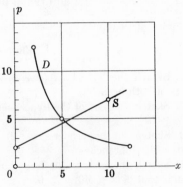

FIGURE 1–17

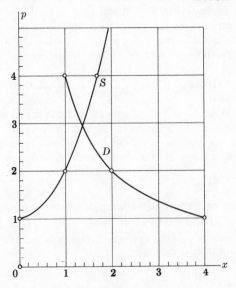

FIGURE 1–18

EXAMPLE 1–16. Find the market equilibrium price geometrically if the demand law is $px = 4$, $(1 \leqq x \leqq 4)$, and the supply law is $p = 1 + x^2$. Compute the equilibrium quantity from the demand law and verify the results in the supply law.

The demand and supply curves are shown in Fig. 1–18. A fair estimate is that $p = 3$; then $x = 4/3$. As the check, $1 + (16/9) = 2.8$. A better estimate would have been that $p = 2.9$. Then $x = 4/2.9 = 1.38$, and $1 + (1.38)^2 = 2.90$ affords the check.

EXAMPLE 1–17. If the demand law is $(x + 20)(p + 10) = 400$ and the supply law is $x = 2p - 7$, determine geometrically and algebraically the market equilibrium price and quantity.

The lines $p = -10$ and $x = -20$ are the asymptotes. The values of p given in the table below are computed from

$$p = \frac{400}{x + 20} - 10 = \frac{200 - 10x}{x + 20}.$$

x	0	20	+10	−10
p	10	0	10/3	30

The supply line is easily drawn; the diagram (Fig. 1–19) suggests a solution near $x = 5$, $p = 6$:

$$p = \frac{200 - 10x}{x + 20} = \frac{x + 7}{2},$$

$$400 - 20x = x^2 + 27x + 140,$$

$$x^2 + 47x - 260 = 0.$$

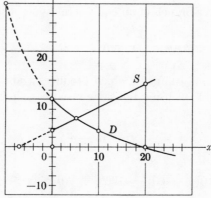

FIGURE 1–19

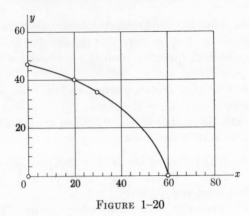

FIGURE 1–20

The above result factors as follows:

$$x^2 + 47x - 260 = (x - 5)(x + 52).$$

Hence the algebraic solution is also $x = 5$, $p = 6$.

Production curve. The parabola and equilateral hyperbola can be used to represent economic situations other than supply and demand functions. One such situation involves the production of two goods by the same firm, using common supplies of labor and raw materials. The two commodities, for example, might be similar but of different quality. If the quantities produced are x and y, then there must be a functional relationship $\phi(x, y) = 0$ between them, such that as x increases, y decreases. Here y is a single-valued, monotonically decreasing function of x, that is, $y = f(x)$; and x is a similar function of y, that is, $x = g(y)$. In the "normal" case it is known that the *production transformation curve*, $\phi(x, y) = 0$, is concave* to the origin (Fig. 1–20). Such curves may be parabolic or may be given as part of the lower branch of an equilateral hyperbola of the type

$$(x - h)(y - k) = a^2, \qquad (x < h, y > 0).$$

EXAMPLE 1–18. A company which produces x and y amounts of steel of two different grades, using the same resources, finds it could use either of the equations

$$y = 45 - \frac{x^2}{80}$$

or

$$(x - 80)(y - 60) = 1200, \qquad (0 \leqq x \leqq 80, y \geqq 0)$$

---

* The subject of concavity is discussed in Section 2–10.

for the production transformation function. (a) Show that both these curves pass through the three points corresponding to $x = 0$, $y = 0$, $x = 20$, but give different values of y for $x = 30$. (b) Sketch the equilateral hyperbola, showing the asymptotes and that part of the curve which is significant.

(a) For the parabola, if $x = 0$, $y = 45$; if $x = 20$, $y = 40$; and if $y = 0$, $x = \sqrt{45 \times 80} = 60$. If $x = 30$, $y = 33\frac{3}{4}$. The equation of the hyperbola can be written

$$y = 60 - \frac{1200}{80 - x} = 60 \cdot \frac{x - 60}{x - 80}.$$

If $x = 0$, $y = 45$; if $x = 20$, $y = 40$; and if $y = 0$, $x = 60$. If $x = 30$, $y = 36$. Hence the conclusions of part (a) are verified.

(b) The asymptotes are $x = 80$, $y = 60$. The curve has two branches, but only that part of the lower branch where x and y are both positive is significant. The points in part (a) are used to draw the curves (Fig. 1–20).

Many other types of curves can be used as demand and supply curves, or to represent other useful economic functions, and these will be introduced periodically as the subject develops.

Exercise Group 1–6

1. Determine the market equilibrium price and quantity, first geometrically and then algebraically, if the demand law is $px = 30$ and the supply law is $3p - x = 9$.

2. Determine the market equilibrium price and quantity, first geometrically and then algebraically, if the demand law is $px = 30$ and the supply law is $4p - x = 12$.

3. If the demand law is $(x + 10)(p + 20) = 300$ and the supply law is $x = 2p - 8$, find the equilibrium price and quantity, geometrically and algebraically.

4. If the demand law is $(x + 6)(p + 12) = 144$ and the supply law is $p = 2 + (x/2)$, find the equilibrium price and quantity, geometrically and algebraically.

5. Determine the market equilibrium price and quantity (geometrically only) if the demand law is $p = 30/x$ and the supply law is $p = 3 + (x^2/4)$.

6. Determine the market equilibrium price and quantity (geometrically only) if the demand law is $p = [300/(x + 10)] - 20$ and the supply law is

$$p = 4 + \frac{x^2}{2}.$$

7. (a) Show that the parabola $y = 2 - (x^2/8)$ and the equilateral hyperbola $(x - 6)(y - 3) = 6$ pass through the same three points corresponding to

$x = 0$, $x = 2$, and $x = 4$, but that they give different values of y for $x = 1$ and $x = 3$. (b) Sketch the equilateral hyperbola, showing the asymptotes and that part of the curve corresponding to $x < 6$ and $y < 3$. Compare this with the graph of the complete parabola.

8. (a) Show that the parabola $y = \frac{1}{4}x^2 - x + 4$ and the equilateral hyperbola $(x + 2)(y - 2) = 4$ give the same values of y for $x = 0$ and $x = 2$, but different values of y for $x = 4$ and $x = -2$. Show that the values of y are the same *only* for the values mentioned above. (b) Sketch the equilateral hyperbola, showing the asymptotes and that part of the curve corresponding to $x > -2$ and $y > 2$. Compare this with the graph of the parabola for the same range of values for x and y.

9. A company which produces x and y amounts of steel of two different grades, using the same resources, finds that its production transformation curve is given by

$$y = 20 - \frac{300}{30 - x}, \qquad (x < 30).$$

(a) Draw the production transformation curve. (b) What are the largest amounts of x and y that can be produced? (c) If the company finds that the demand for its grade x steel is twice that for grade y, what amounts should it produce?

10. A company manufactures two grades of candy from the same resources. If x and y represent the quantities produced (in tons), the production transformation curve is given by $(x - 24)(y - 36) = 240$, $(x < 24)$. (a) Draw this curve. (b) If the demand for grade x candy is two-thirds that for grade y, what amounts should be produced?

1–10 Effect of taxation on market equilibrium. If the government imposes a tax on a given commodity, the price to the consumer will increase and the demand decrease. Consider the effect upon market equilibrium under the following assumptions: (1) under pure competition the consumers' demand depends upon the price alone, that is, the demand function does not change; (2) the producers adjust the supply curve to the new price which includes the tax; (3) a tax of t monetary units is imposed upon each unit of quantity produced (e.g., stamp taxes.)

First (following Marshall's method), consider the supply law in the form where quantity is the independent variable and price the dependent variable. Since p is the price per unit quantity and t the tax per unit quantity, a supply law $p = F(x)$ before taxation becomes $p_1 = F(x) + t$ after taxation. If the demand law is $p = f(x)$, then the equilibrium point $E(x, p)$ is found as in Section 1–4. The new equilibrium point, after taxation, is $E_1(x_1, p_1)$, where (x_1, p_1) is the solution of the equations

$$p_1 = f(x), \qquad p_1 = F(x) + t.$$

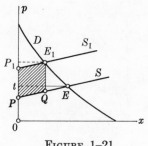

FIGURE 1–21

Geometrically, this is equivalent to moving the original supply curve upward t units. Except in the case where the supply is constant (that is, where the price does not depend upon the quantity produced), the increase in price is less than the amount of the tax (Fig. 1–21).

Second, if the original supply law is in the form $x = G(p)$, it may be possible to solve for p in a convenient form. If not, the supply law after taxation, $p_1 - t = F(x)$, shows that the quantity supplied is $x = G(p_1 - t)$. This equation can be combined with the equation for the demand law to determine the new equilibrium conditions.

A subsidy may be considered as a negative tax. The supply curve is moved downward the amount of the subsidy, and the price to the consumer decreases while the demand increases.

The total revenue T received by the government is tx_1, where x_1 is the new equilibrium quantity; this total may be represented by the area of a rectangle of dimensions t and x_1. If the supply law is linear, the total revenue may also be represented by the area of the parallelogram PQE_1P_1 shown in Fig. 1–21. From this diagram we observe that the tax may be large enough to "kill" the market by reducing the demand to the vanishing point. If the government is interested in taxation for revenue purposes, the question of what tax will give the greatest revenue becomes pertinent. (This question is considered further in Section 3–5.)

EXAMPLE 1–19.   The demand law is $3p + 2x = 27$ and the supply law is $6p - 2x = 9$. (Cf. Example 1–4 and Fig. 1–3.)   (a) If a tax of 3/2 per unit is imposed, find the new equilibrium price and quantity and the total government revenue.   (b) If a subsidy of 1 per unit is granted, find the new equilibrium price and quantity and the total government expenditure.

The problem without taxation was solved earlier and the equilibrium point found to be $E(7\frac{1}{2}, 4)$.

(a) With an additive tax of 3/2, the demand and supply laws can be written

$$p_1 = 9 - \tfrac{2}{3}x \quad \text{and} \quad p_1 = \tfrac{3}{2} + \tfrac{1}{3}x + \tfrac{3}{2} = 3 + \tfrac{1}{3}x.$$

Simultaneous solution of these equations gives

$$p_1 = 9 - \tfrac{2}{3}x = 3 + \tfrac{1}{3}x \quad \text{and} \quad x_1 = 6, \quad p_1 = 5.$$

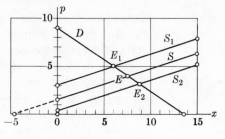

FIGURE 1–22

The increase in price is 1 unit, or 2/3 of the tax. The total government revenue is the product of the new demand and the tax, or $T = 6 \cdot \frac{3}{2} = 9$.

(b) The demand and supply laws can be written

$$p_2 = 9 - \tfrac{2}{3}x \qquad \text{and} \qquad p_2 = \tfrac{3}{2} + \tfrac{1}{3}x - 1 = \tfrac{1}{2} + \tfrac{1}{3}x.$$

Simultaneous solution of these equations gives

$$p_2 = 9 - \frac{2}{3}x = \frac{1}{2} + \frac{x}{3} \qquad \text{and} \qquad x_2 = \frac{17}{2}, \qquad p_2 = \frac{10}{3}.$$

The decrease in price is 2/3 unit, or 2/3 of the subsidy. The total government expenditure is the product of the subsidy and the new demand, or $S = 1 \cdot (17/2)$. All these results are in agreement with the equilibrium points E, E_1, and E_2 shown in Fig. 1–22.

EXAMPLE 1–20. The demand and supply laws before taxation are

$$\text{D:}\ \ 9x + 4p = 40; \qquad \text{S:}\ \ 9x = p^2 - 4.$$

If a tax of 3 units is added to the price, what are the new equilibrium price and quantity?

The problem without taxation was considered in Example 1–11. With the tax, the equations become

$$p_1 = \frac{40 - 9x}{4} = \sqrt{9x + 4} + 3$$

or

$$x = \frac{40 - 4p_1}{9} = \frac{(p_1 - 3)^2 - 4}{9},$$

depending on whether the supply law is or is not solved for p, as suggested in Section 1–10. If the second method is completed, then

$$40 - 4p_1 = p_1^2 - 6p_1 + 5,$$

$$p_1^2 - 2p_1 - 35 = 0,$$

$$p_1 = 1 + \sqrt{1 + 35} = 7 \quad \text{and} \quad x_1 = \frac{40 - 28}{9} = \frac{4}{3}.$$

It is easy to verify that these values satisfy the equations given by the first method. (It is suggested that the reader solve the equations directly and show the geometric solution in a diagram similar to Fig. 1–12.)

EXAMPLE 1–21. If the demand and supply laws are

$$\text{D: } \quad p = 16 - x^2; \qquad \text{S: } \quad p = 4 + x,$$

the equilibrium point is $(3, 7)$ (see problem 4, Exercise Group 1–4). What amount of subsidy is required to lower the price from 7 to 5 units?

With the subsidy, the equations become

$$p_1 = 5 = 16 - x^2 = 4 + x - s,$$

where s is the amount of the subsidy. Hence $x = \sqrt{11}$ and $s = x - 1 = \sqrt{11} - 1 = 2.32$. The results are shown geometrically in Fig. 1–23.

A second type of tax (e.g., sales tax) occurs when the price is increased at a fixed rate, usually expressed in per cent. If the original supply law is $p = F(x)$, then $p_1 = p(1 + r) = F(x)(1 + r)$, where r is the tax rate. The equivalent additive tax t can then be written

$$t = rp = rF(x) = \frac{rp_1}{1 + r},$$

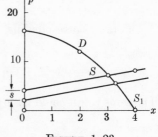

FIGURE 1–23

where p is the price from the original supply law. Problems concerning market equilibrium $E_1(x_1, p_1)$ and the total government tax $T = tx_1$ can be solved by the method used in the previous case. The new supply curve is related to the old curve through the multiplication of each ordinate by the factor $1 + r$. Both curves have the same intercept (which is for a negative value of x) on the x-axis.

EXAMPLE 1–22. The demand law is $3p + 2x = 27$ and the supply law is $6p - 2x = 9$. (Cf. Example 1–19 and Fig. 1–22.) If a 20% tax

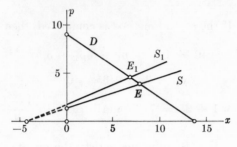

FIGURE 1–24

per unit is imposed, find the new equilibrium price and the total government revenue.

If the tax is 20%, or 1/5 of the original price, the demand and supply laws can be written

$$p_1 = 9 - \frac{2}{3}x_1 \quad \text{and} \quad p_1 = \left(\frac{3}{2} + \frac{x_1}{3}\right)\frac{6}{5},$$

Simultaneous solution of these equations yields

$$p_1 = 9 - \frac{2}{3}x_1 = \frac{9}{5} + \frac{2}{5}x_1,$$

$$\frac{16}{15}x_1 = \frac{36}{5},$$

$$x_1 = \frac{36}{5} \cdot \frac{15}{16} = \frac{27}{4} = 6.75,$$

$$p_1 = 9 - \frac{2}{3} \cdot \frac{27}{4} = \frac{9}{2} = 4.5.$$

The tax t corresponding to the *supply* x_1 is $p/5$, where

$$p = \frac{3}{2} + \frac{1}{3} \cdot \frac{27}{4} = \frac{15}{4}, \quad \text{or} \quad t = \frac{3}{4}.$$

The same result could have been obtained from

$$t = \frac{rp_1}{1 + r} = \frac{\frac{1}{5} \cdot \frac{9}{2}}{\frac{6}{5}} = \frac{3}{4}.$$

Since 27/4 units are subject to this tax, the government revenue is $T = 27/4 \cdot 3/4 = 81/16$. All these results are in agreement with Fig. 1–24, which shows the demand line and the supply lines before and after taxation.

EXERCISE GROUP 1–7

1. If the demand law is $p = 4 - 2x$ and the supply law is $p = 2 + x$, (a) find the increase in price and the government revenue if an additive tax of $\frac{1}{2}$ per unit is imposed; (b) find the decrease in price and the government expenditure if a subsidy of $\frac{1}{2}$ per unit is granted. Illustrate the results geometrically.

2. The demand law is $p = 10 - 2x$ and the supply law is $p = (3x/2) + 1$. Find the new equilibrium price and quantity (a) if an additive tax of 2 per unit is imposed, and (b) if a subsidy of 1 per unit is granted. Illustrate geometrically.

3. If the demand law is $p = 4 - 2x$ and the supply law is $p = 2 + x$, find the increase in price and the government revenue if a 20% tax is imposed upon the original selling price. Illustrate geometrically.

4. The demand law is $p = 10 - 2x$ and the supply law is $p = (3x/2) + 1$. Find the new equilibrium price and quantity if a 25% sales tax is imposed. Illustrate geometrically.

5. (a) If the demand law is $x = 10 - p$ and the supply law is $x = 2p - 5$, what additive tax will increase the price by 2 units? (b) What subsidy will decrease the price by 1 unit? Illustrate geometrically.

6. For the demand and supply laws $3p + 2x = 27$, $6p - 2x = 9$, respectively (Example 1–19), show that the increase in price is always $\frac{2}{3}$ of the tax.

7. If the demand law is $2p + 3x = 10$, the supply law is $x = 4p - 6$, and the tax is $t = 1$, find the new equilibrium price and quantity and the total government revenue. In illustrating the results geometrically, show, by shading, a parallelogram whose area is the total government revenue.

8. If the demand law is $x = 130 - 4p$ and the supply law is

$$p = 10 + \frac{x}{5} + \frac{x^2}{100},$$

find the new equilibrium point, (a) if a tax $t = 5$ is imposed, and (b) if a subsidy of $s = 5$ is granted.

9. If the demand law is $x = 16 - 2p$, the supply law is $4x = 4p + p^2$, and the tax is $t = 2$, what are the equilibrium price and quantity? Illustrate geometrically.

10. If the demand and supply laws are $p = 39 - 3x^2$ and $p = 9x + 9$, respectively, what tax will raise the equilibrium price by 3? What subsidy will lower the equilibrium price by 3?

1–11 Taxation for two commodities. If the demands for two related commodities depend upon the prices of both, and if taxes of t_1 and t_2, respectively, are imposed on unit quantity of the commodities, then an analysis similar to that made in the preceding section can be used to determine the market equilibrium prices and quantities. (See also Section 1–5.) Since the case of linear demand and supply functions is considered here, it is convenient to express the prices p and q in terms of the quantities x and y. After imposition of the taxes, the four equations are

$$p = p_0 - mx + ay, \tag{1-24}$$

$$q = q_0 + bx - ny, \tag{1-25}$$

$$p = P_0 + Mx + Ay + t_1, \tag{1-26}$$

$$q = Q_0 + Bx + Ny + t_2, \tag{1-27}$$

where p_0, m, q_0, n and P_0, M, Q_0, N are positive.

EXAMPLE 1–23. From Example 1–6 the demand laws for two commodities are

$$x = 5 - p + q, \qquad y = 10 - p - q,$$

and the supply laws are

$$x = -5 + p + q, \qquad y = -2 - p + 2q.$$

An additive tax of $\frac{1}{2}$ per unit is imposed on the first commodity and a subsidy of $\frac{1}{2}$ per unit is granted the second commodity. Find the market equilibrium prices and quantities and the net government revenue.

If the first method (Section 1–10) is used, each pair is solved for p and q and in the supply equations the tax and subsidy are taken into account. The resulting equations (subscripts unnecessary) are

D: $p = \frac{1}{2}(15 - x - y)$, $q = \frac{1}{2}(5 + x - y)$;

S: $p = \frac{1}{3}(8 + 2x - y) + \frac{1}{2}$, $q = \frac{1}{3}(7 + x + y) - \frac{1}{2}$.

If the second method (Section 1–10) is used, the demand equations remain as given and the supply equations are written

$$x = -5 + (p - \tfrac{1}{2}) + (q + \tfrac{1}{2}), \qquad y = -2 - (p - \tfrac{1}{2}) + 2(q + \tfrac{1}{2}).$$

The solution is obtained from the second method:

$$x = 5 - p + q = -5 + p + q, \qquad \text{or} \qquad p = 5,$$

$$y = 10 - p - q = -\tfrac{1}{2} - p + 2q, \qquad \text{or} \qquad q = \tfrac{7}{2},$$

and these values give $x = 7/2$, $y = 3/2$. The equations given by the first method may be used as a check. The net government revenue is

$$t_1 x - sy = \tfrac{1}{2} \cdot \tfrac{7}{2} - \tfrac{1}{2} \cdot \tfrac{3}{2} = 1.$$

For a single commodity, imposition of a tax always raises the price. It might be suspected that imposition of taxes on two commodities would raise the prices of both, but this is not always the case. It is possible to tax both articles and decrease both prices; this is known as *Edgeworth's paradox* and is illustrated here by an example due to H. Hotelling.* (Since only a special case is considered here, some details are omitted.)

EXAMPLE 1–24. The demand and supply equations are

$$\text{D:} \quad \begin{aligned} x &= 4 - 10p + 7q, \\ y &= 3 + 7p - 5q, \end{aligned} \qquad \text{S:} \quad \begin{aligned} x &= 7 + p - q, \\ y &= -27 - p + 2q. \end{aligned}$$

The alternative forms are

$$\text{D:} \quad \begin{aligned} p &= 41 - 5x - 7y, \\ q &= 58 - 7x - 10y, \end{aligned} \qquad \text{S:} \quad \begin{aligned} p &= 13 + 2x + y, \\ q &= 20 + x + y. \end{aligned}$$

Note that the demand equations are "normal" for all p and all q, and for $y < 41/7$ and $x < 58/7$. The supply equations are "normal" for $q > 7$ (so that $7 - q$ is negative) and for all p, and for all x and y. The equilibrium prices are found to be $p = 219/13$, $q = 306/13 > 7$, and the values of the quantities are $x = 4/13$, $y = 42/13$. The problem, then, is at least "significant."

Suppose that a tax $t_1 = 13$ is imposed on each unit of the first commodity but that no tax is imposed on the second commodity. The new supply equations are

$$x = 7 + (p - 13) - q, \qquad y = -27 - (p - 13) + 2q,$$

and the new equilibrium equations are

$$x = 4 - 10p + 7q = -6 + p - q,$$
$$y = 3 + 7p - 5q = -14 - p + 2q,$$

or

$$-11p + 8q = -10,$$
$$8p - 7q = -17.$$

Solutions of the above equations (using determinants) are

---

* "Edgeworth's Taxation Paradox," *Journal of Political Economy*, pp. 577–616, especially pp. 602–603, 1932.

$$p = \frac{\begin{vmatrix} -10 & 8 \\ -17 & -7 \end{vmatrix}}{13} = \frac{70 + 136}{13} = \frac{206}{13}, \qquad 1 \text{ } less \text{ than the original } p,$$

$$q = \frac{\begin{vmatrix} -11 & -10 \\ 8 & -17 \end{vmatrix}}{13} = \frac{187 + 80}{13} = \frac{267}{13}, \qquad 3 \text{ } less \text{ than the original } q.$$

Perhaps there are no two real commodities that would satisfy these laws, but this example shows how intuition may be misleading in economic situations involving many variables.

EXERCISE GROUP 1–8*

1. For the demand and supply equations of Example 1–24 (Hotelling's), verify the equilibrium data given. If taxes $t_1 = 5$ and $t_2 = 1$ are imposed, find the corresponding changes in prices.

2. If the demand equations are

$$p = 4 - x + y, \qquad q = 4 + x - 2y,$$

and the supply equations are

$$4p = 7 + 2x - y, \qquad 2q = y + 1,$$

find the new equilibrium prices and the change in prices if taxes $t_1 = 1$ and $t_2 = 1$ are imposed (cf. problem 5, Exercise Group 1–3).

3. Demand and supply laws are

$$\text{D:} \quad \begin{aligned} x &= 4 - 2p + q, \\ y &= 20 + p - 5q, \end{aligned} \qquad \text{S:} \quad \begin{aligned} x &= 4p, \\ y &= -1 + 6q, \end{aligned}$$

and taxes $t_1 = \frac{1}{2}$ and $t_2 = \frac{2}{3}$ are imposed. Find the change in prices (cf. problem 2, Exercise Group 1–3).

4. Demand and supply laws are

$$\text{D:} \quad \begin{aligned} p &= 54 - x - 2y, \\ q &= 77 - x - 3y, \end{aligned} \qquad \text{S:} \quad \begin{aligned} x &= -6 + 2p - q, \\ y &= -3 - 3p + 2q, \end{aligned}$$

and taxes t_1 and t_2, respectively, are imposed. Find the new market equilibrium prices in terms of t_1 and t_2. Show that if $t_2 = 0$, both prices are *lowered* by the imposition of the tax t_1.

---

* The number of problems has been kept small because each takes considerable time to complete.

CHAPTER 2

INTRODUCTION TO DIFFERENTIAL CALCULUS*

2–1 The real number system. The reader is doubtless familiar with *real numbers*. He has learned how they are related through the concepts of equality and "less than" and knows how to perform the usual algebraic operations upon these numbers. These relations and operations are based upon axioms,† which include (1) *axioms of order* for making precise the concepts of *equality, less than* or *greater than, between* and *extension,* and (2) *axioms of addition and multiplication,* upon which the algebraic operations are based. Properties of two special numbers, *zero* and *one,* are included in such axioms and the inverse operations, *subtraction* and *division,* are introduced.

Magnitudes which obey both of the above sets of axioms are said to be *measurable.* A number of such magnitudes have already been discussed; e.g., quantity of goods, prices and other monetary concepts, land, labor, and time. In each of these magnitudes there is a natural unit corresponding to the existence of the number *one.* In economics there are also conceptual magnitudes which obey the axioms of order but for which the "additive" property, that is, the existence of a natural unit of measure, is lacking. Examples of such concepts are taste, preference, and satisfaction. For the present, only measurable magnitudes will be considered. (Other types of magnitudes will be discussed in Chapter 6.) For measurable magnitudes considerable use has been made of the one-to-one correspondence between real numbers and points on a line, that is, the *axiom of linear measure.* This correspondence is the basis for analytic geometry, in which geometric language is used to express algebraic ideas.

One further concept needed in connection with the real number system is the *limit concept.* The real numbers and the real line have no "gaps" in them. There are real numbers, such as π, which intrinsically depend upon the limit concept and which cannot be defined by purely algebraic processes. In order to include such numbers in the real number system,

---

* For further study of the calculus the reader should consult any standard text. These texts are usually written for students of mathematics, science, or engineering and require some knowledge of trigonometry at the later stages. (See references listed in Section 7–8 of this book.)

† See, for example, Whyburn and Daus, *Algebra for College Students*, Prentice-Hall, 1955, or *Universal Mathematics*, Part I, written under the auspices of the Department of Mathematics, University of Kansas, 1954.

an *axiom of continuity* is used. This axiom is stated after several preliminary ideas are discussed.

DEFINITION. *A set of real numbers is bounded above by the real number M, provided every number of the set is less than or equal to M.*

No attempt is made here to give a formal definition of "a set of real numbers," but it is implied that the set contains at least one number and that the elements of the set are known. The numbers of the set may be given explicitly or they may be described by a rule of formation. If the elements of the set are designated by $x_1, x_2, x_3, \ldots, x_n, \ldots$ or $\{x\}$, then the set is bounded above by M if $x \leq M$ for every x in the set. If M is an upper bound of a set, then any number greater than M is also an upper bound. (There may be upper bounds smaller than M.)

DEFINITION. *The least upper bound* (lub) *of a set of real numbers is the upper bound which is less than any other upper bound.*

The axiom of continuity, also referred to as the *least upper bound axiom*, now follows.

AXIOM. *If a set of real numbers has an upper bound, then it has a least upper bound.*

The real number system is by definition the totality of numbers which obey *the axioms of order, the axioms of addition and multiplication, and the axiom of continuity.* The last axiom guarantees that the real number system has no "gaps" in it. The set of all infinite decimal fractions is a well-known model of the real number system, that is, it is a set of numbers that satisfies all the axioms given above. Any two infinite decimals can be compared by comparing their digits; the usual rules of arithmetic manipulation apply (see Section 2–2), and since any infinite decimal is bounded, its value may be identified with the least upper bound of its successive approximations. Since, from algebra, every rational number is equivalent to a terminating or repeating decimal fraction, the real number system contains infinitely many numbers that are not rational, namely, those which involve nonterminating and nonrepeating decimals.

An independent variable x is referred to as a *continuous variable* when it is free to assume all values on an interval of the real number scale.

EXAMPLE 2–1. (a) The infinite set of numbers

$$\left\{1, \frac{1}{2}, \frac{1}{3}, \ldots, \frac{1}{n}, \ldots\right\},$$

where n is a positive integer, has the least upper bound 1. If we define the *greatest lower bound* of a set as the largest number which is less than or equal to every number in the set, then zero, a number which does not belong to the set, is the greatest lower bound.

(b) The infinite decimal fraction 0.333 ... may be thought of as the least upper bound of the set 0.3, 0.33, 0.333, etc. This least upper bound is 1/3.

(c) Consider the infinite decimal fraction 0.323323332..., where the law of formation is: write one 3, then one 2, then two 3's and one 2, then three 3's and one 2, and continue by successively increasing the number of 3's by one. This infinite decimal can be thought of as the least upper bound of its successive decimal approximations. Since every such approximation is less than 0.33, the least upper bound axiom states it has a least upper bound. No other way of writing it is apparent, however.

(d) From the study of geometric progressions, we know that the infinite set of numbers

$$s_1 = 1, \qquad s_2 = 1 + \frac{1}{2}, \qquad s_3 = 1 + \frac{1}{2} + \frac{1}{4}, \qquad \cdots,$$

$$s_n = 1 + \frac{1}{2} + \frac{1}{4} + \cdots + \frac{1}{2^{n-1}}, \qquad \cdots$$

has the least upper bound 2. It is not difficult to show that the infinite set

$$V_1 = \frac{1}{1^2}, \qquad V_2 = \frac{1}{1^2} + \frac{1}{2^2}, \qquad V_3 = \frac{1}{1^2} + \frac{1}{2^2} + \frac{1}{3^2}, \qquad \cdots,$$

$$V_n = \frac{1}{1^2} + \frac{1}{2^2} + \cdots + \frac{1}{n^2}, \qquad \cdots$$

has the number 2 as an upper bound.* It is more difficult to show that its least upper bound is the irrational number $\pi^2/6$.

2–2 Limits and continuity. A *sequence* of real numbers is an ordered set of real numbers, and this ordering is conveniently indicated by natural numbers used as subscripts. All the sets given in Example 2–1 are sequences. A sequence is *monotonically increasing* if every element of the sequence is greater than its predecessor in the given ordering; in parts (b) and (c) of Example 2–1 all the sequences are of this type. For example, the infinite set

$$x_1 = 0.32, \qquad x_2 = 0.32332, \qquad x_3 = 0.323323332, \qquad \cdots$$

is a monotonically increasing sequence.

---

* See Whyburn and Daus, *Algebra for College Students*, p. 231.

Limit of a sequence. A sequence $\{x_n\}$ has a constant L as its limit ($\lim x_n = L$) if the absolute value of the difference of x_n and L becomes and remains less than any preassigned value of $h > 0$, no matter how small, if n is sufficiently large. Briefly, $|x_n - L| < h$, for all $n > N$, where N is fixed when h is known.

A relation between the notion of a limit and the axiom of continuity is indicated by the following theorem:

THEOREM. *Every bounded, monotonically increasing sequence of real numbers has a limit which is its least upper bound.*

Proof. In Fig. 2–1, let M be the least upper bound, as implied by the axiom of continuity. Then $x_n \leqq M$ for all n. Let N be a number arbitrarily near M, but less than M. By making n large enough, $N < x_n \leqq M$; otherwise N, with $N < M$, would be an upper bound. But this is impossible, since M is the least upper bound. Thus $|x_n - M|$ becomes and remains arbitrarily small, and hence $\lim x_n = M$.

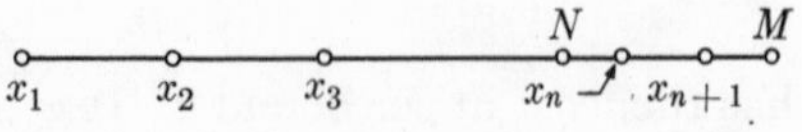

It is true that every real number can be approximated by an infinite decimal fraction which can be considered as a bounded, monotonically increasing sequence of real numbers. (No proof is given here.)

FIGURE 2–1

Limit of an independent variable. If x is a continuous independent variable, that is, if x is free to take on any value in a stated interval, and if a is a given constant, then the limit of x is a ($\lim x = a$ or $x \to a$) if $|x - a|$ *becomes and remains less than any preassigned value* of h, where $h > 0$. The totality of real numbers such that $a - h < x < a + h$ is called a *neighborhood of* a. The definition of $\lim x = a$ means that x remains in such a neighborhood.

Limit of the dependent variable. We say that y is a single-valued real function of a real variable x if for every x in a given interval there corresponds a definite real number y. Let a be in the given interval. The limit of $y = f(x)$ as $x \to a$ is defined as follows: if b is a given constant, then

$$\lim_{x \to a} f(x) = b,$$

provided $|f(x) - b|$ *can be made less than any preassigned positive number k (no matter how small) by making* $|x - a|$ *small enough.*

If $f(x)$ is defined for every x in a neighborhood of a, and if $\lim_{x \to a} f(x) = b$, *then $f(x)$ is said to be continuous at the point $x = a$, provided $f(a) = b$.* If a function is continuous at every point of a given interval, it is *continuous in the interval.*

Concept of infinity. If the independent variable x becomes larger than any positive number K, no matter how large K is selected, then x does not approach a limit in the sense defined above. This idea is expressed by saying "x becomes infinite" or "x tends to infinity" ($x \to \infty$ or $x \to +\infty$). If x is negative and $|x| \to \infty$, x tends to minus infinity ($x \to -\infty$).

If the dependent variable $y = f(x)$ becomes larger than any positive number K (no matter how large the value of K) as $x \to a$, then $f(x)$ does not approach a limit in the sense defined earlier; this idea is expressed by saying "$f(x)$ becomes infinite." If $f(x)$ is negative and $|f(x)| \to \infty$, $f(x)$ tends to minus infinity, that is, $f(x) \to -\infty$. However, it is not always known beforehand for a given function what happens to $f(x)$ as $x \to a$, and it has become customary to write $\lim_{x \to a} |f(x)| = \infty$ to mean that the limit does not exist, but it has been found that $|f(x)|$ becomes and remains greater than any preassigned number (no matter how large) when x is taken near enough to a. The simplest example is $f(x) = 1/x$. Not only is it undefined for $x = 0$, but as $x \to 0$, $f(x)$ can be made arbitrarily large by making x positive and arbitrarily small. This can be expressed by writing

$$\lim_{x \to 0^+} \frac{1}{x} = \infty.$$

Laws of limits.

Law 1. *The limit of a sum is the sum of the limits.*

Law 2. *The limit of a product is the product of the limits.*

Law 3. *The limit of a quotient is the quotient of the limits, provided the limit of the denominator is not zero.*

These laws can be expressed symbolically as follows: if $\lim_{x \to a} f(x) = A$, and $\lim_{x \to a} g(x) = B$, then

1. $\lim_{x \to a} [f(x) + g(x)] = A + B,$

2. $\lim_{x \to a} [f(x)g(x)] = AB,$

3. $\lim_{x \to a} \left[\dfrac{f(x)}{g(x)} \right] = \dfrac{A}{B},$ provided $B \neq 0.$

The exception in Law 3 is more important than the rule, as becomes apparent when the fundamentals of the calculus are developed.

These three laws seem intuitively plausible and are accepted without formal proof in this introductory course, but an indication of the method of proof is given. Consider the second law. Write $f(x) = A + h$, $g(x) = B + k$, so that $f(x)g(x) = AB + Ak + Bh + hk$. Then by making h and k small enough, $f(x)g(x)$ can be made as near AB as desired. The third law can be proved from the second by first considering $G(x) = 1/[g(x)]$ and applying the second law to $g(x)G(x)$, and then to $f(x)G(x)$.

These laws are a basis for the statement that functions obtained from the continuous independent variable x by means of the algebraic operations of addition, subtraction, multiplication, and division (division by zero excluded)—namely, polynomials and the quotients of two polynomials—are *continuous* in some appropriate interval. There are, of course, many other continuous functions, such as those obtained through the operation of extracting roots, with proper conventions used to obtain real single-valued functions. The exponential and logarithmic functions discussed later in this chapter are also continuous.

EXAMPLE 2–2. Consider the function

$$f(x) = \frac{x^2 - 4}{x - 2} \qquad (x \neq 2), \qquad f(2) = 6.$$

Note that it is necessary to define $f(2)$ if $f(x)$ is to be defined for all x. If $x \neq 2$, the laws of limits show that

$$\lim_{x \to 2} f(x) = \lim_{x \to 2} x + 2 = 4.$$

Hence this particular function is not continuous at $x = 2$, since $f(2) = 6$. However, if the given function had been defined as above for $x \neq 2$, and with $f(2) = 4$ instead of $f(2) = 6$, then the function would be continuous at $x = 2$. In light of our other statements it would also be continuous for all x. The graph of the second function is a straight line; that of the first function is this same straight line with a single point $(2, 4)$ omitted and replaced by the point $(2, 6)$.

2–3 Difference quotient and derivative. The functions treated hereafter are single-valued and continuous for the interval under consideration. Let $y = f(x)$, let x_0 be a fixed value of x, and let $f(x_0) = y_0$. Then x can be written in the form $x = x_0 + \Delta x$, where Δx (read, "delta x") is a single symbol denoting a "change in x" and may be considered as an independent variable. The statements

$$\lim x = x_0, \qquad x \to x_0, \qquad \Delta x \to 0, \qquad \lim \Delta x = 0$$

are equivalent.

The dependent variable y can be written in the form

$$y = f(x_0 + \Delta x) = y_0 + \Delta y,$$

where Δy represents the change in y due to a change in x. If the function is continuous at $x = x_0$, then $\Delta y \to 0$ when $\Delta x \to 0$. Now $\Delta x = x - x_0$, and $\Delta y = y - y_0 = f(x_0 + \Delta x) - f(x_0)$. The quotient of Δy by Δx is called the *difference quotient*, and can be written in a number of ways:

$$\frac{\Delta y}{\Delta x} = \frac{y - y_0}{x - x_0} = \frac{f(x) - f(x_0)}{x - x_0} = \frac{f(x_0 + \Delta x) - f(x_0)}{\Delta x}.$$

Geometrically, the difference quotient represents the slope of the secant PQ (Fig. 2–2), joining $P(x_0, y_0)$ to a neighboring point on the curve $Q(x_0 + \Delta x, y_0 + \Delta y)$. Algebraically, it is a function of the independent variable Δx and also depends upon the constant x_0.

The $\lim_{\Delta x \to 0} \Delta y / \Delta x$ (if it exists) is defined as the *derivative of y with respect to x at $x = x_0$*. Several convenient notations are

$$y'(x_0) = f'(x_0) = \frac{dy}{dx}\bigg|_{x=x_0} = \lim_{\Delta x \to 0} \frac{\Delta y}{\Delta x}.$$

If this limit exists for every x_0 in some interval, the subscript may be omitted from x_0. During the process of finding the limit, x is considered fixed and Δx is the independent variable. The definition is written

$$y' \equiv f'(x) \equiv \frac{dy}{dx} = \lim_{\Delta x \to 0} \frac{\Delta y}{\Delta x} \equiv \lim_{\Delta x \to 0} \frac{f(x + \Delta x) - f(x)}{\Delta x}.$$

The term "derivative" arises from the fact that another function $f'(x)$ is derived from the function $f(x)$.

Geometrically, the derivative represents the limiting position of the secant as Q moves along the curve until it coincides with P. This limiting secant is called the *tangent to the curve at P*, and the slope of the curve at P is defined to be the slope of this tangent line. If a given function is monotonically decreasing, then $\Delta y / \Delta x$ and dy/dx are negative (since y decreases as x increases).

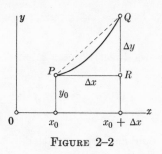

FIGURE 2–2

The calculation of derivatives depends upon the laws of limits. Since the limit of the denominator of $\Delta y / \Delta x$ is zero, Law 3 cannot be applied directly. If the limit of Δy were not also zero, the limit of the quotient would not exist. If the function is continuous, then $\lim \Delta y = 0$. The limit of the quotient $\Delta y / \Delta x$ is sought by transforming this fraction to an equivalent one having a denominator whose limit is not zero. The particular transformation used depends on the nature of the function f.

Before studying the laws of differentiation, it is well to point out that when $\lim_{\Delta x \to 0} \Delta y / \Delta x$ does exist, the function is continuous. Thus, if the derivative can be found, it follows that the original function is continuous.

THEOREM. *If $f(x)$ has a derivative for a fixed x, then $f(x)$ is continuous for this x.*

Proof. Write the identity

$$\Delta y \equiv \frac{\Delta y}{\Delta x} \cdot \Delta x,$$

and pass to the limit as $\Delta x \to 0$, using Law 2 assumed earlier. Then

$$\lim_{\Delta x \to 0} \Delta y = \lim_{\Delta x \to 0} \frac{\Delta y}{\Delta x} \cdot \lim_{\Delta x \to 0} \Delta x = \frac{dy}{dx} \cdot 0 = 0.$$

Hence $f(x)$ is continuous for the given x.

EXAMPLE 2-3. Let $y = f(x) = x^2 - x - 2$, and consider the fixed value x_0. Then

$$\frac{\Delta y}{\Delta x} = \frac{f(x_0 + \Delta x) - f(x_0)}{\Delta x}$$

$$= \frac{[(x_0 + \Delta x)^2 - (x_0 + \Delta x) - 2] - [x_0^2 - x_0 - 2]}{\Delta x}.$$

After expanding and collecting terms, we divide numerator and denominator by Δx to find a form of the difference quotient where the limit of the denominator is not zero:

$$\frac{\Delta y}{\Delta x} = \frac{2x_0 (\Delta x) + (\Delta x)^2 - \Delta x}{\Delta x} = \frac{(2x_0 - 1) + \Delta x}{1}.$$

Since $\Delta x \to 0$, the law of the limit of a sum shows directly that

$$\frac{dy}{dx}\bigg|_{x=x_0} = \lim_{\Delta x \to 0} \frac{\Delta y}{\Delta x} = 2x_0 - 1,$$

and this limit is valid for all x_0. The subscript could have been omitted and

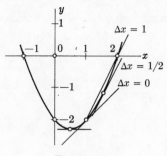

FIGURE 2–3

the result written

$$y = x^2 - x - 2, \quad \frac{dy}{dx} = 2x - 1.$$

The above procedure illustrates the "delta process."

Since the function $f(x) = x^2 - x - 2$ has a derivative for every x, it is continuous for every x. Figure 2–3 shows the parabola and secants corresponding to $\Delta x = 1, \frac{1}{2}, 0$, when $x_0 = 1$.

EXERCISE GROUP 2–1

1. (a) What is the limit of the repeating decimal $0.1111\ldots$? [*Hint:* The sum of an infinite geometric progression is $a/(1 - r)$.] (b) Does the infinite decimal $0.101101110\ldots$ (where the law of formation is one 1 and one zero, two 1's and one zero, and continues by successively increasing the number of 1's by one) have a limit? Explain. (c) Show that the limit in (b) lies between $1/10$ and $1/9$; between $101/1000$ and $102/1000$.

2. (a) What is the limit of the repeating decimal $0.3636\ldots$? (b) An infinite decimal is formed by writing one 3 and one 6, one 3 and two 6's, and continues by successively increasing the number of 6's by one, thus: $0.363663666\ldots$ Does this infinite decimal have a limit? Explain. (c) Find several upper bounds for the number in (b).

3. What are the limits of the following sequences?

(a) $x_1 = 1, \quad x_2 = 1 - \frac{1}{2}, \quad x_3 = 1 - \frac{1}{2} + \frac{1}{4}, \cdots,$

$$x_n = 1 - \frac{1}{2} + \frac{1}{4} - \cdots (-1)^{n-1} \frac{1}{2^{n-1}}, \cdots.$$

(b) $x_1 = \frac{2}{3}, \quad x_2 = \frac{2}{3} + \frac{4}{9}, \quad x_3 = \frac{2}{3} + \frac{4}{9} + \frac{8}{27}, \cdots,$

$$x_n = \frac{2}{3} + \frac{4}{9} + \cdots + \left(\frac{2}{3}\right)^n, \cdots.$$

(c) $x_1 = \frac{2}{3}, \quad x_2 = \frac{2}{3} - \frac{4}{9}, \quad x_3 = \frac{2}{3} - \frac{4}{9} + \frac{8}{27}, \cdots,$

$$x_n = \frac{2}{3} - \frac{4}{9} + \cdots (-1)^{n-1} \left(\frac{2}{3}\right)^n, \cdots.$$

4. (a) If $f(x) = (x^2 - 9)/(x - 3)$, $x \neq 3$, how should $f(3)$ be defined in order that $f(x)$ be continuous at $x = 3$? (b) If $f(x) = (x^2 + 9)/(x - 3)$, $x \neq 3$, is it possible to define $f(3)$ so as to make $f(x)$ continuous at $x = 3$? Explain.

5. Using the laws of limits, evaluate the following:

(a) $\lim\limits_{x \to 2} 5x^2 - 10x.$ (b) $\lim\limits_{x \to 2} (x^2 - 1)(x - 3).$

(c) $\lim\limits_{x \to 1} \dfrac{x^2 + 6x}{2x + 3}.$ (d) $\lim\limits_{x \to 0} \dfrac{3x + 5}{4x + 8}.$ (e) $\lim\limits_{x \to 1/2} \dfrac{2x + 5}{4x}.$

6. Do the following limits exist? Explain.

(a) $\lim\limits_{x \to 0} \dfrac{2x + 5}{4x}.$ (b) $\lim\limits_{x \to \infty} \dfrac{2x + 5}{4x}.$

(c) $\lim\limits_{x \to \infty} \dfrac{3x + 5}{4x + 8}.$ (d) $\lim\limits_{x \to -2} \dfrac{3x + 5}{4x + 8}.$

7. (a) If $y = f(x) = 3 + 2x - x^2$, find the difference quotient at $x_0 = 1$ in terms of Δx. (b) Evaluate this difference quotient for $\Delta x = 1, \frac{1}{2}, \frac{1}{4}, 0$, and show the corresponding curve and secants in a diagram. (c) Find the derivative of y with respect to x for $x_0 = 1$ and for any x.

8. (a) If $y = f(x) = x^2 - 2x - 3$, use the delta process to find dy/dx. (b) Evaluate this derivative for $x = 0$, $x = 1$, $x = 3$, and show the corresponding curve and tangent lines in a diagram.

9. (a) If $y = f(x) = 16/x$, find the difference quotient at $x_0 = 4$ in terms of Δx. [Note that $f(4 + \Delta x) = 16/(4 + \Delta x)$.] (b) Evaluate this difference quotient for $\Delta x = 4, 2, 0$, and show the corresponding curve and secants in a diagram. (c) Find the derivative of y with respect to x for $x_0 = 4$ and for any x.

10. If $y = 6/x$, use the delta process to find dy/dx. Evaluate this derivative for $x = 1, 2, 3, 6$, and show the corresponding curve and tangent lines in a diagram.

2–4 General laws of differentiation. There are laws of differentiation which are valid for all functions. The simpler laws will be considered first, then the rules of differentiation for specific functions will be derived in Section 2–5 and further general laws considered in Section 2–6. In all cases the delta process plays a dominant role, although after the rules have been derived it is seldom used.

Derivative of a sum. If $y = u + v$, where u and v are functions of x which have derivatives, then

$$\frac{dy}{dx} = \frac{du}{dx} + \frac{dv}{dx}. \tag{2–1}$$

Proof. A change of Δx in x will produce a change in u of Δu, in v of Δv, and in y of Δy, where

$$\Delta y = (u + \Delta u) + (v + \Delta v) - u - v = \Delta u + \Delta v.$$

Hence the difference quotient is

$$\frac{\Delta y}{\Delta x} = \frac{\Delta u}{\Delta x} + \frac{\Delta v}{\Delta x},$$

and the derivative is

$$\frac{dy}{dx} = \lim_{\Delta x \to 0} \frac{\Delta y}{\Delta x} = \lim_{\Delta x \to 0} \left(\frac{\Delta u}{\Delta x} + \frac{\Delta v}{\Delta x}\right) = \frac{du}{dx} + \frac{dv}{dx}.$$

The proof involves the definition of derivatives and the law of the limit of a sum.

Equation (2–1) is often written

$$\frac{d}{dx}[f(x) + g(x)] = f'(x) + g'(x),$$

and is stated: "The derivative of a sum is the sum of derivatives." Similar statements apply to the difference of two terms and to the sum or difference of any finite number of terms.

Derivative of a product. If $y = uv$, where u and v are functions of x which have derivatives, then

$$\frac{dy}{dx} = u\frac{dv}{dx} + v\frac{du}{dx}. \tag{2–2}$$

The derivative of a product of two functions is the first function multiplied by the derivative of the second function plus the second function multiplied by the derivative of the first function.

A proof of formula (2–2) using the u-v notation, similar to that given for Eq. 2–1, is left as an exercise (problem 3, Exercise Group 2–2). To illustrate an alternative notation and a useful type of proof needed later, we proceed in a different manner.

Equation (2–2) is often written in the form

$$\frac{d}{dx}[f(x)g(x)] = f(x)g'(x) + g(x)f'(x).$$

If $y = f(x)g(x)$, then a change in x of Δx will produce a change in y of Δy, where

$$\Delta y = f(x + \Delta x)g(x + \Delta x) - f(x)g(x)$$

$$= f(x + \Delta x)[g(x + \Delta x) - g(x)] + g(x)[f(x + \Delta x) - f(x)].$$

This last form was obtained by subtracting and then adding $f(x + \Delta x)g(x)$ and collecting terms. Hence the difference quotient is

$$\frac{\Delta y}{\Delta x} = f(x + \Delta x)\left[\frac{g(x + \Delta x) - g(x)}{\Delta x}\right] + g(x)\left[\frac{f(x + \Delta x) - f(x)}{\Delta x}\right],$$

and the derivative is found by permitting $\Delta x \to 0$. The two fractions become $g'(x)$ and $f'(x)$ in the limit, and $f(x + \Delta x) \to f(x)$. Using the limit of a product and the limit of a sum, we obtain

$$\frac{dy}{dx} = f(x)g'(x) + g(x)f'(x).$$

Derivative of a quotient. If $y = u/v$, where u and v are differentiable functions of x, and if x is restricted so that $v(x) \neq 0$, then

$$\frac{dy}{dx} = \frac{v\,(du/dx) - u\,(dv/dx)}{v^2}. \tag{2-3}$$

The derivative of a quotient is the denominator multiplied by the derivative of the numerator minus the numerator multiplied by the derivative of the denominator, all divided by the square of the denominator.

Proof. A change in x of Δx will produce a change in u of Δu, in v of Δv, and in y of Δy. Thus

$$\Delta y = \frac{u + \Delta u}{v + \Delta v} \cdot \frac{u}{v} = \frac{uv + v\,\Delta u - uv - u\,\Delta v}{v(v + \Delta v)},$$

where the uv terms cancel. Hence the difference quotient can be written

$$\frac{\Delta y}{\Delta x} = \frac{v\,(\Delta u/\Delta x) - u\,(\Delta v/\Delta x)}{v(v + \Delta v)},$$

and

$$\frac{dy}{dx} = \lim_{\Delta x \to 0} \frac{\Delta y}{\Delta x} = \frac{v\,(du/dx) - u\,(dv/dx)}{v^2}.$$

In the proof it was necessary to use the fact that as $\Delta x \to 0$, Δu and $\Delta v \to 0$ (continuity), and also the laws concerning the limits of products, sums, and quotients (including the limitation on this last law).

2–5 Differentiation of special functions. *The derivative of a constant is zero:*

$$\frac{dc}{dx} = 0. \tag{2-4}$$

Proof. If $y = c$, a change in x produces no change in y, that is, Δy is always zero. Hence

$$\frac{dy}{dx} = \lim_{\Delta x \to 0} \frac{\Delta y}{\Delta x} = \lim_{\Delta x \to 0} \frac{0}{\Delta x} = 0.$$

Equation (2–4) is consistent with the geometric interpretation that $y = c$ is a straight line parallel to the x-axis, with slope zero.

$$\text{If} \quad y = x, \quad \text{then} \quad \frac{dy}{dx} = 1. \tag{2–5}$$

Proof.

$$\frac{\Delta y}{\Delta x} = \frac{(x + \Delta x) - x}{\Delta x} = 1 \qquad \text{(independent of } \Delta x\text{)}.$$

Hence

$$\frac{dy}{dx} = \lim_{\Delta x \to 0} 1 = 1.$$

Equation (2–5) is consistent with the geometric interpretation that $y = x$ is a straight line through the origin, with slope 1.

$$\text{If} \quad y = x^n \quad (n \text{ a positive integer}), \quad \text{then} \quad \frac{dy}{dx} = nx^{n-1}. \tag{2–6}$$

Proof. The proof depends upon the binomial theorem. It has been said that Newton invented the binomial theorem so that he could invent the calculus, but whether or not this statement is true is unimportant. The important fact is that the proof of the binomial theorem is based upon mathematical induction, and this implies that n is a positive integer. In general,

$$(a + b)^n = a^n + na^{n-1}b + \frac{n(n-1)}{1 \cdot 2} a^{n-2}b^2 + \cdots + b^n.$$

The above theorem is used in the special form

$$(x + \Delta x)^n = x^n + nx^{n-1}\, \Delta x + (\Delta x)^2 \, [\cdots],$$

where the bracketed dots indicate a finite number of terms of no immediate interest. A change of Δx in x produces a change Δy in y such that

$$\Delta y = (x + \Delta x)^n - x^n$$

$$= x^n + nx^{n-1}\, \Delta x + (\Delta x)^2 \, [\cdots] - x^n.$$

The terms involving x^n cancel, and the difference quotient becomes

$$\frac{\Delta y}{\Delta x} = nx^{n-1} + \Delta x \, [\cdots].$$

The quantity in brackets is a sum of a finite number of terms and has a limit, say B, as $\Delta x \to 0$. Hence

$$\frac{dy}{dx} = nx^{n-1} + 0 \cdot B = nx^{n-1}.$$

The general laws of differentiation of Section 2–4, together with the equations of this section, provide a basis for the differentiation of polynomials, products of polynomials (without forming one polynomial), and quotients of polynomials. For example,

$$\frac{d[cf(x)]}{dx} = cf'(x) + 0 \cdot f(x) = cf'(x).$$

The derivative of a constant times a function is the constant times the derivative of the function.

$$\frac{d[1/x^m]}{dx} = \frac{(x^m \cdot 0) - (1 \cdot mx^{m-1})}{x^{2m}} = \frac{-m}{x^{m+1}}, \qquad (m \text{ a positive integer}).$$

The last example above shows that Eq. (2–6) is also valid *if n is a negative integer;* for if $y = x^{-m}$, where m is a positive integer, and $n = -m$, then

$$y = x^{-m} = \frac{1}{x^m},$$

$$\frac{dy}{dx} = \frac{-m}{x^{m+1}} = -mx^{-m-1} = nx^{n-1}.$$

EXAMPLE 2–4. If $y = x^2 - x - 2$, find y' and the values of x and y for which $y' = 0$.

$$y' = 2x - 1.$$

If $y' = 0$, then

$$2x = 1, \quad x = \tfrac{1}{2}, \qquad y = \tfrac{1}{4} - \tfrac{1}{2} - 2 = -2\tfrac{1}{4}.$$

EXAMPLE 2–5. If $y = 16/x$, find the slope of the curve at $x = 4$.

$$y = \frac{16}{x} = 16x^{-1}, \qquad \frac{dy}{dx} = -16x^{-2} = -\frac{16}{x^2},$$

from Eq. (2–6). If $x = 4$, dy/dx (or the slope) is -1.

EXAMPLE 2–6. If $y = (x^2 + 2x)(1 - x^2)$, find dy/dx.
Using the product formula (Eq. 2–2),

$$\frac{dy}{dx} = (x^2 + 2x)(-2x) + (1 - x^2)(2x + 2)$$

$$= -2x^3 - 4x^2 + 2x + 2 - 2x^3 - 2x^2$$

$$= -4x^3 - 6x^2 + 2x + 2.$$

The same result could have been obtained from the fact that

$$y = -x^4 - 2x^3 + x^2 + 2x.$$

EXAMPLE 2–7. If $y = 2x/(1 - x^2)$, find dy/dx.
Using the quotient formula (Eq. 2–3),

$$\frac{dy}{dx} = \frac{(1 - x^2)2 - 2x(-2x)}{(1 - x^2)^2} = \frac{2x^2 + 2}{(1 - x^2)^2}, \qquad (x^2 \neq 1).$$

If $x^2 \to 1$, then $dy/dx \to \infty$.

EXERCISE GROUP 2–2

1. For each of the following find dy/dx and the values of x and y for which $dy/dx = 0$:
   (a) $y = 5x^2 - 10x$.   (b) $y = 3 + 2x - x^2$.   (c) $y = x^2 - 2x - 3$.
2. For each of the following find dy/dx and the values of x and y for which $dy/dx = 0$:
   (a) $y = x^3 - 3x$.   (b) $y = x^3 + 6x$.   (c) $y = x^3 - 2x^2 + x - 4$.
3. If $y = uv$, where u and v are functions of x which have derivatives, derive the formula for dy/dx, retaining the u and v notation.
4. If $y = (x^2 - 1)(x - 3)$, find dy/dx in two ways and reduce the results to the same form.
5. If $y = (x^2 - 1)(x^2 + 2x + 1)$, find dy/dx in two ways and reduce the results to the same form.
6. (a) If $y = 6/x$, find the slope where $x = 3$. (b) If $y = 25/x^2$, find the slope where $x = 3$.
7. Find dy/dx for each of the following:

   (a) $y = \dfrac{2}{1 - x}.$ (b) $y = \dfrac{2x + 5}{4x}.$ (c) $y = \dfrac{3x + 5}{4x + 8}.$

8. Find dy/dx for each of the following:

   (a) $y = \dfrac{2}{x^2 + 1}.$ (b) $y = \dfrac{2x}{x^2 + 1}.$ (c) $y = \dfrac{2x^2}{x^2 + 1}.$

2–6 Chain rule of differentiation. If $y = f(u)$ is a differentiable function of u, and $u = g(x)$ is a differentiable function of x, then

$$\frac{dy}{dx} = \frac{dy}{du} \cdot \frac{du}{dx} = \frac{df(u)}{du} \cdot \frac{dg(x)}{dx} .$$

Before proceeding with the proof, we give two simple examples.

EXAMPLE 2–8. If $y = u^3$ and $u = 1 - x$, the chain rule shows that

$$\frac{dy}{dx} = 3u^2 \, (-1) = -3(1 - x)^2.$$

If the chain rule is to be combined with another rule of differentiation, the notation may be changed but the fundamental idea remains the same. Thus if $y = uv$, where u is a function of s and s is a function of x, and where v is a function of t and t is a function of x, then

$$\frac{dy}{dx} = u \frac{dv}{dx} + v \frac{du}{dx} ,$$

where, in accordance with the chain rule,

$$\frac{dv}{dx} = \frac{dv}{dt} \cdot \frac{dt}{dx} \quad \text{and} \quad \frac{du}{dx} = \frac{du}{ds} \cdot \frac{ds}{dx} .$$

EXAMPLE 2–9. If $y = uv$, where $u = s^3$ and $s = 1 - x$, and if $v = t^2$, where $t = 1 + x^2$, so that $y = (1 - x)^3(1 + x^2)^2$, then

$$\frac{dy}{dx} = u \frac{dv}{dt} \cdot \frac{dt}{dx} + v \frac{du}{ds} \cdot \frac{ds}{dx}$$

$$= s^3(2t)(2x) + t^2(3s^2) \, (-1) = s^2 t(4xs - 3t)$$

$$= (1 - x)^2(1 + x^2)[4x(1 - x) - 3 - 3x^2]$$

$$= (1 - x)^2(1 + x^2) \, (-7x^2 + 4x - 3).$$

Proof. A change of Δx in x produces a change in u of Δu, and this change in u produces a change in y of Δy. The difference quotient can be written in the form

$$\frac{\Delta y}{\Delta x} = \frac{\Delta y}{\Delta u} \cdot \frac{\Delta u}{\Delta x} , \qquad (\Delta u \neq 0).$$

Hence, by passing to the limit,

$$\frac{dy}{dx} = \frac{dy}{du} \cdot \frac{du}{dx} ,$$

where

$$\frac{dy}{du} = \frac{df(u)}{du} \quad \text{and} \quad \frac{dy}{dx} = \frac{dg(x)}{dx}.$$

This proof is valid if $\Delta u \neq 0$ when $\Delta x \neq 0$, and hence would apply when $u = g(x)$ is a monotonically increasing or decreasing function* in a neighborhood of the fixed x. A more complete proof follows.

Let $y = f(u)$ and $u = g(x)$ determine y as a function of x; that is, $y = F(x)$. Consider the derivative where $x = x_0$ and let $u_0 = g(x_0)$. From the hypotheses it is known that

$$\frac{du}{dx}\bigg|_{x_0} = g'(x_0) \quad \text{and} \quad \frac{dy}{du}\bigg|_{u_0} = f'(u_0)$$

exist. Define the function $h(u)$ as follows:

$$h(u_0) = 0, \tag{2–7}$$

$$h(u) = \frac{\Delta y}{\Delta u} - f'(u_0), \quad (u \neq u_0). \tag{2–8}$$

The function $h(u)$ is continuous at $u = u_0$, since

$$\lim_{u \to u_0} h(u) = 0 = h(u_0).$$

Solving Eq. (2–8) for Δy, we obtain

$$\Delta y = [h(u) + f'(u_0)] \, \Delta u.$$

Then

$$\frac{\Delta y}{\Delta x} = [h(u) + f'(u_0)] \frac{\Delta u}{\Delta x}.$$

On passing to the limit,

$$\frac{dy}{dx}\bigg|_{x_0} = f'(u_0) \frac{du}{dx}\bigg|_{x_0},$$

which, except for changes in notation, completes the proof.

Derivative of x^n, where n is a fraction. We now show that the formula for the derivative of x^n is valid when n is a rational fraction p/q, where p and q are integers. First, consider the case when $p = 1$.

---

* This hypothesis is usually satisfied by the functions considered here. The second proof is much more difficult to follow and might be omitted at a first reading.

Case 1. If $y = x^{1/q}$, then $x = y^q$, from the definition of a unit fraction exponent. Then, using the chain rule and solving for dy/dx,

$$\frac{dx}{dx} = 1 = qy^{q-1}\frac{dy}{dx} = q(x^{1/q})^{q-1}\frac{dy}{dx},$$

$$\frac{dy}{dx} = \frac{1}{q}(x^{1/q})^{1-q} = \frac{1}{q}x^{(1/q)-1}$$

$$= nx^{n-1}, \quad \text{if } n = \frac{1}{q}.$$

It is understood that the formula is valid when x is so restricted that y is real, and that $x^{1/q}$ is interpreted as a single-valued function of x. For example, if $y = x^{1/2}$, y is defined for $x \geqq 0$, and $x^{1/2}$ is interpreted as the positive square root of x. Furthermore, the formula does not apply directly at $x = 0$, since $dy/dx = 1/(2\sqrt{x})$ is not defined at $x = 0$. However, as $x \to 0$, $y' \to \infty$. Thus the tangent to the curve is vertical, and hence the result is valid for all $x \geqq 0$.

Case 2. If $y = x^{p/q} = (x^{1/q})^p$, let $u = x^{1/q}$, so that $y = u^p$. The chain rule of differentiation and the result just proved show that

$$\frac{dy}{dx} = \frac{dy}{du}\cdot\frac{dy}{dx} = pu^{p-1}\cdot\frac{1}{q}x^{(1/q)-1}$$

$$= \frac{p}{q}x^{[(p-1)/q]+(1/q)-1} = \frac{p}{q}x^{(p/q)-1}$$

$$= nx^{n-1}, \quad \text{where } n = \frac{p}{q},$$

which completes the proof.

$$\text{If } y = x^n, \quad \text{then } \frac{dy}{dx} = nx^{n-1} \quad \text{for all rational } n. \tag{2-9}$$

This equation also shows that when y is real and single-valued for the rational exponent $n = p/q$, the function is continuous (theorem of Section 2–3). When needed, formula (2–9) is assumed valid for irrational values of n.

Derivative of the inverse function. If the functional relationship between x and y is solved for x in terms of y, that is, $x = F(y)$, rather than for y in terms of x, that is, $y = f(x)$, it may happen that the function F is simpler than the function f and easier to differentiate. In this case the following general rule is useful.

If the differentiable function $x = F(y)$ defines y as a single-valued continuous function of x[that is, $y = f(x)$] in some interval, then

$$\frac{dy}{dx} = \frac{1}{dx/dy} \quad \text{or} \quad \frac{df(x)}{dx} = \frac{1}{dF(y)/dy}, \qquad (F'(y) \neq 0). \quad (2\text{–}10)$$

Proof.

$$\frac{dy}{dx} = \lim_{\Delta x \to 0} \frac{\Delta y}{\Delta x} = \lim_{\Delta y \to 0} \frac{1}{\Delta x/\Delta y} = \frac{1}{dx/dy}, \qquad \left(\frac{dx}{dy} \neq 0\right).$$

The law of the limit of a quotient is used, as well as the fact that $\Delta y \to 0$ when $\Delta x \to 0$ (continuity).

EXAMPLE 2–10. If $x = y^2 - 1$, find dy/dx and describe the interval of x for which the result is valid. Illustrate geometrically.

Although x is a single-valued function of y, y is a two-valued function of x. To apply the rules of the calculus, the positive value of y is selected, so that

$$y = \sqrt{x + 1}.$$

$$\frac{dy}{dx} = \frac{1}{dx/dy} = \frac{1}{2y} = \frac{1}{2\sqrt{x+1}},$$

$$(y > 0, x > -1).$$

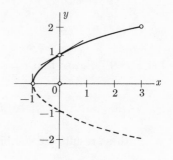

FIGURE 2–4

The value of $y = 0$ must be excluded, and $x > -1$ in order to make y real. The slope can be found at any point on the upper branch of this parabola if either x or y is given. Figure 2–4 shows the curve and the tangent line where $x = 0$.

2–7 Techniques of differentiation. If $y = f(u)$ and $u = g(x)$, then $y = f[g(x)] = F(x)$. Such a function of x is called a *composite function* or a *function of a function.* In many differentiation problems the functions f and g are not given, and it is part of the solution to determine what auxiliary variable u should be introduced. Furthermore, since a given function of x may involve the usual algebraic operations as well as the concept of a function of a function, further intermediate variables and substitutions may be introduced. The formulas of differentiation given here are adequate for problems which involve algebraic operations only.

EXAMPLE 2–11. If $y = (1 + x^2)^3$, find dy/dx.
Let $u = 1 + x^2$, so that $y = u^3$. Then

$$\frac{dy}{dx} = \frac{dy}{du} \cdot \frac{du}{dx} = 3u^2 \cdot 2x = 6x(1 + x^2)^2.$$

EXAMPLE 2–12. If $y = \sqrt{9 + 4x}$, find dy/dx and discuss the interval for which the formula is valid.

Let $u = 9 + 4x$, so that $y = u^{1/2}$. Then

$$\frac{dy}{dx} = \frac{1}{2} u^{-1/2} \cdot 4 = \frac{2}{\sqrt{9 + 4x}}.$$

The formula applies only if $9 + 4x > 0$, or $x > -9/4$. At $x = -9/4$, $y = 0$, and the slope is infinite.

EXAMPLE 2–13. If $y = x\sqrt{1 - x}$, find and discuss dy/dx.

First solution. Consider $y = xv$, where $v = \sqrt{1 - x}$.

$$y' = x\frac{dv}{dx} + v \cdot 1.$$

Let $z = 1 - x$, so that $v = z^{1/2}$. Then

$$\frac{dv}{dx} = \frac{dv}{dz} \cdot \frac{dz}{dx} = \frac{1}{2} z^{-1/2} (-1).$$

When these results are combined, we have

$$y' = \frac{-x}{2\sqrt{1 - x}} + \sqrt{1 - x}$$

$$= \frac{-x + 2 - 2x}{2\sqrt{1 - x}} = \frac{2 - 3x}{2\sqrt{1 - x}}.$$

Second solution.

$$y = \sqrt{x^2 - x^3} = u^{1/2}, \qquad \text{where } u = x^2 - x^3;$$

$$\frac{dy}{dx} = \frac{dy}{du} \cdot \frac{du}{dx} = \frac{1}{2} u^{-1/2}(2x - 3x^2)$$

$$= \frac{2x - 3x^2}{2\sqrt{x^2 - x^3}} = \frac{2 - 3x}{2\sqrt{1 - x}}.$$

Discussion. The original function and the derivative are real only if $x \leqq 1$; y is positive if x is positive, and negative if x is negative; $y = 0$ if $x = 0$ or 1. The derivative is not defined for $x = 1$, but as $x \to 1$, $y' \to \infty$. The derivative is zero if $x = \frac{2}{3}$, positive if $x < \frac{2}{3}$, and negative for $\frac{2}{3} < x < 1$.

EXAMPLE 2–14. If $y = x^2/\sqrt{1-x}$, $(x < 1)$, find dy/dx.

$$y = \frac{x^2}{\sqrt{1-x}} = \frac{u}{v}, \qquad \text{where} \quad u = x^2 \quad \text{and} \quad v = \sqrt{1-x}.$$

If $1 - x = z$, then $v = z^{1/2}$ and

$$\frac{dv}{dx} = \frac{dv}{dz} \cdot \frac{dz}{dx} = \frac{z^{-1/2}(-1)}{2} = \frac{-1}{2\sqrt{1-x}}.$$

Hence

$$\frac{dy}{dx} = \frac{\sqrt{1-x}\,(2x) - x^2\,[-1/(2\sqrt{1-x})]}{1-x}$$

$$= \frac{4(1-x)x + x^2}{2(1-x)^{3/2}}$$

$$= \frac{4x - 3x^2}{2(1-x)^{3/2}}.$$

EXERCISE GROUP 2–3*

1. If $y = (1 - x^2)^3$, find y' in two ways and reduce the results to the same form.

2. If $y = (1 + x^2)^{-3}$, find y' and evaluate it for $x = -1$.

3. If $y = [1/(1+x)^2] + [1/(1-x)^2]$, find y' in two ways and reduce the results to the same form.

4. For each of the following functions, find the derivative and discuss the nature of the function and the derivative in a neighborhood of the origin. (a) $x^{3/2}$. (b) $x^{2/3}$. (c) $x^{-1/2}$. (d) $x^{1/3}$.

5. If $y = 6x^{1.3}$, find $dy/dx \equiv y'$. Also find dy'/dx.

6. If $y = 20/x^{0.4}$, find $y' \equiv dy/dx$ and find dy'/dx.

7. If $y = (1 + x^2)(1 - x)^2$, find dy/dx in two ways and reduce the results to the same form.

8. If $y = (1 + x^2)^2/(1 + x)$, find dy/dx.

9. If $y = (9 + 6x)^{3/2}$, find dy/dx and discuss the interval for which the formula is valid.

10. If $y = 1/\sqrt{8 + 2x}$, find dy/dx and discuss the interval for which the formula is valid.

---

* It is expected that this Exercise Group will require two distinct assignments, the first selected from problems 1 through 8 and the second from problems 9 through 14.

11. If $y = x/\sqrt{1 + x}$, find dy/dx and prove that it is positive for all values of x for which y is defined.

12. If $y = x\sqrt{2 - x^2}$, find the values of x for which $dy/dx = 0$ and the value of dy/dx when $x = 0$.

13. If $x = 4 - y^2$, find dy/dx by first finding dx/dy, and describe the interval of x for which the result is valid. Illustrate geometrically.

14. If $x = y^2 - 2y$, find dy/dx by first finding dx/dy, and describe the interval of x for which the result is valid. Illustrate geometrically.

2–8 Implicit differentiation. When the relationship between the variables is given in implicit form ($\phi(x, y) = 0$), it may not be desirable or convenient to solve for y in terms of x. In general, the implicit equation determines one or more single-valued functions: $y = f(x)$. To find dy/dx for one of these functions, the given function may be differentiated implicitly and the resulting equation solved for dy/dx. The procedure is illustrated by several examples.

EXAMPLE 2–15. If $x^2y - 100 = 0$, dy/dx could be found by first solving for y:

$$y = 100x^{-2}, \qquad y' = -200x^{-3}.$$

To illustrate the implicit differentiation procedure, the given function is differentiated directly. Thus

$$x^2 \frac{dy}{dx} + 2xy = 0, \qquad \text{or} \quad \frac{dy}{dx} = -\frac{2y}{x}, \qquad (x \neq 0).$$

It is a simple matter to show that the two forms of dy/dx are equivalent. If the given function is $xy^2 - 80 = 0$, the first term is a product with the factor y^2 treated as a function of a function (the square of y, where y is a function of x). Hence

$$x \cdot 2y \frac{dy}{dx} + 1 \cdot y^2 = 0, \qquad \text{or} \quad \frac{dy}{dx} = -\frac{y}{2x}, \qquad (xy \neq 0).$$

In these simple examples explicit and implicit differentiation can be used and the two results are shown to be equivalent (problem 1, Exercise Group 2–4). Each of the curves passes through the point $(5, 4)$. From the implicit form of the derivatives, the slope of the first curve at this point is $-8/5$, that of the second is $-4/10$.

EXAMPLE 2–16. Find where the slope of the curve $4x^2 + 2xy + y^2 = 12$ is zero and where it is infinite.

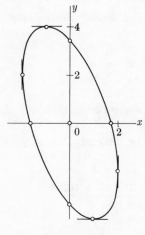

FIGURE 2–5

To find dy/dx, the given expression is differentiated term by term:

$$8x + 2x\frac{dy}{dx} + 2y + 2y\frac{dy}{dx} = 0,$$

$$(x + y)\frac{dy}{dx} = -(4x + y),$$

$$\frac{dy}{dx} = -\frac{4x + y}{x + y}.$$

If $dy/dx = 0$, $y = -4x$ and $4x^2 - 8x^2 + 16x^2 = 12$; $x^2 = 1$. Hence there are two points where the tangent line is horizontal: $(1, -4)$, $(-1, 4)$. If $dy/dx = \infty$, $y = -x$ and $4x^2 - 2x^2 + x^2 = 12$; $x^2 = 4$. There are two points where the tangent line is vertical: $(2, -2)$, $(-2, 2)$. These four points, together with the intercepts $x = 0$, $y = \pm\sqrt{12}$; $y = 0$, $x = \pm\sqrt{3}$, provide sufficient data for a sketch of the curve (Fig. 2–5).

2–9 Derivatives of higher order. If $y = f(x)$, its first derivative is another function of x, represented by y', by $f'(x)$, or by dy/dx. The second derivative of y with respect to x is defined as the *derivative of the first derivative* and is represented by y'', $f''(x)$, or d^2y/dx^2. Note the special positions of the superscripts. They are part of the notation and do *not* indicate multiplication or exponents. Higher derivatives such as

$$y''' \equiv \frac{d^3y}{dx^3}, \qquad y^{(iv)}, \qquad \ldots$$

are similarly defined.

If y is given explicitly in terms of x, the rules of differentiation apply directly.

EXAMPLE 2–17. Evaluate the derivatives of $x^3 - 3x^2 + 4$ for $x = 2$.

$$f(x) = x^3 - 3x^2 + 4, \qquad f(2) = 8 - 12 + 4 = 0,$$
$$f'(x) = 3x^2 - 6x, \qquad f'(2) = 12 - 12 = 0,$$
$$f''(x) = 6x - 6, \qquad f''(2) = 6,$$
$$f'''(x) = 6, \qquad f'''(2) = 6.$$

All higher derivatives vanish identically.

EXAMPLE 2–18. Determine where the first and second derivatives of $y = 2x/(1 + x^2)$ vanish.

$$y' = \frac{(1 + x^2)(2) - (2x)(2x)}{(1 + x^2)^2} = \frac{2 - 2x^2}{(1 + x^2)^2},$$

and $y' = 0$ if $x^2 = 1$, or $x = 1$ and -1; the corresponding values of y are 1 and -1, respectively.

In finding y'', it should be recognized that the denominator of y' is a function of a function.

$$y'' = \frac{(1 + x^2)^2 (-4x) - (2 - 2x^2)(2)(1 + x^2)(2x)}{(1 + x^2)^4}$$

$$= \frac{-4x(1 + x^2) - 4x(2 - 2x^2)}{(1 + x^2)^3} = \frac{4x(x^2 - 3)}{(1 + x^2)^3}.$$

Hence $y'' = 0$ for the points $(0, 0)$, $(\sqrt{3}, \sqrt{3}/2)$, $(-\sqrt{3}, -\sqrt{3}/2)$.

If y is given implicitly, the first derivative is, in general, a function of both x and y, say $y' = \phi_1(x, y)$. To find y'', ϕ_1 is differentiated term by term to obtain a result that involves x, y, and y'. If y' is replaced by its value ϕ_1, then $y'' = \phi_2(x, y)$ is obtained. The procedure is illustrated by two examples.

EXAMPLE 2–19. In Example 2–15 it was found that when $x^2y = 100$, $dy/dx = -(2y/x)$. Hence

$$\frac{d^2y}{dx^2} = -\frac{x \cdot 2\,(dy/dx) - 2y \cdot 1}{x^2} = -\frac{2x\,[-(2y/x)] - 2y}{x^2} = \frac{+6y}{x^2}.$$

This result agrees with that obtained by explicit differentiation.

EXAMPLE 2–20. If $x^2 + y^2 = 4$, find y' and y''.

$$2x + 2y\frac{dy}{dx} = 0, \quad \text{so that} \quad \frac{dy}{dx} = -\frac{x}{y},$$

$$\frac{d^2y}{dx^2} = -\frac{y(1) - x\,(dy/dx)}{y^2} = -\frac{y + (x^2/y)}{y^2} = -\frac{x^2 + y^2}{y^3} = -\frac{4}{y^3}.$$

These results show that $y' = 0$ if $x = 0$, $y' = \infty$ if $y = 0$, and y'' is never zero. They may be verified by explicit differentiation of

$$y = \sqrt{4 - x^2}, \quad (|x| \leq 2).$$

Exercise Group 2–4

1. If $xy^2 = 80$, show that the forms of y' and y'' obtained by implicit and explicit differentiation are equivalent.

2. If $x^2y = 25$, show that the forms of y' and y'' obtained by implicit and explicit differentiation are equivalent.

3. If $y = x^3 - 6x^2 + 9x$, evaluate all derivatives for $x = 1$ and $x = 3$.

4. If $y = x^3 - 9x^2 + 24x - 18$, evaluate y, y', and y'' for $x = 1, 2, 3, 4$. Put the results in tabular form.

5. If $y = (4 - x^2)^3$, find all the values of x for which $y'' = 0$.

6. If $y = 2/(1 + x^2)$, find d^2y/dx^2.

7. If $y = (2x + 5)/4x$, find d^2y/dx^2.

8. If $f(x) = 2x/(1 - x^2)$, show that $f'(x)$ is always positive, and that $f''(x)$ is negative if $x > 1$ and positive if $x < -1$. What can be said about f'' between -1 and $+1$?

9. If $y^2 = 4 + x$ and $y \geqq 0$, find d^2y/dx^2 using both explicit and implicit differentiation. Show that the two forms are equivalent.

10. If $x = y^2 - 2y$, find d^2y/dx^2 in terms of y. Note that although $dy/dx = 1/(dx/dy)$, a similar relation does *not* hold for second derivatives.

11. If $y = \sqrt{4 - x^2}$, find y'' and show that this result and that given in Example 2–20 are equivalent.

12. If $4x^2 - 2xy + y^2 = 48$, find the coordinates of the points where the slope is zero and where it is infinite. Use those points and the intercepts to sketch the curve.

2–10 Curve tracing. An approximate graph of the curve $y = f(x)$ can be obtained by assigning values to x, computing the values of y, and joining the corresponding points by a smooth curve in the order of increasing x. Additional information about the curve can be obtained by evaluating $y' = f'(x)$ and $y'' = f''(x)$ at the computed points. If this is done, the number of points needed to draw the curve can often be reduced. No single rule can be given to determine what values of x to use, but there are certain points that are especially useful. These are the points where the curve crosses the axes, those where $y' = 0$, and those where $y'' = 0$. Not only are these points important, but the values of y, y', and y'' at any point give useful information about the curve.

The geometric interpretation of $y'(a)$ as the slope of the curve at the point $x = a$ has been mentioned. The derivative is the rate of change of y with respect to x. Hence:

If the slope is positive, y increases as x increases, and the curve is rising.

If the slope is negative, y decreases as x increases, and the curve is falling.

A small piece of the tangent line, with slope $f'(a)$, near the point $(a, f(a))$ can be drawn to assist in sketching the curve. The given point is one point on the tangent line; a second point can be found as described in Section 1–3.

EXAMPLE 2–21. Sketch the parabola $y = x^2 - x - 2$, making use of the intercepts, the slope at these points, and the point where $y' = 0$.

$$y = x^2 - x - 2 = (x + 1)(x - 2),$$

$$y' = 2x - 1, \quad y'' = 2.$$

Consequently, the values of x that should be considered are $x = 0, -1, 2, \frac{1}{2}$. The results are put in tabular form and used in Fig. 2–6.

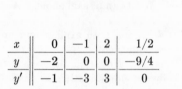

x	0	−1	2	1/2
y	−2	0	0	−9/4
y'	−1	−3	3	0

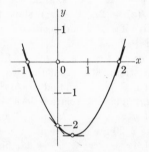

FIGURE 2–6

EXAMPLE 2–22. Draw the demand curve $p = \sqrt{9 - x}$, (p and x both positive).

$$p = \sqrt{9 - x} = u^{1/2}, \quad u = 9 - x, \quad (0 \leqq x \leqq 9),$$

$$\frac{dp}{dx} = \frac{1}{2} u^{-1/2} (-1) = \frac{-1}{2\sqrt{9 - x}}.$$

Since the derivative never vanishes, it is convenient to use the intercepts and the points where $x = 5$ and $x = 8$ (Fig. 2–7).

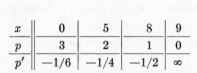

x	0	5	8	9
p	3	2	1	0
p'	−1/6	−1/4	−1/2	∞

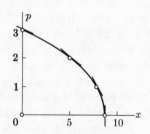

FIGURE 2–7

EXAMPLE 2–23. Sketch the demand curve $p = 8/x^{3/2}$, using the points and slopes corresponding to $x = 1$ and $x = 4$. Also use the asymptotes of the curve.

$$p = 8x^{-3/2}, \qquad \frac{dp}{dx} = -12x^{-5/2} = -\frac{12}{x^{5/2}} \quad \text{(always negative)}.$$

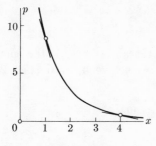

x	0	∞	1	4
p	∞	0	8	1
p'			-12	$-3/8$

FIGURE 2–8

The value of y'' at $x = a$, that is, $f''(a)$, is the rate of change of the slope at the point and hence indicates by its sign whether the slope is increasing or decreasing as x increases.

If $f''(a)$ is positive, the slope is increasing as x increases. In this case, the curve is *concave upward* in the neighborhood of the point and lies above the tangent line.

If $f''(a)$ is negative, the slope is decreasing as x increases. Here, the curve is *concave downward* in the neighborhood of the point and lies below the tangent line.

A point where the concavity changes, that is, a point where the curve crosses the tangent line, is called a *point of inflection.*

In Example 2–21, $y'' = 2$, and hence the curve is always concave upward (Fig. 2–6). In Example 2–22,

$$p'' = -\frac{1}{4} \cdot \frac{1}{(\sqrt{9 - x})^3}.$$

Hence, for $0 \leqq x \leqq 9$, $p'' < 0$ and the curve is concave downward (Fig. 2–7). In Example 2–23, $p'' = 30x^{-7/2}$, and the curve is concave upward (Fig. 2–8).

EXAMPLE 2–24. Sketch the curve $y = x^3 - 3x^2 + 4$. The data are given in tabular form.

$$y' = 3x^2 - 6x = 3x(x - 2), \qquad y'' = 6x - 6 = 6(x - 1).$$

Discussion. The points where $x = 0$ and those where $y' = 0$, and the point for which $y'' = 0$ are found first. Since $f(2) = 0$ and $f'(2) = 0$, it follows that $y = 0$ is tangent to the curve at $x = 2$. The point of tangency corresponds to the fact that $f(x) = 0$ has a double root at $x = 2$, and hence that $(x - 2)^2$ will be a factor of $f(x)$. The third factor of $f(x)$ can be found by dividing $x^3 - 3x^2 + 4$ by $(x - 2)^2$ to find

$$y = (x - 2)^2(x + 1).$$

The point where $x = 3$ is used for completeness. If $x < 1$, the curve is concave downward; if $x > 1$, the curve is concave upward (Fig. 2-9).

x	y	y'	y''
0	4	0	-6
1	2	-3	0
2	0	0	6
-1	0	9	12
3	4	9	$+$

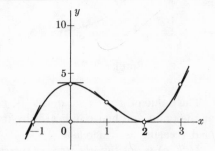

FIGURE 2-9

EXAMPLE 2-25. Sketch the curve $y = x^3 + 3x + 5$.

$$y' = 3x^2 + 3 > 0 \qquad \text{for all } x,$$

$$y'' = 6x.$$

x	y	y'	y''
0	5	3	0
1	9	6	$+$
-1	1	6	$-$

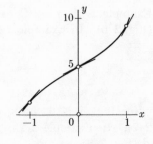

FIGURE 2-10

The determination of x so that $y = 0$ is not convenient. The slope is always positive; the curve is concave downward if $x < 0$, concave upward if $x > 0$, and has a point of inflection at $(0, 5)$ (Fig. 2-10).

EXERCISE GROUP 2–5

For each of the following equations draw the curve by using points, slope, and concavity. Use the important points and as few others as may be required. Put data in tabular form.

1. $y = 3 + 2x - x^2$.
2. $y = 3x^2 - 10x + 3$.
3. D: $p = \sqrt{16 - x}$, $(0 \leq x \leq 4)$.
4. S: $p = 2 + \sqrt{x + 4}$, $(0 \leq x \leq 5)$.
5. D: $p = 100/x^2$.
6. D: $p = [8/(x + 2)] - 1$, $(x \geq 0, p \geq 0)$.
7. $y = x^3 - 6x^2 + 9x$.
8. $y = x^3 - 3x^2 + 20$.
9. $y = x^3 + \frac{1}{4}x + 1$.
10. $y = 8/(4 - x^2)$.

2–11 Maximum and minimum points. All functions considered in this section and their various derivatives are assumed continuous in some interval. This hypothesis is valid when only algebraic operations are involved or if the derivatives exist.

DEFINITION 1.   *$f(x)$ has an absolute maximum at $x = x_0$, provided that $f(x_0) \geq f(x)$ for every x in the given interval $a \leq x \leq b$.*

DEFINITION 2. *$f(x)$ has a relative maximum at $x = x_0$, provided that $f(x_0) \geq f(x)$ for every x in some neighborhood of x_0, that is, in a subinterval $x_0 - \Delta x < x < x_0 + \Delta x$ which is contained in the given interval.*

Necessary condition.   If $f(x)$ has a relative maximum at x_0 and if $f'(x_0)$ exists, then $f'(x_0) = 0$.

Proof. In proceeding from $P_1(x_0 - \Delta x, y_1)$ to $P_0(x_0, y_0)$, the changes Δy and Δx are both positive (Fig. 2–11) and the difference quotient is positive; in proceeding from the point P_0 to $P_2(x_0 + \Delta x, y_2)$, the change in y is negative. Since $f'(x_0)$ exists and is

$$\lim_{\Delta x \to 0} \frac{\Delta y}{\Delta x},$$

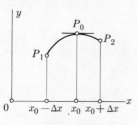

FIGURE 2–11

it follows that this limit is ≥ 0 if $P_1 \to P_0$ but this limit ≤ 0 if $P_2 \to P_0$. Hence $f'(x_0) = 0$.

Statements analogous to Definitions 1 and 2 and to the necessary condition give notions of an *absolute minimum* and a *relative minimum*. If the function has a maximum or a minimum it must be either at an end point of the interval or at a point where $f'(x_0) = 0$. Such points are called *critical points*. If the function is evaluated at the end points and at all the critical points, the absolute maximum and absolute minimum are readily found from these values.

Figure 2-12 shows the graph of a function defined in the interval $0 \leqq x \leqq 3$. There is an absolute maximum at A, a relative maximum at C, a relative minimum at B, and an absolute minimum at D. If the function had been defined for the interval $0 \leqq x \leqq 2$ only, there would be an absolute minimum at B. Figure 2-12 corresponds to the function

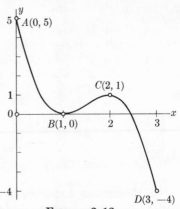

$$y = (x - 1)^2(5 - 2x),$$

$$(0 \leqq x \leqq 3).$$

FIGURE 2-12

The condition that $f'(x_0) = 0$ is a *necessary* condition for $f(x)$ to have a relative maximum or minimum, but it is *not* sufficient. If $f'(x_0) = 0$, the function $f(x)$ might have a *maximum* or a *minimum*, or *neither*. It is important to have criteria for determining which of these situations occurs.

Sufficient conditions for an extremum. Three criteria for determining sufficient conditions, each useful for different situations, now follow (with specific application to Examples 2-21, 2-22, and 2-23).

(1) Use Definition 2. It may be possible to show by algebraic means that $f(x_0) \geqq f(x)$ for all x in some neighborhood of x_0 [or that $f(x_0) \leqq f(x)$] and thereby determine that the point is a maximum (or a minimum).

(2) Use $f'(x)$. If $f'(x)$ changes algebraic sign from $+$ to $-$ as x increases from some value less than x_0 to a value greater than x_0, then $f(x)$ has a relative maximum at x_0; if the sign changes from $-$ to $+$, then $f(x)$ has a relative minimum.

(3) Use $f''(x)$. If $f'(x_0) = 0$ and $f''(x_0) < 0$, the curve is concave downward and $f(x)$ has a relative maximum; if $f''(x_0) > 0$, the curve is concave upward and $f(x)$ has a relative minimum.

EXAMPLE 2-26. (See Example 2-21 and Fig. 2-6.) $y = x^2 - x - 2$.

$$y' = 2x - 1, \qquad y'' = 2 > 0,$$

$$y = (x - 1/2)^2 - 9/4 \quad \text{(method of completing the square)}.$$

(3) The critical point is $x = 1/2$ and $y'' > 0$, and (2) y' changes sign from $-$ to $+$ as x passes through the critical point with increasing x:

each shows that $x = 1/2$ corresponds to a relative minimum for y. (1) The last form of y shows that $f(1/2) = -9/4$ is a relative minimum for y. Since there are no end points and only one critical point, $-9/4$ is the absolute minimum for y.

EXAMPLE 2–27. (See Example 2–22 and Fig. 2–7.)

$$p = \sqrt{9 - x}, \qquad (0 \leqq x \leqq 9);$$

$$\frac{dp}{dx} = -\frac{1}{2\sqrt{9 - x}}.$$

There are no critical points. The largest value p can have is 3 at the end point $x = 0$, and the smallest value is zero at the end point $x = 9$.

EXAMPLE 2–28. (See Example 2–23 and Fig. 2–8.) $p = 8/x^{3/2}, (x > 0)$.

$$\frac{dp}{dx} = -12x^{-5/2}.$$

There are no critical points and no actual end points. The smaller the positive value x becomes, the larger p becomes; and the larger x becomes, the smaller p becomes.

2–12 Points of inflection. If, in applying criterion (3) of the preceding section for a relative maximum or minimum, it is found that $f''(x_0) = 0$, *the test fails;* nothing definite can be concluded about $f(x)$, and tests (1) or (2) must be applied. For example, if $f(x) = x^4$, then $f'(x) = 4x^3$, and as x passes through the critical value $x = 0$, $f'(x)$ changes sign from $-$ to $+$. Hence, $f(0) = 0$ is the minimum value of $f(x)$. This is verified by test (1), since any value of $x \neq 0$ makes $x^4 > 0$. In this case, $f''(x) = 12x^2$ and $f''(0) = 0$. On the other hand, if $f(x) = x^3$, then $f'(x) = 3x^2$, $f''(x) = 6x$, and $f''(0) = 0$. This function has neither a maximum nor a minimum at $x = 0$, since $f'(x)$ is always positive and $f(x) = x^3$ changes from a negative to a positive value as x changes from a negative to a positive value.

If $f''(x_0) = 0$, the curve may have a point of inflection, that is, a point where the concavity changes. Hence to find the points of inflection, it is *necessary* to find the points where $f''(x_0) = 0$ and it is *sufficient* to show that $f''(x)$ changes sign in the neighborhoods of such points. For example, if $f(x) = x^3$, $f''(x) = 6x$. Since $f''(x)$ changes sign as x passes through $x = 0$, the curve has a point of inflection where $x = 0$.

EXAMPLE 2–29. (See Example 2–24 and Fig. 2–9.) $y = x^3 - 3x^2 + 4$.

$$y' = 3x(x - 2), \qquad y'' = 6(x - 1).$$

There are two critical points: $(x = 0, y = 4)$, $(x = 2, y = 0)$. If $x = 0$, $y'' = -6$, and hence there is a *relative maximum* at the corresponding point; if $x = 2$, $y'' = +6$, and there is a *relative minimum*. If $x \to +\infty$, $y \to +\infty$, and if $x \to -\infty$, $y \to -\infty$; hence these relative extremes are *not* absolute extremes. The same conclusions could have been reached by applying criterion (2) to $y' = 3x(x - 2)$. If $x < 0$, $y' > 0$; if $0 < x < 2$, $y' < 0$; and if $x > 2$, $y' > 0$.

The point $x = 1$, $y = 2$ is a point of inflection, since $y''(1) = 0$ and $y''(x)$ changes sign as x passes through the value 1.

EXAMPLE 2–30. (See Example 2–25 and Fig. 2–10.) $y = x^3 + 3x + 5$.

$$y' = 3x^2 + 3 > 0 \quad \text{for all } x, \qquad y'' = 6x.$$

It follows that there is no *relative* (or *absolute*) maximum or minimum. There is a point of inflection at $x = 0$, $y = 5$, since y'' changes sign if x does. If the equation were to represent a supply curve with the restriction $x \geqq 0$, then $y = 5$ would be the *absolute minimum*.

EXAMPLE 2–31. Discuss and sketch the curve $y = 8x/(x^2 + 4)$. Locate the maximum and minimum points and the points of inflection.

$$y' = \frac{8(4 - x^2)}{(x^2 + 4)^2}, \qquad y'' = \frac{16x(x^2 - 12)}{(x^2 + 4)^3}.$$

The data are put in tabular form. The curve is symmetric with respect to the origin, since changing the sign of x merely changes the sign of y. Hence negative values of x need not be entered in the table. [The point $x = 6$ was included to indicate proper scales (Fig. 2–13).]

x	y	y'	y''	Remark
0	0	2	0	Inflection
2	2	0	$-$	Absolute maximum
-2	-2	0	$+$	Absolute minimum
$\sqrt{12}$	$\sqrt{3}$	$-1/4$	0	Inflection
6	6/5		$+$	Concave upward
∞	0			Horizontal asymptote

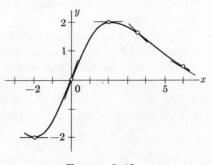

FIGURE 2–13

EXERCISE GROUP 2–6*

Discuss and sketch the curves in problems 1 through 7. Locate the maximum and minimum points and the points of inflection. Put the results in tabular form.

1. $y = x^3 - 6x^2 + 9x$.
2. $y = x^3 - 3x^2 + 20$.
3. $y = x^3 - 2x^2 + 10$.
4. $y = x^2(36 - x^2)$. Is there an absolute maximum? Explain.
5. $4y = x^3(x + 4)$. Is there an absolute maximum or an absolute minimum? Explain.
6. $y = 2x/(x^2 + 1)$.
7. $y = x^2/(x^2 + 1)$.
8. Prove that the circle $x^2 + y^2 = 4$ has no point of inflection.
9. Prove that the equilateral hyperbola $(x + 2)(y + 3) = 6$ has no point of inflection.
10. Prove that the parabola $y = ax^2 + bx + c$ has either an absolute maximum or an absolute minimum, but has no point of inflection.

2–13 Exponents and logarithms.

Exponents. The fundamental definitions and laws of exponents follow. The base a is a positive number different from zero and 1; the exponents are real.

DEFINITIONS.

$$a^0 = 1, \qquad a^{-k} = \frac{1}{a^k}, \qquad a^{1/q} = \sqrt[q]{a}.$$

It is assumed that for every n, there is a number $N = a^n$ which is positive, and conversely, if N is given, that there exists a corresponding exponent n.

Law I: $\qquad a^m a^n = a^{m+n}$,

Law II: $\qquad \dfrac{a^m}{a^n} = a^{m-n}$,

Law III: $\qquad (a^m)^k = a^{mk}$.

The graph of the curve $y = a^x$ is not difficult to construct from points. If $a > 1$, the curve passes through the point $(0, 1)$ and is everywhere monotonically increasing. As $x \to -\infty$, $y \to 0$. Figure 2–14 shows the graphs for $a = 2$ and $a = 3/2$. (If $a = 10$, it would be desirable to select a smaller y unit.)

---

* Because each of problems 1 through 7 is long and the graphs are all essentially different, two assignments might be spent on this Exercise Group.

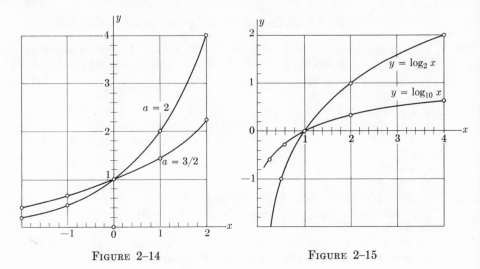

FIGURE 2–14   FIGURE 2–15

Logarithms. The definition and fundamental laws of logarithms follow.

DEFINITION. If $M = a^m$, then $m = \log_a M$.

Law Ia: $\log (M \cdot N) = \log M + \log N$,

Law IIa: $\log \dfrac{M}{N} = \log M - \log N$,

Law IIIa: $\log M^k = k \log M$.

The base a has been omitted from the notation, since these laws are valid for all bases under consideration. Familiarity with the use of tables of common logarithms is assumed. These tables are also tables of exponentials of the form $10^x = N$, where $x = \log_{10} N$.

The equation $y = a^x$ is equivalent to $x = \log_a y$, and either equation is represented by the curves in Fig. 2–14. The functions $y = a^x$ and $y = \log_a x$ are inverse functions; that is, the graph of the second can be obtained from that of the first by interchanging x and y. If the units on both axes are equal, this inversion can be accomplished by a mechanical reflection on the line $y = x$. The graphs of the curves $y = \log_2 x$ and $\log_{10} x$, $(0 < x \leqq 4)$, are shown in Fig. 2–15. If $a > 1$, the fundamental characteristics of the graph of $\log_a x$ are (1) the curve is defined only if $x > 0$, and (2) the curve is monotonically increasing. If $x = 1$, $\log x = 0$; if $x > 1$, $\log x$ is positive; and if $0 < x < 1$, $\log x$ is negative and approaches $-\infty$ as $x \to 0$.

The equation $y = ax^n$ is equivalent to $\log y = \log a + n \log x$.   If new variables, defined by $X = \log x$, $Y = \log y$, are introduced, the equation is linear in the new variables and its graph is a straight line. A demand function in the form of a generalized hyperbola $p = a/x^b$, where a and b are positive constants, becomes

$$\log p = \log a - b \log x,$$

or

$$P = A - bX,$$

where $P = \log p$, $A = \log a$, $X = \log x$.

EXAMPLE 2–32. Sketch the demand curve $p = 8/(x^{1.5})$, ($\frac{1}{2} \leqq x \leqq 6$), and the corresponding straight line obtained by introducing new variables $P = \log p$, $X = \log x$.

The new equation is $\log p = \log 8 - 1.5 \log x$, or

$$P = 0.9031 - 1.5X.$$

The computations are made by using a four-place table and then rounding off. Since more points are obtained than are actually needed, the extra points serve as checks (Figs. 2–16 and 2–17).

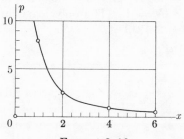

FIGURE 2–16

x	X	P	p
0.5	−0.3010	1.3546	22.6
1	0.0	0.9031	8.0
2	+0.3010	0.4516	2.8
4	0.6020	0.0	1.0
6	0.7782	9.7327 − 10, or −0.2673	0.54

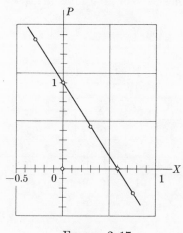

FIGURE 2–17

As a second illustration of logarithms and exponents consider Pareto's law of distribution of incomes,* which can be stated as follows:

The number of individuals N from a given population whose income exceeds x is given by the law

$$N = \frac{a}{x^b}.$$

It is recognized that this law can be applied only in the case where the income is sufficiently large, that is, for above-subsistence income. Pareto felt that the value of b was approximately 1.5. It has been found that the exponent varies from population to population, but that 1.5 is indeed a crude approximation for its value. It is remarkable that statistical data does indicate that this is an appropriate empirical law. In logarithmic form Pareto's law is

$$\log N = \log a - b \log x, \quad \text{or} \quad Y = A - bX,$$

where $Y = \log N$, $A = \log a$, and $X = \log x$.

EXAMPLE 2–33. In a given population the number of individuals whose income exceeds x (in convenient units) is

$$N = \frac{10{,}000}{x^{1.75}}.$$

Plot the curve obtained by setting $Y = \log N$, and $X = \log x$, using the points where $x = 4, 1, 0.4$ and where $N = 1$. [The only logarithm needed from the table is $\log 4 = 0.60$ (Fig. 2–18).]

$$\log N = 4 - 1.75 \log x,$$

or

$$Y = 4 - 1.75X.$$

x	N	X	$Y = \log N$
4		0.60	2.95
1		0	4
0.4		−0.40	4.70
	1	2.29	0

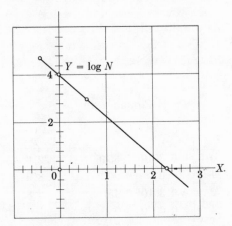

FIGURE 2–18

* Vilfredo Pareto, *Cours d'Economic Politique*, 1897. For a more detailed discussion of this law, see H. T. Davis, *The Theory of Econometrics*, Principia Press, 1941.

Change of base. In addition to the laws of exponents and logarithms previously stated, there is another law that plays a role in the calculus. If a given number M is written in the two forms

$$M = a^x = b^z,$$

then $x = \log_a M$ and $z = \log_b M$. If it is necessary to change from one form to the other, we take logarithms of the members of the above equation, first using the base a and then the base b:

$$x = z \log_a b \qquad \text{and} \qquad x \log_b a = z.$$

Then we have

$$\text{Law IVa:}\quad \log_a M = (\log_a b)\log_b M = \left(\frac{1}{\log_b a}\right)\log_b M,$$

where $\log_a b$ is a constant and $\log_b a$ is its reciprocal. Law IVa, or its exponential form,

$$\text{Law IV:}\quad a^x = b^{x\log_b a},$$

is known as the *law of change of base.*

Two bases are in common use, the base 10 and the base e, where e is an irrational number to be defined presently. A decimal approximation to four places is $e = 2.7183$. In this text, we now adopt the convention that "$\log M$" means the common logarithm of M (base is 10), and "$\ln M$" the natural logarithm of M (base is e). (Short tables appear in the Appendix. In view of Law IVa, one table would be sufficient, but it is convenient to have both available.) Laws IVa and IV take the special forms

$$\log M = 0.4343 \ln M, \qquad \ln M = 2.3026 \log M,$$
$$10^x = e^{2.3026x}.$$

The short table of natural logarithms gives $\ln N$ for $1 < N < 10$. Any number M can be written in the form $M = N \times 10^k$, where $1 < N < 10$ and k is a positive or negative integer. Hence, $\ln M = \ln N + k(2.3026)$, and $\ln M$ can be found. If $\ln M$ is given, and is not a decimal fraction between zero and 2.3026, the above operation is reversed.

EXAMPLE 2–34. (a) Find the natural logarithm of 2.43, 24.3, and 0.243 directly from the table, and by using the table of common logarithms together with the law of change of base. (b) Find the number (in two ways) if its natural logarithm is 0.9010, and if it is 3.9010.

(a)

Direct reading:

$$\ln 2.43 \ = \ 0.8879,$$
$$\ln 24.3 \ = \ 0.8879 + 2.3026 = 3.1905,$$
$$\ln 0.243 = 0.8879 - 2.3026 = -1.4147 = 8.5853 - 10.$$

Using the table of common logarithms with the law of change of base:

$$\ln 2.43 \ = \ 2.3026 \log 2.43 \qquad = 2.3026(0.3856) = 0.8879,$$
$$\ln 24.3 \ = \ 2.3026(1.3856) \qquad = 3.1905,$$
$$\ln 0.243 = 2.3026(9.3856 - 10) = 2.3026\,(-0.6144) = -1.4147.$$

(b)

$$\ln N \ = \ 0.9010, \quad N = 2.462 \qquad \text{(direct reading and interpolation)},$$
$$\log N = 0.4343(0.9010) = 0.3913, \qquad N = 2.462.$$

$$\ln N = 3.9010,$$
$$\ln N/10 = 3.9010 - 2.3026 = 1.5984, \qquad N = 10 \times 4.945 = 49.45,$$
$$\log N \ = 0.4343(3.9010) = 1.6942, \qquad N = 49.46 \quad \text{(check)}.$$

EXERCISE GROUP 2–7

1. Draw the graphs of the curves $y = 3^x$ and $y = \log_3 x$ in the same diagram.

2. Sketch the demand curve $p = 8/x^{4/3}$, $(1 \leqq x \leqq 8)$, and the corresponding straight line obtained by introducing new variables $P = \log p$, $X = \log x$. Put the data in tabular form, showing x, X, P, and p.

3. Proceed as in problem 2 for $p = 4/x^{2/3}$, $(\frac{1}{8} \leqq x \leqq 8)$.

4. If the demand law is $p = 17.6/x^{1.43}$, (a) find p if $x = 2$, and (b) find x if $p = 5$. First write the law in logarithmic form.

5. In a certain group the number of individuals whose income exceeds x is given by $N = (8 \times 10^8)/x^{3/2}$. (a) How many have an income exceeding \$1600? (b) How many have an income between \$1600 and \$3600? (c) What is the lowest income of the wealthiest 800 individuals? The calculations can all be made without using logarithms.

6. The Pareto distribution of incomes for a given population is $N = 5000/x^{1.60}$. Plot the curve obtained by setting $Y = \log N$ and $X = \log x$, using the points where $x = 2$, 1, 0.2, and where $N = 1$. The only logarithm needed is $\log 2 = 0.30$.

7. The Pareto distribution of incomes for a given population was found to be $N = (1.9 \times 10^{12})/x^{1.70}$. (a) How many have an income exceeding \$50,000? (b) How many have incomes between \$25,000 and \$50,000? (c) What is the lowest income of the first million people with highest incomes? (d) Draw the line corresponding to plotting $\log N$ against $\log x$.

8. (a) Write 2^x as a power of 10; as a power of e. (b) Write $(0.2)^x$ as a power of 10; as a power of e.

9. Use two different methods to find the natural logarithm of each of the following numbers: 8.76, 876, 0.0876.

10. Find the numbers whose natural logarithms are the following. Solve the problem in two ways. 2.1702, −2.1702, 4.1702, −4.1702.

2–14 Derivatives of exponential and logarithmic functions. The family of curves $y = a^x$ all pass through the point $x = 0$, $y = 1$, but have slopes at this point which depend on the value of a. The slope at this point could be approximated by the difference quotient, using a very small value of x. To emphasize the fact that a is variable, it will be replaced by the symbol u; and to emphasize that x is to approach zero, it will be replaced by the symbol Δx. The slope at $(0, 1)$ is

$$\lim_{\Delta x \to 0} \frac{u^{\Delta x} - 1}{\Delta x} = G(u), \qquad (2\text{–}11)$$

a function which depends upon the value of u. It is easily observed that if u is near 1, the slope is nearly 0, and if u is very large, the slope is large. We assume that there is some value of u for which the slope $G(u) = 1$, and this value of u is defined as the number e. That is, the number e is defined by

$$\lim_{\Delta x \to 0} \frac{e^{\Delta x} - 1}{\Delta x} = 1. \qquad (2\text{–}12)$$

To obtain a rough idea of the size of e, Eq. (2–11) can be approximated for $u = 2$, $u = 3$, and $\Delta x = 0.01$. An estimate of e can then be found by interpolation. The computations are made by means of logarithms, and the results put in tabular form:

		u	$G(u)$
$\log 2 = 0.3010,$	$\log 3 = 0.4771,$		
$0.01 \log 2 = 0.0030,$	$0.01 \log 3 = 0.0048,$	2	0.7
$2^{0.01} = 1.007,$	$3^{0.01} = 1.011,$	e	1.0
$e = 2 + \frac{3}{4}.$		3	1.1

The approximation so obtained is slightly large. It is known from the calculus that e can be expressed as an infinite series which is bounded and monotonically increasing, and hence has a limit:

$$e = 1 + 1 + \frac{1}{2!} + \frac{1}{3!} + \cdots + \frac{1}{n!} + \cdots = 2.7183.$$

The definition of e given in Eq. (2–12) is the basis of the proof that

$$\text{if} \quad y = e^x, \quad \text{then} \quad \frac{dy}{dx} = e^x. \qquad (2\text{–}13)$$

Proof.
$$\Delta y = e^{x+\Delta x} - e^x = e^x(e^{\Delta x} - 1),$$

$$\frac{\Delta y}{\Delta x} = e^x \frac{e^{\Delta x} - 1}{\Delta x},$$

$$\frac{dy}{dx} = \lim_{\Delta x \to 0} \frac{\Delta y}{\Delta x} = e^x \cdot 1 = e^x.$$

If $y = e^{kx}$, then

$$\frac{dy}{dx} = ke^{kx}. \tag{2-14}$$

This is an immediate consequence of the chain rule of differentiation. Let $u = kx$, so that $y = e^u$. Then

$$\frac{dy}{dx} = \frac{dy}{du} \cdot \frac{du}{dx} = e^u \cdot k = ke^{kx}.$$

Since $10^x = e^{2.3026x}$, then

$$\frac{d(10^x)}{dx} = 2.3026 \times 10^x. \tag{2-15}$$

The simplicity of Eq. (2–13) over Eq. (2–15) explains why the base e, rather than the base 10, is used in the calculus.

The chain rule of differentiation shows that if u is a function of x, and

$$\text{if} \quad y = e^u, \quad \text{then} \quad \frac{dy}{dx} = e^u \cdot \frac{du}{dx}, \tag{2-13a}$$

since $dy/du = e^u$. It is important to recognize that although the variables are not always called x, u and y, the same type of formula applies. For example, if $z = e^y$, where y is a function of x, then $dz/dx = e^y \, (dy/dx)$.

$$\frac{d \ln x}{dx} = \frac{1}{x}. \tag{2-16}$$

Proof. If $y = \ln x$, then $x = e^y$, and

$$\frac{dy}{dx} = \frac{1}{dx/dy} = \frac{1}{e^y} = \frac{1}{x}, \quad (x > 0).$$

The chain rule of differentiation shows that if u is a function of x, and

$$\text{if} \quad y = \ln u, \quad \text{then} \quad \frac{dy}{dx} = \frac{1}{u} \frac{du}{dx}, \tag{2-16a}$$

since $dy/du = 1/u$. Again, even though the variables are not always called x, u, and y, the same type of formula applies. For example, if $z = \ln y$, where y is a function of x, then $dz/dx = (1/y)\,(dy/dx)$. If $y = 1 + 3x^2$, then

$$\frac{dy}{dx} = 6x \quad\text{and}\quad \frac{dz}{dx} = \frac{6x}{1 + 3x^2}.$$

A formula for $d\,(\log x)/dx$ could be derived, but it is not needed. Formulas (2–13) and (2–16) are fundamental and, together with the other laws of differentiation, provide a basis for solving calculus problems involving logarithmic functions.

EXAMPLE 2–35. The equation

$$p = Ae^{-kx},\ (x \geqq 0, A > 0, k > 0),$$

satisfies the conditions for a demand function. The expression

$$\frac{dp}{dx} = -Ake^{-kx}$$

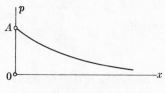

FIGURE 2–19

is always negative, that is, the function is positive and monotonically decreasing. The second derivative is written

$$\frac{d^2p}{dx^2} = Ak^2 e^{-kx}.$$

Since p' and p'' never vanish, the curve (Fig. 2–19) has no relative maximum or minimum points and no points of inflection. The absolute maximum occurs at the end point $x = 0$, namely, $p = A$. The curve is concave upward.

EXAMPLE 2–36. The equation

$$p = A + B \ln (1 + x),$$

$(x > 0;\ A \text{ and } B \text{ positive})$, satisfies the conditions for a supply function. Since the logarithm of a number between zero and 1 is negative, the function $\ln (1 + x)$ is used rather than $\ln x$:

$$\frac{dp}{dx} = \frac{B}{1 + x},\qquad \frac{d^2p}{dx^2} = \frac{-B}{(1 + x)^2}.$$

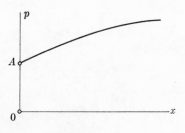

FIGURE 2–20

There are no relative maximum or minimum points and no points of inflection. The curve is concave downward (Fig. 2–20).

EXAMPLE 2-37. The curve $y = e^{-x^2/2}$ plays an important role in the theory of probability and statistics.

$$\frac{dy}{dx} = -xe^{-x^2/2}, \qquad \frac{d^2y}{dx^2} = -x\left(-xe^{-x^2/2}\right) - e^{-x^2/2} = e^{-x^2/2}(x^2 - 1).$$

The curve is symmetric with respect to the y-axis (Fig. 2-21).

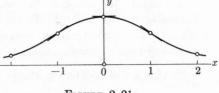

x	y	y'	y''	Remark
0	1	0	—	Absolute maximum
1	0.6	−0.6	0	Inflection
2	0.14		+	Concave upward
∞	0			

FIGURE 2-21

Logarithmic differentiation. If $y = f(x)$, then

$$\ln y = \ln f(x) = F(x).$$

Frequently it is more convenient to differentiate $F(x)$ than $f(x)$, especially when the laws of logarithms are used to simplify the form of $F(x)$. It must be borne in mind that $\ln y$ is a function of a function and is differentiated accordingly:

$$\frac{1}{y} \cdot \frac{dy}{dx} = F'(x),$$

or   (2-17)

$$\frac{dy}{dx} = yF'(x).$$

This process, known as *logarithmic differentiation*, is illustrated by the function $y = e^{-x^2/2}$:

$$\ln y = \frac{-x^2}{2},$$

$$\frac{1}{y} \cdot \frac{dy}{dx} = -x, \quad \text{or} \quad \frac{dy}{dx} = -xy = -xe^{-x^2/2}.$$

The second derivative may be found in several ways:
If $y' = -xy$, then

$$y'' = -xy' - y = x^2y - y = y(x^2 - 1).$$

If $-y' = xe^{-x^2/2}$, then

$$\ln(-y') = \ln x - \frac{x^2}{2},$$

$$\frac{-1}{-y'} \cdot \frac{d^2y}{dx^2} = \frac{1}{x} - x = \frac{1-x^2}{x},$$

$$\frac{d^2y}{dx^2} = \frac{1-x^2}{x}\, y' = \frac{1-x^2}{x}\,(-xy) = y(x^2-1).$$

EXAMPLE 2–38. If $p = (9-x)^{1/2}$, find dp/dx.

$$\ln p = \frac{1}{2}\ln(9-x),$$

$$\frac{1}{p} \cdot \frac{dp}{dx} = \frac{1}{2} \cdot \frac{-1}{9-x},$$

$$\frac{dp}{dx} = \frac{-(9-x)^{1/2}}{2(9-x)} = \frac{-1}{2(9-x)^{1/2}}.$$

EXAMPLE 2–39. If the revenue $R = x\sqrt{9-x}$, find dR/dx, using logarithmic differentiation, and sketch the revenue curve. Consider the points where R and R' are zero. (See Section 3–4.)

$$R = x(9-x)^{1/2}, \qquad (0 \leqq x \leqq 9),$$

$$\ln R = \ln x + \frac{1}{2}\ln(9-x),$$

$$\frac{1}{R} \cdot \frac{dR}{dx} = \frac{1}{x} + \frac{1}{2} \cdot \frac{-1}{9-x} = \frac{18-3x}{2x(9-x)},$$

$$\frac{dR}{dx} = \frac{3(6-x)}{2x(9-x)} \cdot x(9-x)^{1/2} = \frac{3}{2} \cdot \frac{6-x}{\sqrt{9-x}}.$$

The curve (Fig. 2–22) is sketched from the following data:

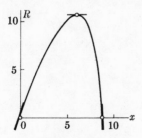

FIGURE 2–22

x	0	6	9
R	0	10.4	0
R'	3	0	∞

EXERCISE GROUP 2-8

1. (a) Sketch the curve $y = e^x$, $(-1 \leq x \leq 1)$, using the value of $e = 2.7$. Draw the tangent line at the point $(0, 1)$ and estimate its slope from the diagram. (b) Sketch the curve $y = \ln x$, $(1/e \leq x \leq e)$, and the tangent line at the point $(1, 0)$. Estimate the slope of this tangent line from the diagram.

2. Find the derivative of each of the following functions and evaluate them where $x = 0$:

(a) $e^{x/4}$,   (b) e^{-4x},   (c) e^{x^2-2x},   (d) 10^{-x^2}

3. Using logarithmic differentiation, find y' for each of the following:

(a) $y = e^{-4x}$,   (b) $y = 10^{-x^2}$,

(c) $y = \sqrt{4 - x^2}$,   (d) $y = x\sqrt{4 - x}$.

4. For (a) $y = 1/(3e^{x^2})$, and (b) $y = 1/(3 + e^{x^2})$, find y' directly and then by logarithmic differentiation. Reduce both answers to the same form.

5. Sketch the demand curve $p = 8e^{-x/4}$, $(0 \leq x \leq 8)$, from a consideration of p, p', and p''.

6. Sketch the curve $y = e^{x^2/2}$, $(-2 \leq x \leq 2)$, from a consideration of y, y', and y''.

7. Sketch the curve $y = \ln (1 + x)^{3/2}$, $(0 \leq x \leq 9)$, from a consideration of y, y', and y'' and using as few points as possible.

8. Sketch the curve $y = \ln (1 + x^2)$, showing the absolute minimum point and the points of inflection.

9. Sketch the demand curve $p = \sqrt{9 - 2x}$ from a consideration of p and p'. Find p' by logarithmic differentiation.

10. Sketch the demand curve $p = \sqrt{9 - x^2}$ from a consideration of p and p'. Find p' by logarithmic differentiation.

11. Sketch the curve $R = x\sqrt{9 - 2x}$ from a consideration of the points where R and R' are zero. Find R' by logarithmic differentiation (x and R are positive).

12. Sketch the curve $R = x\sqrt{9 - x^2}$ from a consideration of the points where R and R' are zero. Find R' by logarithmic differentiation (x and R are positive).

CHAPTER 3

APPLICATIONS OF DIFFERENTIAL CALCULUS

3-1 Elasticity of demand. Recognition that demand for some commodities is more sensitive to price change than demand for others has led economists to consider the ratio of the *relative* change in demand to the *relative* change in price, called the *elasticity of demand*.* Roughly speaking, if an increase in demand of $r\%$ corresponds to a decrease in price of $s\%$, then the elasticity of demand with respect to price is approximately $-r/s$. More precisely, if the demand is regarded as a function of the price, and a change in demand of Δx corresponds to a change in price of Δp, then the *elasticity of demand with respect to price* [represented by Ex/Ep, or by the Greek letter η (eta)] is given by

$$\eta = \frac{Ex}{Ep} = \lim_{\Delta p \to 0} \frac{\Delta x/x}{\Delta p/p} = \frac{p}{x} \cdot \frac{dx}{dp}. \tag{3-1}$$

We note that η may be considered as a function of p (or of x) and that, in general, it varies from point to point along the demand curve.

Equation (3-1) may be put into two alternative forms:

$$\frac{Ex}{Ep} = \frac{p/x}{dp/dx}, \tag{3-2}$$

a form useful when p is expressed in terms of x, and

$$\frac{Ex}{Ep} = \frac{d(\ln x)}{d(\ln p)} = \frac{dX}{dP}, \tag{3-3}$$

where $X = \ln x$ and $P = \ln p$. Equation (3-3) is useful when the demand function has a simple logarithmic form. Its validity can be shown by using

---

* The concept can be traced back to A. A. Cournot. Its importance has been questioned by some modern economists (see, for example, P. A. Samuelson, *Foundations of Economic Analysis*, Harvard University Press, 1947) on the grounds that the laws of economics are fundamentally qualitative and ordinal rather than quantitative. Other economists defend the importance of the concept on the basis that the laws of economics are at least statistically quantitative and that relative rather than absolute changes play an extremely important role in statistics.

the chain rule and the derivative law for the inverse function:

$$\frac{dX}{dP} = \frac{dX}{dx} \cdot \frac{dx}{dp} \cdot \frac{dp}{dP} = \frac{(dX/dx)(dx/dp)}{dP/dp}$$

$$= \frac{(1/x)(dx/dp)}{1/p} = \frac{p}{x} \cdot \frac{dx}{dp} = \frac{Ex}{Ep},$$

from Eq. (3–1).

EXAMPLE 3–1. Consider the demand function $x = 18 - 2p^2$ at the point where $p = 2$, $x = 10$. If the price decreases by 5%, determine the *relative* increase in demand, and hence an approximation to the elasticity of demand. Compare this result with the elasticity of demand with respect to price* at the given point.

The new price is $p_1 = 2 - 2(0.05) = 1.9$, and the new demand is $x_1 = 18 - 2(3.61) = 10.78$, so that the increase in demand is 0.78 and the relative increase in demand is $0.78/10 = 7.8\%$. The approximation to the elasticity of demand is

$$\frac{7.8\%}{-5\%} = -1.56.$$

By Eq. (3–1), the elasticity of demand is

$$\eta = \frac{Ex}{Ep} = \frac{p}{x} \cdot \frac{dx}{dp} = \frac{p}{x}(-4p) = -\frac{4p^2}{x}$$

$$= \frac{-4p^2}{18 - 2p^2} = -\frac{2(18 - x)}{x}.$$

Any one of the various forms can be used to show that $\eta = -1.60$. Or we may solve the given demand law for p or use implicit differentiation to obtain the same results from Eq. (3–2):

$$2p^2 = 18 - x,$$

$$4p\,\frac{dp}{dx} = -1,$$

$$\frac{Ex}{Ep} = \frac{p/x}{-1/(4p)} = \frac{-4p^2}{x}, \qquad \text{as before.}$$

* The words "with respect to price" are generally omitted if no misunderstanding can occur.

This particular demand law does not lend itself readily to the use of Eq. (3–3), but logarithmic differentiation is found useful:

$$\ln x = \ln (18 - 2p^2),$$

$$\frac{1}{x} \cdot \frac{dx}{dp} = \frac{-4p}{18 - 2p^2}.$$

If the above equation is multiplied by p, then

$$\frac{p}{x} \cdot \frac{dx}{dp} = \frac{Ex}{Ep} = \frac{-4p^2}{18 - 2p^2}, \qquad \text{as before.}$$

EXAMPLE 3–2. The demand curve is the equilateral hyperbola $p = 8/(2 + x)$, $(0 \le x \le 6)$. Find the elasticity of demand with respect to price at the end points of the given interval. Sketch the demand curve.

The vertical asymptote $x = -2$, the horizontal asymptote $p = 0$, and the two points $(0, 4)$, $(6, 1)$ provide sufficient data for the sketch (Fig. 3–1). The value of η is found from Eq. (3–2):

$$\frac{dp}{dx} = \frac{-8}{(2 + x)^2},$$

$$\frac{Ex}{Ep} = \frac{1}{x} \cdot \frac{8/(2 + x)}{-8/(2 + x)^2} = -\frac{2 + x}{x}.$$

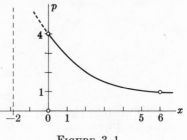

FIGURE 3–1

At $x = 0$, $Ex/Ep = -\infty$; at $x = 6$, $Ex/Ep = -4/3$. The given demand law may be solved for x, and η found from Eq. (3–1):

$$x = \frac{8 - 2p}{p},$$

$$\frac{dx}{dp} = \frac{p(-2) - (8 - 2p)(1)}{p^2} = -\frac{8}{p^2},$$

$$\frac{Ex}{Ep} = \frac{p}{x}\left(-\frac{8}{p^2}\right) = -\frac{8}{px} = \frac{-8}{8 - 2p} = -\frac{2 + x}{x}.$$

EXAMPLE 3–3. Using Eq. (3–3), find the elasticity of demand with respect to price for the demand law

$$x = \frac{27}{p^3}, \qquad (\tfrac{1}{8} \le x \le 8),$$

and sketch the px and PX curves.

$$\ln x = \ln 27 - 3 \ln p,$$

$$X = 3.30 - 3P,$$

$$\frac{Ex}{Ep} = \frac{dX}{dP} = -3.$$

Note that the slope of the corresponding line is $-1/3$ (Fig. 3–2b).

x	1/8	1	8	27/8
p	6	3	3/2	2

X	2.1	0	−2.1
P	0.4	1.1	1.8

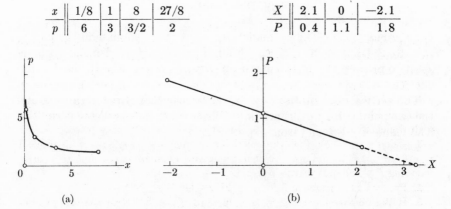

(a)   (b)

FIGURE 3–2

3–2 Constant elasticity of demand. If the demand law is given by a generalized hyperbola in the form

$$x = \frac{a}{p^m},$$

then the elasticity of demand η is the constant $-m$. In terms of approximate relative changes in price and demand, this means that a relative increase of 1% in the price will cause a relative decrease of $m\%$ in the demand.

This demand law was used in Example 3–3. The proof of the general case follows the pattern used in Example 3–3.

If

$$x = \frac{a}{p^m},$$

then

$$\ln x = \ln a - m \ln p,$$

$$X = A - mP,$$

where $X = \ln x$, $A = \ln a$, $P = \ln p$. Thus

$$\frac{Ex}{Ep} = \frac{dX}{dP} = -m.$$

The same result could have been obtained from Eq. (3–1). If we write $x = ap^{-m}$, then

$$\frac{Ex}{Ep} = \frac{p}{x} \cdot \frac{dx}{dp} = \frac{p}{x} \cdot (-m)ap^{-m-1} = -m\,\frac{ap^{-m}}{ap^{-m}} = -m.$$

EXERCISE GROUP 3–1

1. The demand law is $x + p = 10$ near the point $x = 4$, $p = 6$. If the demand increases by 5%, determine the percentage decrease in price, and hence an approximation to the elasticity of demand. Compare the result with the correct value of the elasticity of demand corresponding to $x = 4$.

2. The demand function is $x = 48 - 3p^2$ near the point where $p = 3$, $x = 21$. If the price decreases by 4%, determine the relative increase in demand, and hence an approximation to the elasticity of demand. Compare this with the elasticity of demand with respect to price at the given point.

3. Using Eq. (3–3), find the elasticity of demand with respect to price if $x = 8/p^{3/2}$, ($\frac{1}{8} \leqq x \leqq 8$). Sketch the given demand curve and the corresponding PX line in separate diagrams.

4. Proceed as in problem 3 for $p = 27/x^3$, ($1 \leqq x \leqq 3$).

5. If the demand law is $p = (x - 6)^2$, ($0 \leqq x \leqq 6$), find the elasticity of demand and evaluate it at $x = 3$ and $x = 6$.

6. If the demand law is $p = 10/(x + 1)$, ($0 \leqq x \leqq 4$), find Ex/Ep in several ways. Evaluate it at the end points of the given interval.

7. If the demand law is $p = 1/(1 + x^2)$, find the elasticity of demand, using direct differentiation and using logarithmic differentiation.

8. (a) If the demand law is given in the form $p = 10e^{-x/2}$, find the elasticity of demand. (b) If the demand law is given in the form $p = ae^{-kx}$, prove that $\eta = -1/(kx)$.

9. (a) If the demand law is given in the form $x = 16 - 8 \ln p$, find Ex/Ep. (b) Solve the given law for p and then verify the results in (a).

10. If the demand law is $x = \sqrt{6 - p^2}$ or $x^2 + p^2 = 6$, find the elasticity of demand with respect to price at the point where $p = 2$, using (a) explicit differentiation, and (b) implicit differentiation.

3–3 Cost, average cost, and marginal cost. The *total cost* of producing (and marketing) x units of a commodity is assumed to be a function of x alone, that is, it is independent of other commodities and of time. The total cost is represented by $Q(x)$, and the average cost,* or cost per unit,

---

* The suggestive symbols C and A have been avoided because they are so often used here and elsewhere to represent constants.

by $q(x)$. Thus

$$q(x) = \frac{Q(x)}{x}.$$

The *marginal cost* is defined to be the rate of change of the cost $Q(x)$ with respect to x, and is represented by

$$Q'(x) \equiv \frac{dQ(x)}{dx}, \qquad \text{or simply} \quad Q' \equiv \frac{dQ}{dx}$$

if no confusion can arise. The term "marginal cost" is used in economics because it is represented approximately by the change in total cost for each additional marginal unit of production, that is, $\Delta Q/\Delta x$. The word "marginal" is widely used in economics instead of the mathematical term "derivative of the." Thus *marginal cost is the derivative of the cost.* Similarly, the *marginal average cost* is defined as dq/dx and it may be approximated by $\Delta q/\Delta x$.

Although functions of many types may be used, either theoretically or statistically, to represent the total cost, there are certain natural economic limitations which appear in the "normal" case. (1) If no goods are produced, the total cost is zero or positive, that is, $Q_0 \equiv Q(0) \geqq 0$ (Q_0 is often called the "overhead" cost of production). It is understood that x and Q are always positive (or zero). (2) The total cost must increase as x increases, so that the marginal cost $Q'(x)$ is always positive. (3) The cost of producing an extremely large quantity of any commodity is prohibitive. Ultimately, the cost curve must be concave upward, so that $Q''(x) > 0$. However, in a limited range the curve may be concave downward, corresponding to decreasing marginal cost, and this situation is of most frequent occurrence.

In addition to these economic limitations, we assume, for simplicity, the principles of infinite divisibility and continuity, so that cost functions can be represented by simple continuous functions of types already considered. Several such functions will now be discussed (or will appear in Exercises).

(a) *Linear cost function.*

$$Q = ax + b, \qquad Q' = a;$$

$$q = a + \frac{b}{x}, \qquad q' = -\frac{b}{x^2}.$$

The constants a and b are positive. The graph of the total cost function is a straight line and that of the average cost function is an equilateral hyperbola having the line $q = a$ as its horizontal asymptote (Fig. 3–3). The average cost, continually decreasing as x increases, approaches a

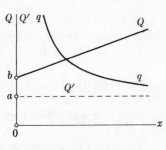
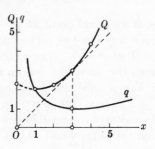

FIGURE 3–3   FIGURE 3–4

constant value, a situation that frequently occurs in industrial plants where large values of x are involved.

(b) *Quadratic cost functions* of the form

$$Q = ax^2 + bx + c$$

are found to be statistically satisfactory, within a limited interval for x, for many manufactured commodities. Since $a > 0$ and $Q' = 2ax + b$, the critical point of the function corresponds to a negative value of x, provided b is also positive. In this case, the x-interval can be started with $x = 0$. This does not mean that quadratic functions with a negative b cannot be used for cost functions, but it does mean that specific limitations on the interval of validity must be determined (Example 3–4).

EXAMPLE 3–4. The parabola

$$Q = \tfrac{1}{4}(x^2 - 2x + 9)$$

was determined* to pass through the three observed points $(2, 9/4)$ $(3, 3)$, $(4, 17/4)$.

Since $Q' = \tfrac{1}{2}(x - 1)$ and $Q'' = \tfrac{1}{2}$, the absolute minimum of Q occurs when $x = 1$, and is 2. Between $x = 0$ and $x = 1$ the function is decreasing (Fig. 3–4). This quadratic function can represent a cost function if and only if $x \geqq 1$; it does not represent a cost function for $0 \leqq x < 1$. The value of $Q(0) = 9/4$ has no economic significance and does *not* represent the overhead cost.

A study of the average cost function yields

$$q = \frac{1}{4}\left(x - 2 + \frac{9}{x}\right), \qquad q' = \frac{1}{4}\left(1 - \frac{9}{x^2}\right), \qquad q'' = \frac{9}{2x^3}.$$

---

* This is equivalent to the problem of solving three simultaneous linear equations in the three unknowns a, b, c.

There is a critical point at $x = 3$, where $q = 1$ and $q'' > 0$. Since q is large for very large or very small x, there is an absolute minimum average cost of 1 at $x = 3$. The average cost curve is also shown in Fig. 3-4, although the details have been omitted.

(c) *Exponential cost functions* and *logarithmic cost functions* involving $\ln (1 + x)$ are useful to represent functions that are always concave upward or always concave downward in a specified interval. (See Example 3-6 and problems 9 and 10 of Exercise Group 3-2.)

(d) *Cubic cost functions* may be used to represent a function whose concavity changes in the given x-interval. Care should be exercised to see that the function has no relative maximum or minimum, that is, that $Q'(x)$ is never zero. It is often found that the tangent at the point of inflection gives a good linear approximation to the cost function, within a limited range.

EXAMPLE 3-5.

$$Q(x) = x^3 - 3x^2 + 15x + 27,$$

$$Q'(x) = 3x^2 - 6x + 15 = 3(x^2 - 2x + 5)$$
$$= 3(x - 1)^2 + 12, \qquad \text{which is never zero,}$$

$$Q''(x) = 6x - 6.$$

x	Q	Q_1
0	27	28
1	40	40
2	53	52
3	72	64

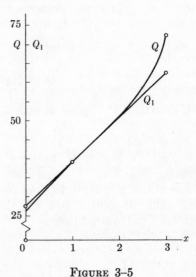

FIGURE 3-5

There is a point of inflection at $x = 1$, $Q = 40$. If $0 \leqq x < 1$, the curve is concave downward, and if $x > 1$, the curve is concave upward.

The slope of the curve at $x = 1$ is $Q'(1) = 12$. The equation of the inflectional tangent line may be found as follows. It has the form

$$Q_1 = 12x + b.$$

Since it must pass through the point (1, 40),

$$40 = 12 + b, \quad \text{or} \quad b = 28.$$

The line $Q_1 = 12x + 28$ is a good approximation to the cost function for the interval $0 \leq x \leq 2$. Figure 3–5 shows both the cubic curve and this line.

The *minimum average cost* can be determined from a consideration of $q(x)$ and its derivatives. [See Example 3–4 and Fig. 3–4. Note the corresponding geometrical situation obtained by drawing the graph of $q(x)$.] Necessary and sufficient conditions for minimum average cost are that $q'(x_0) = 0$ and that $q''(x_0) > 0$. These conditions can be expressed in terms of the total cost function and its derivative as follows:

$$Q = xq, \quad Q' = xq' + q, \quad Q'' = xq'' + q' + q'.$$

Since $q'(x_0) = 0$, it follows that

$$\frac{dQ(x_0)}{dx} = \frac{Q(x_0)}{x_0} \quad \text{and} \quad \frac{d^2Q(x_0)}{dx^2} > 0$$

are also necessary and sufficient conditions that the average cost be a minimum at $x = x_0$. A second geometric interpretation of minimum average cost, corresponding to the above equations, can be given in the total cost diagram (Figs. 3–4 and 3–6). If P is any point on the cost curve, then the slope $Q(x)/x$ of the line OP represents the average cost. Since the curve is ultimately concave upward ($Q''(x) > 0$), it appears intuitively from Fig. 3–6 that there will be a point $M(x_0, Q(x_0))$ such that the slope $Q(x_0)/x_0$ of line OM equals $Q'(x_0)$. For this value of $x = x_0$, $q(x)$ has its minimum value $q(x_0)$. If x_0 does not appear

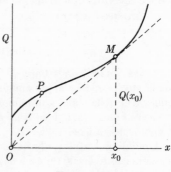

FIGURE 3–6

in the interval for which the total cost function is defined, the minimum average cost may appear at one of the end points of the interval.

EXAMPLE 3–6. Find the minimum average cost if the total cost function is $Q(x) = e^{x/5}$, $(0 \leqq x \leqq 10)$.

$$Q'(x) = \tfrac{1}{5}e^{x/5}, \qquad Q''(x) = \tfrac{1}{25}e^{x/5} > 0.$$

The cost curve is concave upward.

$$q(x) = \frac{e^{x/5}}{x},$$

$$q'(x) = \frac{\tfrac{1}{5}xe^{x/5} - e^{x/5}(1)}{x^2} = \frac{e^{x/5}}{5x^2}(x - 5),$$

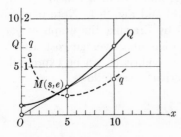

FIGURE 3–7

x	0	5	10	1
$Q(x)$	1	2.7	7.4	1.22
$Q'(x)$	0.2	0.54	1.5	
$q(x)$	∞	0.54	0.74	1.22
$q'(x)$		0		

and $q(x)$ has a critical point at $x = 5$. Since the slope changes from $-$ to $+$ as x increases through the value 5, there is a minimum value (absolute minimum) of $q(x) = 0.54$, which is consistent with the fact that the line joining the origin to the point $M(5, e)$ is tangent to the total cost curve. The corresponding curves are shown in the same diagram (Fig. 3–7), but since the variation in $q(x)$ near the critical point is small, units of different size are used for Q and q.

EXERCISE GROUP 3–2

1. It was found, over a ten-year period, that the cost of producing a certain grade of steel could be approximated by $Q = 56x + 182$, where Q is expressed in millions of dollars and x in millions of tons. Draw the total cost and average cost curves. Show that there is no minimum average cost, but that the average cost approaches a fixed value.

2. A building contractor has a fixed overhead expense of $25,000 a year, and other costs run to $6000 for each house he builds. (a) Express the total cost and average cost as functions of the number of houses built in a year. (b) Draw the total cost and average cost curves. (c) What is the smallest number of houses he must build in a year so that his average cost is less than $6400?

3. If the total cost function is $Q = 4 + 2x + x^2$, (a) find the minimum average cost, and (b) draw the cost and average cost curves.

4. If the total cost function is $Q = (1/50)x^2 + 6x + 200$, $(0 \leqq x \leqq 200)$, find the minimum average cost. Draw the total cost and average cost curves in different diagrams, using appropriate scale units.

5. (a) For what values of x is $Q = x^2 - 2x + 4$ an appropriate cost function? (b) Find the minimum average cost. (c) Draw appropriate diagrams.

6. Show that the total cost function $Q = \sqrt{x + 8}$, $(0 \leqq x \leqq 8)$, always has decreasing marginal cost and decreasing average cost.

7. If the total cost function is $Q = x^3 + x + 8$, (a) find the minimum average cost, (b) find the equation of the tangent line at the point of inflection, and (c) compare the graphs of the cost curve and the line between $x = 0$ and $x = 2$.

8. (a) Show that the equation $Q = x^3 - 6x^2 + 14x + 24$ may be used as a cost function. (b) Compare this cost curve with the equation of the tangent line at its point of inflection. (c) From the cost diagram, estimate the value of x which gives the minimum average cost. Do not attempt to solve the problem algebraically. However, it is useful to find the slope Q' at $(4, 48)$ and to compare it with the slope of the line joining the origin to this point.

9. If the cost curve is $Q = 4e^{x/4}$, $(0 \leqq x \leqq 8)$, find the minimum average cost and draw the cost and average cost curves.

10. (a) If the average cost function is $q = 8 + 4e^{-x}$, $(0 \leqq x \leqq 2)$, show that there are maximum and minimum average costs at the end points and that the average cost approaches a fixed value. (b) Sketch the average cost curve. (c) Using the relation $Q = xq$ and the graph of the q-curve, construct the Q-curve mechanically.

3–4 Revenue and marginal revenue. For any given demand function, the *total revenue* $R(x)$ is the product of x, the quantity demanded, and p, the price per unit quantity:

$$R = xp = x\,f(x) = R(x).$$

The *marginal revenue* with respect to demand, R', is defined as the derivative of the revenue:

$$R' = \frac{dR(x)}{dx} = R'(x).$$

(The derivative of R' is represented by R'' and has no other distinctive name.)

The graph of the function $R(x)$ is called the *revenue curve* and that of $R'(x)$ the *marginal revenue curve*. These curves are drawn by the use of intercepts, slopes, maximum and minimum values, and for purposes of comparison, are often drawn in the same diagram with the demand curve, using different vertical scales when necessary. Since x and p are always positive (or zero), so is R, and when either x or p is zero, $R = 0$. The marginal revenue R' may be positive or negative. That part of the marginal revenue curve where R' is negative should be included for those permissible values of x which are determined by the demand function.

We could consider R as a function of the price and define the *marginal revenue with respect to price* as dR/dp. This may be desirable when the demand function is given in the form $x = g(p)$ and when it is not easy to solve for p in terms of x. Since we have adopted the geometric convention that corresponds to taking x as the independent variable, implicit differentiation and the chain rule are used to find dR/dx and d^2R/dx^2 when the demand function is given in the form $x = g(p)$.

EXAMPLE 3–7.

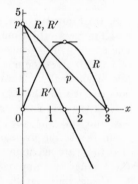

Demand law:
$$3x + 2p = 9,$$
$$p = \frac{9}{2} - \frac{3}{2}\,x;$$

Revenue:
$$R = \frac{9}{2}\,x - \frac{3}{2}\,x^2;$$

Marginal revenue:
$$R' = \frac{9}{2} - 3x,$$
$$R'' = -3.$$

FIGURE 3–8

Here $R = 0$ when $p = 0$ and $x = 3$, and when $x = 0$. There is a critical point $x = 3/2$, and since $R'' < 0$, the revenue curve has an absolute maximum at $x = 3/2$, where $R = 27/8$. The revenue curve, the straight lines corresponding to the demand curve and the marginal revenue curve are all shown in Fig. 3–8, where the same units are used for p, R, and R'.

EXAMPLE 3–8 (Fig. 3–9).

$$p = 6 - x^2, \qquad R = 6x - x^3,$$
$$R' = 6 - 3x^2, \qquad R'' = -6x < 0.$$

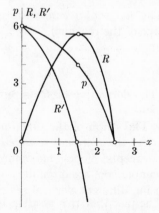

x	p	R	R'
0	6	0	6
$\sqrt{6}$	0	0	-12
$\sqrt{2}$	4	$4\sqrt{2}$ = Max. R	0

FIGURE 3–9

EXAMPLE 3–9 (Fig. 3–10).

$$p = \sqrt{9 - x}, \qquad R = x\sqrt{9 - x} = \sqrt{9x^2 - x^3} = u^{1/2},$$

where $u = 9x^2 - x^3$.

$$R' = \frac{1}{2} \cdot \frac{18x - 3x^2}{\sqrt{9x^2 - x^3}}$$

$$= \frac{3}{2} \cdot \frac{6 - x}{\sqrt{9 - x}} \cdot$$

The data used to draw the three curves are given in tabular form.

x	p	R	R'
0	3	0	3
5	2	10	3/4
8	1	8	-3
9	0	0	∞
6	$\sqrt{3}$	$6\sqrt{3}$	0

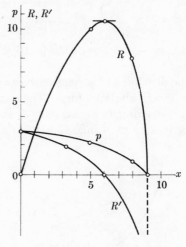

FIGURE 3–10

If the given demand law is solved for x, then

$$x = 9 - p^2, \quad \text{so that} \quad R = 9p - p^3;$$

$$\frac{dR}{dx} = \frac{dR/dp}{dx/dp}, \quad \text{and} \quad \frac{dR}{dx} = 0 \quad \text{when} \quad \frac{dR}{dp} = 0 = 9 - 3p^2.$$

This result leads to the critical point $p = \sqrt{3}$, $x = 6$, obtained before. Since $dx/dp = -2p$,

$$R' = \frac{dR}{dx} = \frac{9 - 3p^2}{-2p}; \qquad \frac{d^2R}{dx^2} = \frac{dR'}{dx} = \frac{dR'/dp}{dx/dp},$$

so that

$$\frac{d^2R}{dx^2} = \frac{[(-2p)(-6p) - (9 - 3p^2)(-2)]/4p^2}{-2p} = \frac{6p^2 + 18}{-8p^3} \cdot$$

The fact that this result is always negative shows that the revenue curve is concave downward.

EXAMPLE 3-10.

$$p = 10e^{-x/2} \qquad \text{(monotonically decreasing)},$$
$$R = 10xe^{-x/2},$$
$$R' = e^{-x/2}(10 - 5x),$$
$$R'' = e^{-x/2}[-5 - \tfrac{1}{2}(10 - 5x)]$$
$$= e^{-x/2}(-10 + \tfrac{5}{2}x).$$

The demand and revenue curves are shown in Fig. 3-11, and the data used are given in tabular form. The marginal revenue R' changes sign at $x = 2$, corresponding to a maximum R, and R'' changes sign at $x = 4$, corresponding to a point of inflection.

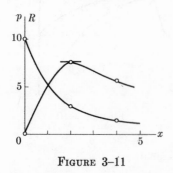

x	p	R	R'	R''
0	10	0	—	—
2	3.7	7.4	0	—
3	2.2	6.6		—
4	1.4	5.6		0

FIGURE 3-11

3-5 Maximum revenue from taxation. If an additive tax is placed upon a commodity in accordance with the conditions of Section 1-10, the total revenue T received by the government is

$$T = tx_1,$$

where x_1 is the equilibrium amount after taxation and t is the tax per unit quantity. The quantities t and x_1 are related through the demand and supply equations

$$\text{D:} \quad p_1 = f(x); \qquad \text{S:} \quad p_1 = F(x) + t.$$

(Since in this section it is not necessary to compare the old and new equilibrium conditions, the subscript on x is dropped.) If the tax t is considered as variable, it is easy to see that if $t = 0$ there is no revenue, and if the tax is large enough so that the demand becomes zero, there is no revenue. Hence, for some intermediate value the revenue T is a maximum. Since

T may be considered as a function either of t alone or of x alone, this maximum can be found by considering the marginal revenue either with respect to t or with respect to x. Since t occurs linearly in the relation between t and x, it is usually better to consider T as a function of x.

EXAMPLE 3–11. In Example 1–22, where the demand and supply functions were

$$3p + 2x = 27, \qquad p = \frac{3}{2} + \frac{x}{3} + t,$$

it was found that

$$x = \frac{15}{2} - t.$$

Hence

$$T = \frac{15}{2} t - t^2, \qquad \frac{dT}{dt} = \frac{15}{2} - 2t, \qquad \frac{d^2T}{dt^2} = -2.$$

The critical value of t is 15/4, and the corresponding values of x, p, and T are $x = 15/4$, $p = 13/2$, and $T_{max} = 225/16$.

EXAMPLE 3–12. If the demand law is $p = 20 - x^2$, and the supply law before imposition of an additive tax of t per unit is $p = 2 + x^2$, find the maximum revenue that can be obtained by the government. Illustrate geometrically.

The relation between t and x, after taxation, is

$$p = 20 - x^2 = 2 + x^2 + t,$$

$$t = 18 - 2x^2.$$

Hence

$$T = tx = 18x - 2x^3,$$

$$\frac{dT}{dx} = 18 - 6x^2.$$

The critical value is $x = \sqrt{3}$ and the other corresponding values are $p = 17$, $t = 12$, and $T_{max} = 12\sqrt{3} \doteq 20.8$.

Figure 3–12 shows the original demand curve, the supply curves corresponding to $t = 0$ and $t = 12$, the revenue curve T, and a parallelogram whose area corresponds to the maximum revenue.

The revenue T could have been expressed as a function of t:

$$T = tx = t\sqrt{\frac{18 - t}{2}} = \sqrt{\frac{18t^2 - t^3}{2}}.$$

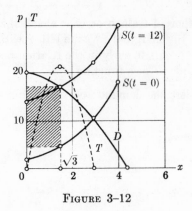

FIGURE 3–12

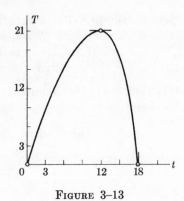

FIGURE 3–13

The corresponding curve is shown in Fig. 3–13.

$$\frac{dT}{dt} = \frac{1}{2}\left(\frac{18t^2 - t^3}{2}\right)^{-1/2}\left(\frac{36t - 3t^2}{2}\right) = \frac{3}{4}\left(\frac{18 - t}{2}\right)^{-1/2}(12 - t).$$

The critical value of $t = 12$ yields $x = \sqrt{3}$ and $T = 12\sqrt{3}$, as before, but the first solution is the simpler one.

EXERCISE GROUP 3–3

1. If the demand law is $3p = 105 - x$, find the maximum revenue. Draw the demand curve and the revenue and marginal revenue curves in the same diagram.

2. If the demand law is $3p + 2x = 27$, find the maximum revenue and draw the revenue curve.

3. If the demand curve is the straight line $(x/x_0) + (p/p_0) = 1$, show that the maximum revenue occurs for $x = x_0/2$ and has the value $p_0x_0/4$.

4. If the demand law is $p = 27 - 3x^2$, find the maximum revenue. Draw the demand curve and the revenue and marginal revenue curves in the same diagram.

5. If the demand law is $p = (10 - x)^2$, $(0 \leqq x \leqq 10)$, find the maximum revenue and draw the revenue curve.

6. If the demand law is $p = \sqrt{27 - x}$, express the revenue in terms of x alone and in terms of p alone. From each of these forms, find the maximum revenue and the corresponding prices and amounts.

7. If the demand law is $p = 8/(4 + x^2)$, determine the maximum revenue. Draw the demand and revenue curves in the same diagram.

8. If the demand law is $p = 8e^{-x/4}$, find the maximum revenue. Draw the demand and revenue curves in the same diagram.

9. If the demand curve is the generalized hyperbola $p = 12/\sqrt{x}$, $(1 \leqq x \leqq 9)$, show that the revenue is a monotonically increasing function of x, and hence has its maximum value at an end point.

10. The demand curve is the equilateral hyperbola $(x + 1)(p + 2) = 18$, x and p positive. Find the maximum revenue and draw the demand and revenue curves in the same diagram.

11. If the demand function is $p = 4 - 2x$ and the supply function is $p = 2 + x$ before an additive tax of t per unit is imposed, find the maximum revenue that can be obtained by the government. Illustrate geometrically.

12. If the demand and supply laws (including the tax) are

$$\text{D:} \quad 5x + 3p = 30; \qquad \text{S:} \quad p = 2 + x + t,$$

find the maximum revenue that the tax will yield. In a single diagram show the demand curve, the supply curves corresponding to $t = 0$ and to the tax that will yield the maximum revenue, and also the curve corresponding to T as a function of x.

13. If the demand law is $p = 39 - 3x^2$ and the supply law is $p = 3 + x^2$, find the maximum revenue obtained by imposing an additive tax of t per unit quantity. Illustrate geometrically, as in Example 3–12.

14. Proceed as in problem 13 for

$$\text{D:} \quad p = 45 - x^2; \qquad \text{S:} \quad p = 6 + 2x + t.$$

3–6 Profit under monopoly. Under a fixed price-demand law, the price the consumer must pay depends only upon the quantity demanded, and it is assumed here that this demand law, $p = f(x)$, is known. A *monopolist* is one who can control the price by regulating the supply of the commodity, so that if the supply is limited, the price is relatively high, and when the supply is increased, the price will decrease. If the monopolist knows the average cost q of producing each commodity as a function of the quantity produced, then the total cost function $Q = Q(x) = qx$. We also assume, "all other things being equal," that the monopolist will control the supply x and consequently the price p, determined by the known demand law, so as to maximize his profit. The revenue he receives is $R = px$, where $p = f(x)$, and the total profit Π is the difference between the total revenue and the total cost:

$$\Pi = R - Q = px - qx.$$

The necessary and sufficient conditions that Π have a relative maximum are

$$\Pi' = 0 \qquad \text{or} \qquad R' = Q',$$

and

$$\Pi'' < 0 \qquad \text{or} \qquad R'' < Q''$$

(where the primes denote differentiation with respect to x). It is further understood that the critical value of x must be in the interval for which the cost and demand functions have economic significance. If the demand law is given in the form $x = g(p)$, and it is not possible or convenient to solve for p in terms of x, the profit may be expressed as a function of p and the problem solved with p as the independent variable. Further, if the solution of the equation $R' = Q'$ requires methods not yet discussed, we can regard x as the independent variable and obtain an approximate solution by finding the point where the graphs of $R'(x)$ and $Q'(x)$ intersect.

EXAMPLE 3–13. Suppose the demand function is $p = 10 - 3x$, so that $R = 10x - 3x^2$, and that the average cost is $q = 3$, so that $Q = 3x$. Then

$$\Pi = 10x - 3x^2 - 3x = 7x - 3x^2,$$

$$\Pi' = 7 - 6x, \qquad \Pi'' = -6.$$

The critical value of x is $7/6$, the critical price is $13/2$, and the maximum profit $\Pi_{max} = 7 \cdot (7/6) - 3 \cdot (49/36) = 49/12$.

If p is considered as the independent variable, then $x = \frac{1}{3}(10 - p)$, $R = \frac{1}{3}(10p - p^2)$, and $Q = 10 - p$, so that

$$\Pi = -\frac{1}{3}\,p^2 + \frac{13}{3}\,p - 10,$$

$$\frac{d\Pi}{dp} = -\frac{2}{3}\,p + \frac{13}{3}, \qquad \frac{d^2\Pi}{dp^2} = -\frac{2}{3}.$$

The critical value of p is $13/2$, and

$$\Pi_{max} = -\frac{1}{3} \cdot \frac{169}{4} + \frac{13}{3} \cdot \frac{13}{2} - 10 = \frac{49}{12},$$

as before.

EXAMPLE 3–14. Suppose that $p = 12 - 4x$ and $Q = x^2 + 2x$. Then

$$R = 12x - 4x^2, \qquad q = x + 2,$$

$$R' = 12 - 8x, \qquad Q' = 2x + 2,$$

$$R'' = -8, \qquad Q'' = 2.$$

The condition $R' = Q'$ yields $12 - 8x = 2x + 2$, or $x = 1$. The condition $R'' < Q''$ is satisfied for all x, so that $x = 1$ corresponds to maximum profit. If $x = 1$, then $p = 8$, $q = 3$, $R = 8$, $Q = 3$, and $\Pi_{max} = 5$.

3–7 Geometric interpretation of maximum profit. Two geometric interpretations of the maximum profit under monopoly, illustrated by Example 3–13 (Figs. 3–14a and b) and Example 3–14 (Figs. 3–15a and b), will now be described.

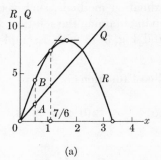

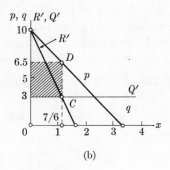

(a)   (b)

FIGURE 3–14

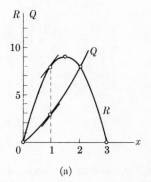

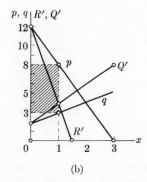

(a)   (b)

FIGURE 3–15

(a) If the revenue and total cost curves are drawn in the same diagram, then the vertical distance between them (AB in Fig. 3–14a) measures the profit corresponding to the quantity x. The maximum length of AB corresponds to the maximum profit. This occurs when $R' = Q'$, or for the value of x where the slopes of the curves are equal, that is, where the tangents at A and B, respectively, are parallel.

(b) If the marginal revenue and marginal cost curves are drawn in the same diagram (Fig. 3–14b), they intersect at a point which gives the critical value of x_0 corresponding to the maximum profit. If the demand curve $p = f(x)$ and the average cost curve $q = Q(x)/x$ are drawn in the same diagram, the ordinate through x_0 meets them in D and C, respectively, so that $CD = p - q$. Since $\Pi = x(p - q)$, the area of the rectangle of height CD and width x_0 represents the maximum profit. More generally, for any given x, the area of the rectangle of width x and height $p - q$ gives the profit. The area of this rectangle is greatest for the value of x_0, where the R'- and Q'-curves intersect.

These devices afford a graphic illustration of the economic situation and also provide a check on the algebraic processes. When the equation

$R' = Q'$ can be solved only by approximation methods, such geometric procedures are a first and important step in obtaining the solution. Figure 3–14 corresponds with Example 3–13 and Fig. 3–15 with Example 3–14. Two further examples are now given.

EXAMPLE 3–15. Let the demand and cost functions be

$$p = 10e^{-x/2} \quad \text{and} \quad Q = 5 + \frac{x}{4}, \quad (0 \leqq x \leqq 4),$$

Then

$$R = 10xe^{-x/2}, \quad R' = 5e^{-x/2}(2 - x), \quad Q' = \frac{1}{4}.$$

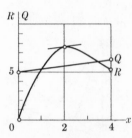

x	p	R	R'
0	10	0	10
2	3.7	7.4	0
4	1.4	5.6	−1.4

FIGURE 3–16

The equation $R' = Q'$ is solved by approximation methods, using geometric procedure (a). The revenue curve (Fig. 3–16) is drawn from the above table, using $e^{-1} = 0.37$, $e^{-2} = 0.14$.

The total cost curve is a straight line of slope $\frac{1}{4}$. The critical point occurs when $R' = \frac{1}{4}$ and hence must be just a little less than $x = 2$. By trial and interpolation from a table of the exponential function, a more accurate value of x_0 is found to be 1.88. The maximum profit is then

$$\Pi_{\max} = 10(1.88)(0.39) - 5.47 = 1.86$$

EXAMPLE 3–16. Let the demand law be $p = (10 - x)^2$, $(0 \leqq x \leqq 10)$, and the cost curve be $Q = 55x - 8x^2$, for the interval for which Q is monotonically increasing. Determine the maximum profit.

$$R = x(10 - x)^2 = x^3 - 20x^2 + 100x$$

$$R' = 3x^2 - 40x + 100 = (x - 10)(3x - 10),$$

$$Q = 55x - 8x^2, \quad Q' = 55 - 16x, \quad q = 55 - 8x.$$

The parabola $Q = 55x - 8x^2$ is monotonically increasing until $x = 55/16$, so that it represents a cost function for $0 \leqq x \leqq 55/16$. Hence in drawing the revenue and cost curves, the diagram (Fig. 3–17) may be limited to this range.

$$\text{II} = x^3 - 20x^2 + 100x - (55x - 8x^2) = x^3 - 12x^2 + 45x,$$

$$\text{II}' = 3x^2 - 24x + 45 = 3(x^2 - 8x + 15) = 3(x - 3)(x - 5),$$

$$\text{II}'' = 6x - 24.$$

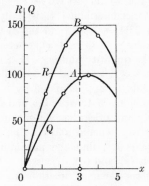

FIGURE 3–17

For $x = 3$, $\text{II}'' = -6 < 0$, and since $x = 3$ is within the permissible range, it corresponds to the maximum profit. (Note that $x = 5$ is not in the permissible range and, further, that II'' is then positive.)

$$\text{II}_{max} = 3(9 - 36 + 45) = 54.$$

The data used in drawing Figs. 3–17 and 3–18 are given in tabular form. Only a small part of the marginal revenue and marginal cost curves are shown (Fig. 3–18) near the point where they intersect. The demand and unit cost curves are shown, and the rectangle of height $p - q = 49 - 31 = 18$ and width $x_0 = 3$ is shaded to represent the maximum profit ($= 54$).

x	p	R	R'	Q	q	Q'
0	100	0	100	0	55	55
2	64	128		78		
3	49	147	7	93	31	7
10/3	400/9	148	0			
4	36	144		92	23	

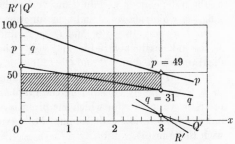

FIGURE 3–18

EXERCISE GROUP 3–4*

1. If the demand curve is $p = 20 - 4x$ and the average cost is constant, $q = 4$, find the maximum profit. First, consider the profit as a function of x, then as a function of p, and show that both methods lead to the same result.

---

*It is expected that this Exercise Group will require two assignments, even with a selection of problems.

2. If the demand and cost curves are $p = 12 - 4x$ and $Q = 8x - x^2$, $(0 \leqq x \leqq 3)$, find the maximum profit. Consider Π as a function of x and draw the profit curve. In another diagram draw the revenue and cost curves and illustrate the maximum profit geometrically.

3. If the demand and cost functions are $x = 75 - 3p$ and $Q = 100 + 3x$, find the maximum profit. Illustrate the solution geometrically by showing the marginal revenue and marginal cost curves to locate the critical point, and the demand and unit cost curves to show the maximum profit.

4. It was determined statistically that the demand for sugar could be expressed as $p = 2.34 - 1.34x$, and the average cost of production could be expressed as $q = 0.85x - 0.83 + (1/x)$, where x, p, and q are in convenient units. Determine the quantity and price that will maximize the profit.

5. It was determined statistically that the demand and cost of production of steel could be approximated by $p = 250 - 50x$ and $Q = 182 + 56x$, where x is in millions of tons and p and Q are in millions of dollars. Determine the quantity and price that will maximize the profit.

6. If the demand and cost functions are $p = 12 - 5x$, $(0 \leqq x \leqq 2)$, and $Q = x^3 + 3x^2$, find the maximum profit. Illustrate geometrically by both methods (a) and (b), discussed in the text.

7. If the demand function is $p = 20 - x^2$ and the average cost is $q = 5$, find the maximum profit. Illustrate geometrically in each of the following ways: (a) Sketch the profit curve. (b) Sketch the revenue and cost curves in the same diagram. (c) Sketch the demand and average cost curves in the same diagram and, using the critical value of x previously found, show a rectangle which represents the maximum profit.

8. Proceed as in problem 7 for $p = 36 - 2x^2$ and $q = 24$.

9. If $p = \sqrt{8 - x}$ and $Q = 3 + x$, find the maximum profit. Consider p as the independent variable, and verify the result geometrically by means of a diagram which shows R and Q as functions of x.

10. If $p = \sqrt{16 - 3x}$ and $Q = x$, find the maximum profit. Consider p as the independent variable, and verify the result geometrically by means of a diagram which shows R and Q as functions of x.

11. (a) Let the demand and cost functions be $p = \sqrt{9 - x}$ and $Q = x$, $(0 \leqq x \leqq 9)$. By considering the graphs of the revenue and cost curves, estimate the value of x for which the profit is a maximum. (b) Considering p as the independent variable, determine the maximum profit and compare the results with those in (a).

12. If the demand and cost functions are $p = 10/x^{3/4}$ and $Q = 5 + x$, find the quantity and price that will maximize the profit. Use logarithms to solve the equation $R' = Q'$.

13. If the demand law is $p = (x - 6)^2$, $(0 \leqq x \leqq 6)$, and the cost function is

$$Q = \frac{39}{4} x - x^2$$

for the interval for which Q is monotonically increasing, determine the maximum profit. Illustrate geometrically.

14. Proceed as in problem 13 for $p = (10 - x)^2$, $(0 \leqq x \leqq 10)$, and $Q = 51x - 6x^2$.

15. Let the demand and cost functions be $p = 8e^{-x/4}$ and $Q = 3 + (x/2)$, $(0 \leqq x \leqq 8)$. By considering the graphs of the revenue and cost curves, estimate the value of x for which the profit is a maximum and compute the value of the maximum profit.

16. Proceed as in problem 15 for $p = 10e^{-2x}$, $(0 \leqq x \leqq 1)$, and $q = (1/x) + \frac{1}{2}$.

3–8 Effect of taxation on monopoly. The imposition of a tax t per unit quantity upon a commodity produced by a monopolist raises the average cost by t and the total cost by tx. The new equilibrium price and quantity are then obtained by maximizing the profit, using the new cost function $Q_1 = Q + tx$. Hence

$$\Pi = R - Q_1 = R - Q - tx = x(p - q - t).$$

The necessary condition for maximum profit is

$$R' = Q'_1 = Q' + t,$$

while the sufficient condition remains $R'' < Q''$, since t is independent of x. Since the Q'_1 curve is the Q' curve translated upward a distance t, the critical amount produced will be decreased (Fig. 3–19), and hence, for a normal demand law, the price will be increased.

The total revenue received by the government is $T = tx_1$, where x_1 is the critical amount produced after the tax is imposed and T is a function of t which has the value zero if $t = 0$ and if t is just large enough to tax the product out of the market. Hence T has a maximum value which can be obtained in the usual way.

A subsidy s may be considered as a negative tax, and the general analysis remains unchanged. The new marginal cost curve is obtained by lowering the original marginal cost curve a distance equal to the amount of the subsidy; thus, for a normal demand law, the price will be decreased. There is, of course, no theoretical maximum amount the government might expend upon the subsidy.

If the tax imposed is a sales tax based upon the price to the consumer, say $t = rp$, where r is usually expressed in per cent, the profit equation can be obtained as follows. Let p be the price before taxation and p_1 the price after taxation, so that $p_1 = p(1 + r)$. It is the price p_1 that con-

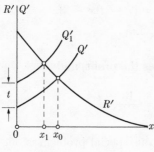

FIGURE 3–19

trols the demand and is used in the demand law, but the price p determines the revenue received by the monopolist. Hence

$$\Pi = R - Q = px - Q = \frac{p_1 x}{1 + r} - Q,$$

where p_1 and Q are functions of x.

EXAMPLE 3-17.   (Cf. Example 3-13 and Fig. 3-14.) (a) Suppose that the demand function is $p = 10 - 3x$, the average cost is $q = 3$, and that a tax of 1 per unit quantity produced is imposed on the monopolist. Find the quantity and price that correspond to the maximum profit. (b) Solve part (a) if the tax is t. Also determine the amount of the tax that maximizes the tax revenue. (c) Solve part (a) if the tax imposed is a 25% sales tax.

(a)
$$p = 10 - 3x, \qquad q_1 = 3 + 1 = 4,$$
$$R = 10x - 3x^2, \qquad Q_1 = 4x,$$
$$R' = 10 - 6x, \qquad Q_1' = 4,$$
$$R'' = -6,$$

$$\Pi = 10x - 3x^2 - 4x = 6x - 3x^2,$$
$$\Pi' = 6 - 6x,$$
$$\Pi'' = -6.$$

The critical value $x = 1$ maximizes Π; $p = 7$ and $\Pi_{\max} = 3$. (These results should be compared with those of Example 3-13.) The profit curve and the R'-Q' diagram are similar to those previously drawn and are left as an exercise.

(b) If the tax is t, $q_1 = 3 + t$ and $Q_1 = (3 + t)x$. Thus

$$\Pi = 10x - 3x^2 - (3 + t)x = (7 - t)x - 3x^2,$$
$$\Pi' = (7 - t) - 6x, \qquad \Pi'' = -6.$$

The critical value $x = (7 - t)/6$ maximizes the profit, and

$$p = 10 - 3\left(\frac{7 - t}{6}\right) = \frac{13 + t}{2},$$

which shows that the increase in price for this special problem is one-half the tax.

$$\Pi_{max} = \frac{(7-t)^2}{6} - 3\frac{(7-t)^2}{36} = \frac{(7-t)^2}{12},$$

$$T = tx = \frac{7t - t^2}{6}, \qquad \frac{dT}{dt} = \frac{7 - 2t}{6}, \qquad \frac{d^2T}{dt^2} = -\frac{2}{6}.$$

Hence the revenue T is a maximum for $t = 7/2$. For this value of t,

$$x = \frac{7}{12}, \qquad p = \frac{33}{4}, \qquad \Pi_{max} = \frac{49}{48}, \qquad T_{max} = \frac{49}{24}.$$

(c) $p_1 = 10 - 3x = p(1.25)$,   or $p = \frac{4}{5}(10 - 3x)$,

$$\Pi = \frac{4}{5}(10 - 3x) \cdot x - 3x = 5x - \frac{12}{5}x^2,$$

$$\Pi' = 5 - \frac{24}{5}x, \qquad \Pi'' < 0.$$

The critical value of x is 25/24. Corresponding to this value, $p_1 = 165/24$, $p = 132/24$, $t = pr = 33/24$, $T = (25/24)(33/24) \doteq 1.43$, and $\Pi_{max} = 125/48 \doteq 2.60$.

EXAMPLE 3–18. (Cf. Example 3–14 and Fig. 3–15.) If $p = 12 - 4x$, $Q = x^2 + 2x$, and an additive tax of t per unit quantity is imposed on the monopolist, determine the change in price, the maximum profit, and the revenue received by the government as functions of t. Then determine the maximum revenue that can be obtained by the government.

$$\Pi = (12x - 4x^2) - (x^2 + 2x + tx) = (10 - t)x - 5x^2,$$

$$\Pi' = (10 - t) - 10x, \qquad \Pi'' = -10 < 0.$$

The critical point $x = 1 - (t/10)$ maximizes the profit, and

$$p = 12 - 4\left(1 - \frac{t}{10}\right) = 8 + 0.4t;$$

hence the increase in price is $0.4t$.

$$\Pi_{max} = (10 - t)\left(1 - \frac{t}{10}\right) - 5\left(1 - \frac{t}{10}\right)^2 = \frac{(10 - t)^2}{20},$$

$$T = t - \frac{t^2}{10}, \qquad \frac{dT}{dt} = 1 - \frac{2t}{10}, \qquad \frac{d^2T}{dt^2} < 0.$$

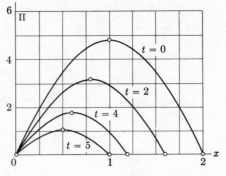

FIGURE 3–20

The critical value is $t = 5$, and $T_{max} = 2.5$. For each value of t, there is a profit curve (a parabola), with intercepts at $x = 0$ and $x = (10 - t)/5$. The highest point is at $x = (10 - t)/10$ and $\Pi = (10 - t)^2/20$. The curves for $t = 0, 2, 4, 5$ are shown in Fig. 3–20.

EXERCISE GROUP 3–5*

1. (a) Suppose that the demand function is $p = 20 - 4x$, the average cost is $q = 4$, and that a tax of $\frac{1}{2}$ per unit quantity produced is imposed on the monopolist. Find the quantity and price that correspond to the maximum profit and find the maximum profit. Illustrate geometrically. (b) Solve part (a), if the tax is t. Also interpret your result for the case where a subsidy is granted. (c) Determine the tax that maximizes the tax revenue, and determine the maximum tax revenue.

2. If $p = 12 - 4x, Q = 8x - x^2$, and an additive tax of t per unit quantity produced is imposed on a monopolist, determine the change in price, the maximum profit, and the revenue received by the government as functions of t. Then determine the maximum revenue that can be obtained by the government.

3. If the demand law is $x = 75 - 3p$ and the total cost function is

$$Q = 100 + 3x,$$

determine the maximum government revenue that can be obtained by the additive tax t for each unit of quantity produced by a monopolist.

4. If the demand law is $p = (10 - x)^2$ and the cost function is

$$Q = 55x - 8x^2,$$

show that the imposition of a tax of 9 per unit quantity produced by a monopolist increases the price by an amount greater than the tax.

---

* It is recommended that two assignments (selections from 1 through 7 and from 8 through 11) be used for this Exercise Group, since the problems are either long or fairly difficult.

5. If the demand and cost functions are $p = \sqrt{24 - x}$ and $Q = x$, and an additive tax of 2 per unit quantity produced is imposed on a monopolist, determine the price and quantity that maximize the profit. (Consider p as the independent variable.)

6. If the demand and cost functions are $p = \sqrt{8 - x}$ and $Q = 3 + x$, and an additive tax of $\frac{1}{2}$ per unit quantity produced is imposed upon a monopolist, determine the price and quantity that maximize the profit. (Consider p as the independent variable.)

7. If the demand and cost functions are $p = 10/x^{3/4}$ and $Q = 5 + x$, and the tax $t = 1$ is added to the average cost of production, determine the quantity and price that maximize the profit. Use logarithms to solve the equation $R' = Q_1'$.

8. Suppose that the demand function is $p = 20 - 4x$ and the average cost is $q = 4$. If a 10% sales tax is imposed on each unit produced by a monopolist, find the quantity and price that correspond to the maximum profit and find the maximum profit.

9. (a) If the demand law is $p = 12 - 5x$ and the cost function is

$$Q = x^3 + 3x^2,$$

determine the change in price due to the imposition of a tax of 2 per unit quantity produced by a monopolist. Find the corresponding profit. (b) Solve part (a) for a subsidy of 1 per unit quantity produced. (c) Solve part (a) for a sales tax of 20%.

10. Complete the three diagrams for part (a) of Example 3–17 (that is, the profit curve, the R-Q diagram, and the R'-Q' diagram showing the rectangle corresponding to maximum profit).

11. If the demand function is $p = 20 - x^2$ and the cost function after taxation is $Q_1 = (5 + t)x$, determine the maximum profit and the government revenue as functions of t. Also determine the value of t that maximizes the government revenue and find the maximum government revenue.

CHAPTER 4

INTRODUCTION TO INTEGRATION

4–1 Differentials. If $y = f(x)$ is a function that has a derivative $f'(x)$ for each x in a given interval $a \leq x \leq b$, and if dx is an independent variable which takes on arbitrary values, then the *differential of y* (written dy) is defined by

$$dy = f'(x)\, dx. \tag{4-1}$$

In earlier discussions Δx was considered as an independent variable; now Δx and dx are related by the equation

$$dx = \Delta x. \tag{4-2}$$

With this notation, the increment of y due to a change of dx in x is given by

$$\Delta y = f(x + dx) - f(x). \tag{4-3}$$

Note that dy and Δy are not identical but are approximately equal when dx is small. Since the derived function $f'(x)$ may be considered as the quotient of *differential* y by *differential* x, the notation dy/dx can therefore represent the derivative. On the other hand,

$$f'(x) = \lim_{dx \to 0} \frac{\Delta y}{dx},$$

and it is in this sense that dy/dx approximates $\Delta y/dx$, and hence Δy approximates dy.

A geometrical interpretation of the foregoing relation is useful (Fig. 4–1). If $P(x, y)$ and $Q(x + dx, y + \Delta y)$ are two points on the curve, with PT tangent to the curve

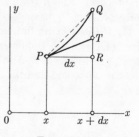

FIGURE 4–1

and PR parallel to the x-axis, then $PR = dx$, $RT = dy$, and $RQ = \Delta y$. The slope of the tangent is dy/dx, independent of the size of dx. The slope of the secant PQ is $\Delta y/dx$ and its limit, as $dx \to 0$, is dy/dx.

EXAMPLE 4–1. Let $y = f(x) = \ln x$, so that $f'(x) = 1/x$. Compare the values of dy and Δy for $x = 2$ and $dx = 0.1$.

$$dy = \frac{1}{x}\, dx = \frac{1}{2}\,(0.1) = 0.050,$$

$$\Delta y = \ln 2.1 - \ln 2 = \ln 1.05 = 0.049.$$

106

4–2 Inverse of differentiation. Indefinite integral. Every formula of differentiation can be written in differential form. The statements

$$\frac{dy}{dx} = F(x) \qquad \text{and} \qquad dy = F(x)\, dx$$

are equivalent. If $F(x)$ is a given continuous function of x in the interval $a \leq x \leq b$, it is natural to ask what the nature of y is, considered as a function of x, say $y = f(x)$. Since $f'(x) = F(x)$, we seek a function $f(x)$ whose derivative is the known function $F(x)$. The process of finding such a function, which is the inverse of differentiation, is known as *integration*. This operation is represented by the integral sign ($\int$) and is defined as follows:

$$\text{If} \quad dy = F(x)\, dx, \qquad \text{then} \quad y = \int F(x)\, dx.$$

[Read: "y is an (indefinite) integral of $F(x)\, dx$."]

Techniques of integration are intrinsically more difficult than those of differentiation, and it is easy to indicate indefinite integrals $\int F(x)\, dx$ for which the corresponding $f(x)$ cannot be expressed in terms of elementary functions of types already studied. This book treats the simpler cases of integration which involve reversing the formulas of differentiation given earlier. We recall that the derivative of a constant is zero, and hence the addition of an arbitrary constant to one function $f(x)$ gives another value for $\int F(x)\, dx$. Thus, if $f(x)$ is any function whose derivative is $F(x)$, then $f(x) + C$, where C is an arbitrary constant, is another such function. Conversely,* if $f(x)$ and $g(x)$ are continuous functions whose derivatives are both equal to $F(x)$, then $f(x) - g(x) = \text{const.}$

The following essential formulas of integration can be verified by differentiation:

$$\int x^n \, dx = \frac{x^{n+1}}{n+1} + C, \qquad (n \neq -1). \tag{4–4}$$

$$\int \frac{dx}{x} = \ln x + C, \qquad (x > 0). \tag{4–5}$$

$$\int e^x \, dx = e^x + C. \tag{4–6}$$

$$\int [F(x) + G(x)]\, dx = \int F(x)\, dx + \int G(x)\, dx. \tag{4–7}$$

---

* A complete proof depends upon a deeper study of the real number system than has been attempted here. See, for example, A. E. Taylor, *Advanced Calculus*, Ginn, 1955, or the article by M. K. Fort, Jr., in *American Mathematical Monthly*, **63**, p. 334, 1956.

$$\int k \, F(x) \, dx = k \int F(x) \, dx. \tag{4-8}$$

Finally, if the substitution $g(x) = u$, $g'(x) \, dx = du$ yields

$$\int F(x) \, dx = \int G(u) \, du,$$

and this new integral can be evaluated, then the original integral can be found.

EXAMPLE 4–2.

$$\int (x^3 - 4x^2 + 6) \, dx = \frac{x^4}{4} - \frac{4x^3}{3} + 6x + C. \tag{4-9}$$

EXAMPLE 4–3.

$$\int \frac{dx}{1 + x} = \int \frac{du}{u} = \ln u + C = \ln (1 + x) + C, \quad (x > -1), \tag{4-10}$$

where the solution was obtained by setting $1 + x = u$ and $dx = du$.

EXAMPLE 4–4.

$$\int e^{kx} \, dx = \frac{e^{kx}}{k} + C. \tag{4-11}$$

Equation (4–11) can be verified by differentiation or by using the substitution $u = kx$, $du = k \, dx$:

$$\int e^{kx} \, dx = \int e^u \frac{du}{k} = \frac{1}{k} e^u + C = \frac{e^{kx}}{k} + C.$$

EXAMPLE 4–5. If $y = x \ln x - x$, then

$$\frac{dy}{dx} = \frac{x}{x} + \ln x - 1 = \ln x.$$

Hence

$$\int \ln x \, dx = x \ln x - x + C. \tag{4-12}$$

($x > 0$ is required for the differentiation of y.)

Many indefinite integrals can be obtained in the manner just illustrated, and differentiation is one of the best ways to verify the result. The method of substitution is especially valuable when the integral contains the square root of a linear function.

EXAMPLE 4–6. To evaluate

$$\int \sqrt{9 - x}\, dx,$$

set $u = \sqrt{9 - x}$ or $x = 9 - u^2$. Then $dx = -2u\, du$, and

$$\int \sqrt{9 - x}\, dx = \int u\, (-2u\, du) = -2\int u^2\, du$$

$$= \frac{-2}{3} u^3 + C = -\frac{2}{3}(9 - x)^{3/2} + C. \quad (4\text{–}13)$$

EXAMPLE 4–7.

$$\int \frac{dx}{\sqrt{9 - x}} = -2\int \frac{u\, du}{u} = -2\sqrt{9 - x} + C, \quad (4\text{–}14)$$

where $u = \sqrt{9 - x}$.

EXERCISE GROUP 4–1

1. If $y = \ln x$, compare the values of dy and Δy where $x = 5$ and dx has the successive values 1, 0.1, 0.01.

2. If $y = [8/(x + 1)] - 2$, compare the values of dy and Δy where $x = 2$ and dx takes the values 1, 1/2, 1/4, 1/10.

3. Compare the values of dy and Δy, if $x = 0.5$ and $dx = 0.1$, for

(a) $y = (1 + x)^2$,   (b) $y = (1 + x)^{1/2}$.

4. If the demand law is $p = 20 - x^2$, compare the elasticity of demand with $(dx/x)/(\Delta p/p)$, where $x = 2$ and $dx = 0.1$.

5. Evaluate the following indefinite integrals:

(a) $\displaystyle \int (x^2 + 6x - 3)\, dx$ (b) $\displaystyle \int \left(x^3 + x + \frac{1}{x} + \frac{1}{x^3} \right) dx$

(c) $\displaystyle \int \left(\sqrt{x} + \frac{1}{\sqrt{x}} \right) dx$ (d) $\displaystyle \int (1 - x)(1 + x)(1 + x^2)\, dx$

6. Evaluate each of the following:

(a) $\displaystyle \int \frac{dx}{2 + x}$ (b) $\displaystyle \int \frac{dx}{1 + 2x}$

(c) $\displaystyle \int e^{-2x}\, dx$ (d) $\displaystyle \int e^{x/2}\, dx$

7. (a) Find the derivative of $x \ln x$, and hence determine

$$\int (1 + \ln x)\, dx.$$

(b) Find the derivative of $x^2 \ln x$, and hence determine

$$\int (x + 2x \ln x)\, dx \qquad \text{and} \qquad \int 2x \ln x\, dx.$$

8. Using the substitution $u = \sqrt{8 - x}$, evaluate the following integrals. Verify by differentiation.

(a) $\displaystyle\int \sqrt{8 - x}\, dx$ (b) $\displaystyle\int x\sqrt{8 - x}\, dx$

(c) $\displaystyle\int \frac{dx}{\sqrt{8 - x}}$ (d) $\displaystyle\int \frac{x\, dx}{\sqrt{8 - x}}$

4–3. Marginal revenue and marginal cost. The constant of integration can be evaluated if the value of the integral is known for one value of x. If the marginal revenue is given as a function of x, the revenues can be found by integration. The initial condition that if the quantity $x = 0$, then the revenue $R = 0$, may be used to evaluate the constant of integration. Several examples follow.

EXAMPLE 4–8. If $R' = dR/dx = (9/2) - 3x$, then

$$R = \frac{9}{2} x - \frac{3x^2}{2} + C,$$

$$0 = \frac{9}{2} \cdot 0 - \frac{3}{2} \cdot 0 + C, \qquad \text{or} \quad C = 0.$$

Hence

$$R = \frac{9}{2} x - \frac{3x^2}{2} \qquad \text{and} \qquad p = \frac{9}{2} - \frac{3}{2} x.$$

EXAMPLE 4–9. If $R' = 100 - 40x + 3x^2$, then

$$R = \int (100 - 40x + 3x^2)\, dx$$
$$= 100x - 20x^2 + x^3 + C = x(10 - x)^2 + C.$$

Since $R = 0$ when $x = 0$, a simple calculation shows that $C = 0$. Hence

$$R = x(10 - x)^2 \qquad \text{and} \qquad p = (10 - x)^2.$$

EXAMPLE 4–10. If

$$R' = \frac{3}{2}\frac{6-x}{\sqrt{9-x}},$$

the procedure is not so direct, but the substitution $u = \sqrt{9-x}$ reduces the integral to one that can be evaluated. In this case, $x = 9 - u^2$ and $dx = -2u\, du$:

$$R = \frac{3}{2}\int \frac{6-x}{\sqrt{9-x}}\, dx = \frac{3}{2}\int \frac{(6-9+u^2)\,(-2u\, du)}{u}$$

$$= \int (9 - 3u^2)\, du = 9u - u^3 + C$$

$$= u(9 - u^2) + C = x\sqrt{9-x} + C.$$

Since $R = 0$ if $x = 0$, then $C = 0$. Hence

$$R = x\sqrt{9-x} \quad \text{and} \quad p = \sqrt{9-x}.$$

The interval for which the given marginal revenue law holds may not always extend to zero. This is the case for the following example.

EXAMPLE 4–11. If the marginal revenue is $R' = (1/x^2) - (1/x)$, and $R(1) = 3$, discuss the revenue curve.

$$R' = \frac{1-x}{x^2}, \qquad R'' = \frac{x-2}{x^3}.$$

The revenue curve has an absolute maximum at $x = 1$ and a point of inflection at $x = 2$.

$$R(x) = \int \left(\frac{1}{x^2} - \frac{1}{x}\right) dx = -\frac{1}{x} - \ln x + C,$$

$$3 = -1 - 0 + C, \quad \text{or} \quad C = 4,$$

$$R(x) = 4 - \frac{1}{x} - \ln x;$$

$$R(\tfrac{1}{2}) = 4 - 2 + 0.69 = 2.69, \qquad R(2) = 4 - \tfrac{1}{2} - 0.69 = 2.81,$$

$$R(\tfrac{1}{4}) = 4 - 4 + 1.38 = 1.38, \qquad R(4) = 4 - \tfrac{1}{4} - 1.38 = 2.37.$$

From these data the curve $R(x)$, $(\tfrac{1}{4} \leq x \leq 4)$, is drawn (Fig. 4–2).

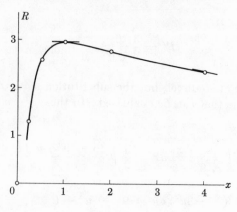

FIGURE 4–2

If the marginal cost function is known, the cost function can be found by integration. The constant of integration can be evaluated if the initial overhead ($Q_0 \geqq 0$) or the value of Q for one x is known.

EXAMPLE 4–12. If $Q' = \frac{2}{5}e^{x/5}$ and $Q(0) = 1$, find $Q(x)$ and $Q(5)$.

$$Q(x) = \frac{2}{5}\int e^{x/5}\,dx = 2e^{x/5} + C,$$

$$1 = 2 + C, \quad \text{or} \quad C = -1,$$

$$Q(x) = 2e^{x/5} - 1, \quad Q(5) = 2e - 1 \doteq 4.44.$$

EXAMPLE 4–13.   If the marginal cost function is $Q' = \frac{1}{2}(x - 1)$, ($x \geqq 1$), and if $Q(1) = 2$, find the cost function. (The limitation $x \geqq 1$ is essential since the marginal cost cannot be negative. To evaluate the constant of integration, a value of Q for some value of $x \geqq 1$ is needed.)

$$Q = \frac{1}{2}\int (x - 1)\,dx = \frac{x^2}{4} - \frac{x}{2} + C,$$

$$2 = \frac{1}{4} - \frac{1}{2} + C, \quad \text{or} \quad C = \frac{9}{4},$$

$$Q(x) = \frac{1}{4}(x^2 - 2x + 9), \quad (x \geqq 1).$$

EXERCISE GROUP 4–2

1. If the marginal revenue is $R' = 12 - 3x$, determine the revenue and demand functions.

2. If the marginal revenue is $R' = 12 - 3x^2$, determine the revenue and demand functions.

3. (a) If the marginal revenue is a constant different from zero, prove that the price is constant. (b) What is the nature of the demand curve if $R' = 0$ and $R(0) \neq 0$?

4. If the marginal revenue function is $R' = 12 - 8x + x^2$, determine the revenue and demand functions. What limitation is placed on x?

5. If the marginal revenue function is $R' = 4 - 6x - 2x^2$, determine the revenue and demand functions.

6. If the marginal cost is $Q' = 3 + 4x^2 + \frac{1}{2}e^{-x}$, and $Q(0) = 5$, find $Q(2)$.

7. (a) If the marginal cost function is $Q' = 2x + 1$, and $Q(1) = 4$, find the cost function. (b) If the marginal cost function is $Q' = 2x - 1$, and $Q(1) = 4$, find the cost function. What can be said about the "initial overhead" in parts (a) and (b)?

8. If the marginal cost is $Q'(x) = \ln x$, ($x \geq 1$), determine the cost function (a) if $Q(1) = 3$, and (b) if $Q(2) = 3$. (For the indefinite integral, see Eq. 4–12.)

9. If the marginal cost is constant, prove that the total cost curve is a straight line.

10. If the marginal revenue is $R' = 3(2 - x)/(2\sqrt{3 - x})$, find the revenue function and draw the revenue curve.

11. If the marginal revenue is $R' = 3(6 - x)/\sqrt{18 - 2x}$, find the revenue function and draw the revenue curve.

12. If the marginal revenue is $R' = (2/x^2) - (1/x)$, and $R(2) = 4$, discuss and draw the revenue curve from $x = \frac{1}{4}$ to $x = 8$.

4–4 The definite integral. Suppose that $F(x)$ is a positive, single-valued, continuous function of x defined in the interval $a \leq x \leq b$ (Fig. 4–3). Let the interval be divided into n equal parts, each of length

$$\Delta x = \frac{b - a}{n},$$

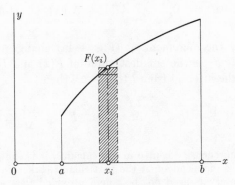

FIGURE 4–3

so that as $n \to \infty$, $\Delta x \to 0$. In each subinterval select some x, $(x = x_i)$, and form the product $F(x_i)\,\Delta x$. Add all such products together to form the sum

$$[F(x_1) + F(x_2) + \cdots + F(x_n)]\,\Delta x = \sum_{i=1}^{i=n} F(x_i)\,\Delta x.$$

(The summation symbol is read: "The sum from $i = 1$ to $i = n$ of F of x_i times Δx.") The definite integral is then given by*

$$\int_a^b F(x)\,dx = \lim_{\Delta x \to 0} \sum_{i=1}^{i=n} F(x_i)\,\Delta x. \qquad (4\text{--}15)$$

(The left member is read: "The integral from a to b of $F(x)\,dx$.") The limit of this sum is also used to define the area bounded by the x-axis, the curve, and the vertical lines $x = a$ and $x = b$:

$$\text{Area}\,\bigg|_a^b = \int_a^b F(x)\,dx. \qquad (4\text{--}16)$$

This geometric interpretation helps us evaluate the definite integral (Eq. 4–15) by means of indefinite integrals.

Let a be fixed and b vary, and for emphasis replace b by t. Then

$$\text{Area}\,\bigg|_a^t = \int_a^t F(x)\,dx = A(t).$$

That is, this variable area is a function of t, represented by $A(t)$, with the special properties

$$A(a) = \text{Area}\,\bigg|_a^a = 0, \qquad A(b) = \text{Area}\,\bigg|_a^b \qquad \text{(total area)}.$$

A change in t by the increment Δt (Fig. 4–4a) changes the area by an increment ΔA. If F_1 is the smallest value of $F(x)$ and F_2 is the largest value of $F(x)$ in the interval from t to $t + \Delta t$, then

$$F_1\,\Delta t \le \Delta A \le F_2\,\Delta t, \qquad \text{or} \qquad F_1 \le \frac{\Delta A}{\Delta t} \le F_2.$$

---

* In a more comprehensive course in the calculus, it is shown that the limit does exist, that it is independent of the particular x_i taken in the subinterval, and that the subintervals need not be equal, provided they all approach zero in the limit.

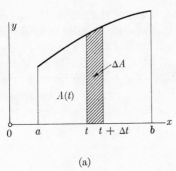

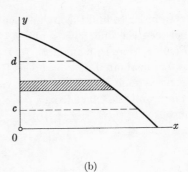

(a) (b)

FIGURE 4–4

Since the function F is continuous, as $\Delta t \to 0$, F_1 and F_2 both approach $F(t)$, and hence

$$\lim_{\Delta t \to 0} \frac{\Delta A}{\Delta t} = \frac{dA(t)}{dt} = F(t).$$

Let $f(t)$ be an indefinite integral of $F(t) \, dt$. Then

$$\frac{df(t)}{dt} = F(t), \quad \text{or} \quad f(t) = \int F(t) \, dt.$$

We have

$$A(t) = f(t) + C,$$

where C is a constant. If $t = a$,

$$A(a) = 0 = f(a) + C,$$

so that $C = -f(a)$ and

$$A(t) = f(t) - f(a).$$

If $t = b$,

$$\text{Area} \Big|_a^b = A(b) = f(b) - f(a).$$

If t is replaced by x, the result may be summarized as follows:

$$\text{Area} \Big|_a^b = \int_a^b F(x) \, dx = f(x) \Big|_a^b = f(b) - f(a), \qquad (4\text{–}17)$$

where $f(x) = \int F(x) \, dx$.

In order to find the area above the x-axis and below the curve $y = F(x)$ between the lines $x = a$ and $x = b$, we first find an indefinite integral of $F(x)\,dx$, that is, a function $f(x)$ whose derivative is $F(x)$. Then the area is $f(x)$ evaluated at $x = b$ less $f(x)$ evaluated at $x = a$. Similarly, if the curve is such that x is a single-valued function of y, the area between the y-axis and the curve from $y = c$ to $y = d$ is $\int_c^d x\,dy$, where x is expressed in terms of y (cf. Fig. 4–4b).

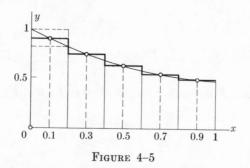

FIGURE 4–5

EXAMPLE 4–14. Using five subintervals, determine an approximation to the area under the curve $y = 1/(1 + x)$ from $x = 0$ to $x = 1$. Verify the result by integration.

The function is monotonically decreasing; if the left ends of the sub-intervals are used for x_i, the result is larger than the area; if the right ends of the subintervals are used, the result is smaller than the area. The mid-points of the subintervals afford a compromise (Fig. 4–5):

$$\text{Area} = 0.2 \left[\frac{1}{1.1} + \frac{1}{1.3} + \frac{1}{1.5} + \frac{1}{1.7} + \frac{1}{1.9} \right]$$

$$= 0.2\,[0.909 + 0.769 + 0.667 + 0.588 + 0.526] \doteq 0.692,$$

$$\text{Area} = \int_0^1 \frac{dx}{1 + x} = \ln (1 + x) \Big|_0^1 = \ln 2 - \ln 1 = 0.693.$$

EXAMPLE 4–15. The integral

$$\int_0^1 e^{-x^2}\,dx$$

is closely related to the "probability integral" but cannot be evaluated in terms of elementary functions. An approximation to this integral can be found by using five subintervals and their midpoints:

$$\int_0^1 e^{-x^2}\, dx \doteq 0.2\,[e^{-0.01} + e^{-0.09} + e^{-0.25} + e^{-0.49} + e^{-0.81}]$$

$$\doteq 0.2\,[0.990 + 0.914 + 0.779 + 0.613 + 0.445] = 0.748.$$

More precise results can be obtained by using more subintervals.

EXAMPLE 4–16.   Find the area between the parabola $R = 4x - x^2$ and the x-axis (Fig. 4–6).

$$A = \int_0^4 (4x - x^2)\, dx = \left(2x^2 - \frac{x^3}{3}\right)\Bigg|_0^4 = \left(32 - \frac{64}{3}\right) - 0 = \frac{32}{3}.$$

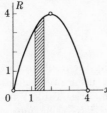

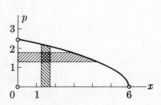

FIGURE 4–6   FIGURE 4–7

EXAMPLE 4–17.   Find the area bounded by the parabola $p = \sqrt{6 - x}$ and the coordinate axes.

Figure 4–7 shows the part of the parabola in the first quadrant, an element of area parallel to the p-axis corresponding to $p\, dx$, and an element of area parallel to the x-axis corresponding to $x\, dp$. If $p = \sqrt{6 - x}$, then $x = 6 - p^2$, and the area can be expressed as

$$A = \int_0^6 p\, dx = \int_0^6 \sqrt{6 - x}\, dx,$$

or

$$A = \int_0^{\sqrt{6}} x\, dp = \int_0^{\sqrt{6}} (6 - p^2)\, dp.$$

Both of the above integrals give $A = 4\sqrt{6}$.

EXERCISE GROUP 4–3

1. (a) Find the area bounded by the parabola $y = 6x - x^2$ and the x-axis.
(b) Find the area bounded by the parabola $y = 9 - (x^2/4)$ and the coordinate axes. Show both parabolas in the same diagram.

2. (a) Find the area bounded by the parabola $y = 5x - x^2$ and the x-axis. (b) Find the area bounded by the parabola $y = (25 - x^2)/4$ and the coordinate axes. Show both parabolas in the same diagram.

3. Evaluate the two integrals of Example 4–17, giving the area bounded by the parabola $p = \sqrt{6 - x}$ and the coordinate axes.

4. Find the area bounded by the parabola $p = \sqrt{9 - 2x}$ and the coordinate axes in two ways. Draw the appropriate diagram.

5. (a) Find the area bounded by the parabola $y = (6 - x)^2$, $(0 \leqq x \leqq 6)$, and the coordinate axes, using $A = \int y \, dx$. (b) Find the same area using $A = \int x \, dy$. Draw the appropriate diagram.

6. (a) Find the area bounded by the parabola $y = (4 - x)^2$, the x-axis, and the line $x = 2$, using $A = \int y \, dx$. (b) Find the same area using $A = \int x \, dy$ and the area of a rectangle. Draw the appropriate diagram.

7. Determine an approximation to

$$\int_1^2 \frac{15 \, dx}{1 + 2x},$$

using five subintervals and their midpoints. Verify the result by integration.

8. Determine an approximation to $\int_0^1 e^{-x} \, dx$, using five subintervals and their midpoints. Verify the results by integration. (Use Table V in Appendix.)

9. (a) Determine an approximation to $\int_0^2 e^{-x^2/2} \, dx$, using four subintervals and their midpoints. (b) Proceed as in part (a), using the left end points and right end points of the same subintervals, and average these results. (Use Table V in Appendix.)

10. Determine an approximation to $\int_1^2 \ln x \, dx$, using five subintervals and their midpoints. Verify the result by integration. ($\int \ln x \, dx = x \ln x - x + C$.)

4–5 Consumers' surplus and producers' surplus.

If a demand curve is given and the market demand x_0 and the corresponding price p_0 are determined in some way—such as under pure competition, under monopoly, or arbitrarily—consumers who would have been willing to pay more than the market price p_0 have gained by the setting of the price at p_0 rather than at the maximum price they would have been willing to pay. Under certain economic assumptions the total consumer gain is represented (Fig. 4–8) by the area above the horizontal line $p = p_0$ and below the demand curve, and is called the *consumers' surplus*.* This surplus is evaluated as the area under the demand curve less the area of the rectangle

---

* For a critique of the significance of this concept, see P. A. Samuelson, *Foundations of Economic Analysis*, pp. 195 ff, Harvard University Press, 1947. The concept is discussed here because it occurs in economic literature and affords a simple illustration of integration applications.

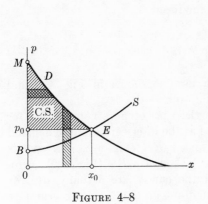

FIGURE 4–8

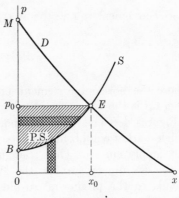

FIGURE 4–9

whose dimensions are x_0 and p_0. Hence, using vertical elements of area shown in Fig. 4–8,

$$\text{C.S.} = \int_0^{x_0} p_D \, dx - (p_0 x_0), \qquad (4\text{–}18)$$

where p_D is a function of x (the subscript is used to emphasize the notion of demand). If the demand law is given in the form $x = g(p)$, the area may be found from the form

$$\text{C.S.} = \int_{p_0}^{M} x \, dp, \qquad (4\text{–}19)$$

where the horizontal element of area used is shown in Fig. 4–8 and where M is the value of p_D corresponding to $x = 0$.

If a supply curve is given and if the amount supplied, x_0, and the corresponding price p_0 are determined in some way, producers who would have been willing to supply the commodity below the price p_0 have gained by the setting of the price at p_0. The total producer gain is represented in Fig. 4–9 by the area below the horizontal line $p = p_0$ and above the supply curve, and is called the *producers' surplus*. This surplus is evaluated as the area of the rectangle whose dimensions are x_0 and p_0 less the area under the supply curve. Hence, using vertical elements of area shown in Fig. 4–9,

$$\text{P.S.} = (p_0 x_0) - \int_0^{x_0} p_S \, dx, \qquad (4\text{–}20)$$

where p_S is a function of x (the subscript is used to emphasize the notion of supply). If the supply law is given in the form $x = G(p)$, it may be more convenient to find the area from the form

$$\text{P.S.} = \int_{B}^{p_0} x \, dp, \tag{4-21}$$

where the horizontal element of area used is shown in Fig. 4–9 and where B is the value of p_S corresponding to $x = 0$.

Figures 4–8 and 4–9 correspond to the case of pure competition for which market equilibrium is determined as the intersection of the demand and supply curves. The "triangular" area p_0EM (Fig. 4–8) corresponds to the consumers' surplus; the "triangular" area p_0BE (Fig. 4–9) corresponds to the producers' surplus. If the curves are actually straight lines, the results may be found without integration. A few examples are now given to illustrate the economic concepts involved and the techniques of integration.

EXAMPLE 4–18. If the demand function is $p = 35 - 2x - x^2$, and if $x_0 = 3$, find the consumers' surplus.

$$p = (7 + x)(5 - x); \quad \text{if} \quad x_0 = 3, p_0 = 20.$$

The demand curve is part of a parabola (Fig. 4–10).

$$\text{C.S.} = \int_{0}^{3} (35 - 2x - x^2) \, dx - 60 = \left(35x - x^2 - \frac{x^3}{3}\right)\Big|_{0}^{3} - 60$$

$$= 105 - 9 - 9 - 60 = 27.$$

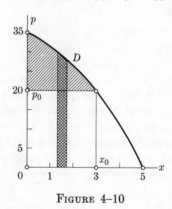

FIGURE 4–10

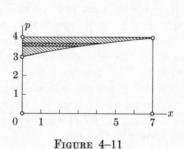

FIGURE 4–11

EXAMPLE 4–19. If the supply curve is $p = \sqrt{9 + x}$, and $x_0 = 7$, find the producers' surplus.

$$\text{If} \quad x_0 = 7, p_0 = 4; \quad \text{if} \quad x = 0, p = 3; \quad x = p^2 - 9.$$

If Eq. (4–21) is used,

$$\text{P.S.} = \int_3^4 (p^2 - 9)\, dp = \left(\frac{p^3}{3} - 9p\right)\Bigg|_3^4 = \frac{64}{3} - 36 - \frac{27}{3} + 27 = \frac{10}{3}$$

(see Fig. 4–11). If Eq. 4–20 is used,

$$\text{P.S.} = 28 - \int_0^7 \sqrt{9 + x}\, dx,$$

which yields the same result.

EXAMPLE 4–20. If the supply curve is $p = 4e^{x/3}$, and $x_0 = 3$, find the producers' surplus.

If $x_0 = 3$, then $p_0 = 4e$. Using Eq. (4–20), we find

$$\text{P.S.} = 12e - 4\int_0^3 e^{x/3}\, dx = 12e - 12e^{x/3}\Bigg|_0^3$$

$$= 12e - 12e + 12 = 12.$$

EXAMPLE 4–21. If the demand curve is the part of the equilateral hyperbola

$$p = \frac{8}{x + 1} - 2 = \frac{6 - 2x}{x + 1}$$

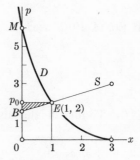

FIGURE 4–12

in the first quadrant, and the supply curve is $p = \frac{1}{2}(x + 3)$, find the consumers' surplus and the producers' surplus under pure competition.

The equilibrium point $E(x_0, p_0)$ is found by solving the given equations simultaneously:

$$\frac{6 - 2x}{x + 1} = \frac{x + 3}{2}, \qquad 12 - 4x = x^2 + 4x + 3,$$

$$x^2 + 8x - 9 = 0, \qquad (x - 1)(x + 9) = 0,$$

so that $x_0 = 1$, $p_0 = 2$. Hence, from Eq. (4–18),

$$\text{C.S.} = \int_0^1 \left(\frac{8}{x + 1} - 2\right) dx - 2 = [8 \ln (x + 1) - 2x]_0^1 - 2$$

$$= 8 \ln 2 - 2 - 0 - 2 = 8(0.693) - 4 = 1.54.$$

The producers' surplus can be found without integration and is represented (Fig. 4–12) by a right triangle whose area is $\frac{1}{2} \cdot \frac{1}{2} \cdot 1 = \frac{1}{4}$.

EXAMPLE 4–22. The demand and supply curves are $p_D = (6 - x)^2$, $(0 \leq x \leq 6)$, and $p_S = 14 + x$, respectively. Find the consumers' surplus (a) if the demand and price are determined under pure competition, and (b) if the demand and price are determined under a monopoly so as to maximize the profit, and the supply function is identified with the marginal cost function.*

(a) Market equilibrium conditions are found from

$$p = (6 - x)^2 = 14 + x$$

to be $x_0 = 2$, $p_0 = 16$. Hence, from Eq. (4–18),

$$\text{C.S.} = \int_0^2 (36 - 12x + x^2)\, dx - 32$$

$$= \left(36x - 6x^2 + \frac{x^3}{3}\right)\Big|_0^2 - 32 = 72 - 24 + \frac{8}{3} - 32 = \frac{56}{3}.$$

If Eq. (4–19) is used, the same result is given by

$$\text{C.S.} = \int_{16}^{36} (6 - p^{1/2})\, dp.$$

(b) To find the demand and price under monopoly, we have

$$R = 36x - 12x^2 + x^3, \qquad Q' = 14 + x,$$

$$R' = 36 - 24x + 3x^2 = 14 + x,$$

$$3x^2 - 25x + 22 = 0,$$

$$(x - 1)(3x - 22) = 0.$$

Hence $x_0 = 1$, $p_0 = 25$, and (from Eq. 4–18)

$$\text{C.S.} = \int_0^1 (36 - 12x + x^2)\, dx - 25 = \frac{16}{3}.$$

---

* For a justification of this identification, see P. A. Samuelson, *Foundations of Economic Analysis*, p. 41. Under certain assumptions of stability, if the price is considered as a fixed parameter and the profit is maximized, then $\Pi = px - Q$ implies $d\,\Pi/dx = 0 = p - (dQ/dx)$, and the marginal cost is the price.

Exercise Group 4–4

1. If the demand law is $p = 85 - 4x - x^2$, find the consumers' surplus (a) if $x_0 = 5$, and (b) if $p_0 = 64$.

2. If the demand law is $p = 39 - 3x^2$, find the consumers' surplus (a) if $x_0 = 5/2$, and (b) if the commodity is free, that is, $p_0 = 0$.

3. If the demand law is $p = \sqrt{9 - x}$ and the demand is fixed at $x_0 = 5$, find the consumers' surplus, using each of the methods corresponding to Eqs. (4–18) and (4–19).

4. If the supply law is $p = (x + 2)^2$ and the price is fixed at $p_0 = 25$, find the producers' surplus, using each of the methods corresponding to Eqs. (4–20) and (4–21).

5. If the demand curve is the equilateral hyperbola $p = 24/(x + 2)$ and the supply curve is the parabola $p = x^2/4$, show by trial that their point of intersection is $(4, 4)$. Find the corresponding consumers' surplus. Draw the appropriate diagram.

6. The quantity demanded and the corresponding price, under pure competition, are determined by the demand and supply laws $p = 16 - x^2$ and $p = 4 + x$, respectively. Determine the corresponding consumers' surplus and producers' surplus. Draw the appropriate diagram.

7. The quantity demanded and the corresponding price, under pure competition, are determined by the demand and supply laws $p = 36 - x^2$ and $p = 6 + (x^2/4)$, respectively. Determine the corresponding consumers' surplus and producers' surplus. Draw the appropriate diagram.

8. The demand and supply laws under pure competition are $p = \frac{1}{4}(9 - x)^2$ and $p = \frac{1}{4}(1 + 3x)$, respectively. If an additive tax of 3 per unit quantity produced is imposed on the commodity, determine the decrease in consumers' surplus. Draw the appropriate diagram.

9. The quantity sold and the corresponding price, under a monopoly, are determined by the demand law $p = 16 - x^2$ and by the marginal cost $Q' = 6 + x$ in such a way as to maximize the profit. Determine the corresponding consumers' surplus.

10. The quantity sold and the corresponding price, under a monopoly, are determined by the demand law $p = 45 - x^2$ and by the marginal cost $Q' = 6 + (x^2/4)$ in such a way as to maximize the profit. Determine the corresponding consumers' surplus.

CHAPTER 5

INTRODUCTION TO PARTIAL DIFFERENTIATION*

5–1 Functions of two independent variables. The study of a single-valued, continuous, and differentiable function of one variable may be extended to functions of several independent variables. In the theory of economics the demand for a commodity often depends not only on the price of the commodity, but also on the prices of related commodities, on income level, and on time. For simplicity and for the convenience of geometric interpretation, our considerations are confined to the static case and, in general, to functions of two independent variables, under the usual assumption "all other things being equal." Extensions to several variables are usually analogous to the extensions in going from one to two independent variables.

The dependent variable z is a single-valued function of the independent variables x and y, that is, $z = f(x, y)$, provided that for each pair of values of x and y in some given region of the xy-plane, there is a rule f which determines a unique value of z. Without attempting to state explicitly what is meant by "continuous" or "differentiable," we shall merely say here that the functions considered are without jumps or gaps, and when limit processes are involved, the limits are assumed to exist.

5–2 Rectangular coordinates and surfaces. Consider three mutually perpendicular lines with a common origin and with convenient scales marked on each line. The xy-plane is usually taken horizontal and the positive z-axis is taken upwards (Fig. 5–1). (These conventions may be changed when convenient.) Letting P be any point in space, we draw PN perpendicular to the xy-plane, and from N we draw NM perpendicular to the x-axis. Corresponding to point P is an ordered triple of signed numbers (x, y, z), where $x = OM$, $y = MN$, $z = NP$, each measured in terms of the appropriate unit. Conversely, for any ordered number triple (x, y, z), the point P is uniquely determined. This one-to-one correspondence between points in space and number triples affords a means of

---

* A more detailed study of partial differentiation and analytic geometry of three dimensions can be found in standard texts on analytic geometry and calculus, such as those listed in Section 7–8 of this book. However, the study of indifference maps in these texts is generally quite meager. The interested reader should consult R. D. G. Allen, *Mathematical Analysis for Economists*, Macmillan, 1939.

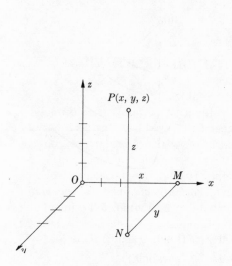

FIGURE 5–1

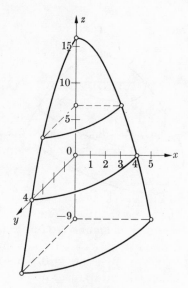

FIGURE 5–2

visualizing the functional relationship $z = f(x, y)$. The totality of points corresponding to all number triples (x, y, z), obtained by assigning all permissible values to x and y and computing the corresponding z values, is called a *surface*. The actual surface could be constructed as a space model. It can be visualized by means of a perspective drawing, in the plane, that shows certain important curvilinear sections of the surface. The plane sections include those made by the three coordinate planes: the xy-, the xz-, and the yz-planes; these are obtained by using the equations $z = 0$, $y = 0$, and $x = 0$, respectively. Other convenient planes for sectioning the surface have equations with $z = $ const.

EXAMPLE 5–1. $z = 16 - x^2 - y^2$.

The units on the x- and y-axes are taken equal, and a smaller unit is selected on the z-axis. The section of the surface by the plane $z = 0$ is the circle $x^2 + y^2 = 16$, which, when drawn in perspective, appears elliptical (Fig. 5–2). The section by the plane $y = 0$ is the parabola $z = 16 - x^2$, and the section by the plane $x = 0$ is a similar parabola. Figure 5–2 also shows the sections corresponding to $z = 7$ and $z = -9$. Only one-fourth of the surface, that part corresponding to $x \geqq 0$, $y \geqq 0$, is indicated. If the additional restriction is made that z be zero or positive, then only that part in the *first octant* is needed. (Note that $z \leqq 16$.)

EXAMPLE 5–2. $z = 9 - x^2 - y$, $(y \geqq 0, z \geqq 0)$.
The following sections are used in sketching the surface:

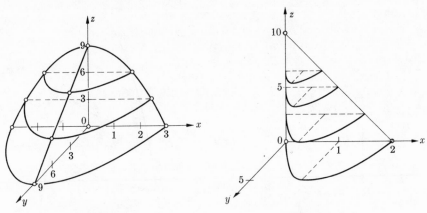

FIGURE 5–3   FIGURE 5–4

$$x = 0, \quad y + z = 9 \qquad \text{(line)},$$
$$y = 0, \quad z = 9 - x^2 \qquad \text{(parabola)},$$
$$z = 0, \quad y = 9 - x^2 \qquad \text{(parabola)}.$$

The section by the plane $z = a$ is a parabola congruent to that by the plane $z = 0$, and moved upward and backward with its vertex on the line $x = 0, y + z = 9$. Figure 5–3 shows the sections for $z = 3$ and $z = 6$; the value of z cannot exceed 9 if y is to remain positive. If parabolic sections are cut from cardboard and mounted at proper heights, a space model can be constructed.

EXAMPLE 5–3. The following function (with a different notation) was considered earlier (Example 3–18):

$$y = 10x - 5x^2 - xz$$

or

$$z = \frac{10x - 5x^2 - y}{x}, \qquad (x > 0, y \geqq 0, z \geqq 0).$$

The sections by the coordinate planes are

$$z = 0, \quad y = 10x - 5x^2 \qquad \text{(parabola)},$$
$$y = 0, \quad z = 10 - 5x \qquad \text{(line)},$$
$$x = 0, \quad y = 0 \qquad \text{(z-axis)}.$$

Every section by a plane $z = a$ gives a parabola $y = (10 - a)x - 5x^2$; y is positive between the values $x = 0$ and $x = 10 - a$, so that a cannot exceed 10. Several such sections are shown in Fig. 5–4.

EXERCISE GROUP 5–1

Discuss the following surfaces and make a perspective sketch of each.

1. Planes: (a) $(x/4) + (y/3) + (z/2) = 1$. (b) $6z = 12 + 3x - 4y$.
   (c) $3z = 3x + 2y - 6$, $(-2 \leqq z \leqq 2)$.
2. Planes: (a) $z = 2x + y$. (b) $z = -2x + y$.
3. Paraboloids: (a) $z = x^2 + y^2$. (b) $z = 25 - x^2 - y^2$.
4. Paraboloids: (a) $9x^2 + 4y^2 = 36z$. (b) $9x^2 + 4y^2 = 9 - z$.
5. Spheres: (a) $x^2 + y^2 + z^2 = 4$. (b) $(x - 2)^2 + y^2 + z^2 = 4$.
6. Cones: (a) $z^2 = x^2 + y^2$. (b) $9y^2 + 4z^2 = 36x^2$, $(0 \leq x \leq 2)$.
7. $z = 16 - x^2 - 2y$, $(y \geqq 0, z \geqq 0)$.
8. $z = 10 - x - y^2$, $(x, y, z$ positive or zero).
9. $x = 8y - 2y^2 - yz$.
10. $x^2 + y^2 - 8x + xz = 0$.

5–3 Indifference maps. The difficulties inherent in drawing a perspective diagram of a surface and the usefulness of taking horizontal sections suggest a second method for representing the function $z = f(x, y)$. For each fixed value of z there is a plane section of the surface, known as an *equilevel curve*. If a number of such curves are projected upon the xy-plane, that is, drawn in the xy-plane and labeled by the corresponding value of z, the family of curves so obtained is called a *contour map*. This map can be used to represent the functional relationship $z = f(x, y)$. In economic theory this diagram is called an *indifference map*, for regardless of what point is taken on a selected curve, the value of z is the same. The assumption that f is single-valued in some region of the xy-plane is equivalent to the fact that no two *indifference curves* intersect in the given region.

The indifference maps for Examples 5–1, 5–2, and 5–3 are readily described and drawn. For $z = 16 - x^2 - y^2$ (Example 5–1), the indifference curves are circles with centers at the origin and radii given by $r = \sqrt{16 - z}$. If $z = 16$, the circle reduces to a single point; as z decreases, the radius increases. The first quadrant diagram is shown in Fig. 5–5.

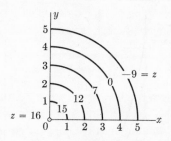

FIGURE 5–5

The contour curves for the surface $z = 9 - x^2 - y$, $(y \geqq 0, z \geqq 0)$, (Example 5–2) are the parabolas $y = (9 - z) - x^2$. These parabolas, subject to the restriction $y \geqq 0$, are shown in Fig. 5–6 for $z = 0, 3, 5, 7, 8, 9$.

The contour map for $y = 10x - 5x^2 - xz$ (Example 5–3) is the set of parabolas $y = (10 - a)x - 5x^2$, and may be visualized by imagining

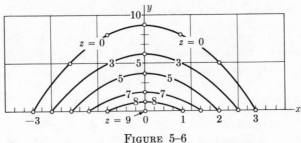

FIGURE 5-6

the parabolas sketched in Fig. 5-4 as projected downward upon the xy-plane (cf. Fig. 3-20).

EXAMPLE 5-4. An example of an equation whose surface is difficult to draw as a space diagram, and whose contour map is more easily drawn, is

$$z = (x + 1)(y + 2), \qquad (x, y, z \text{ positive}).$$

When this is written in the forms

$$y = \frac{z}{x + 1} - 2, \qquad y = \frac{(z - 2) - 2x}{x + 1},$$

we see that each curve is an equilateral hyperbola with the same asymptotes, $x = -1$ and $y = -2$. The intercepts are $x = 0$, $y = z - 2$; $y = 0$, $x = (z - 2)/2$. The contour lines are drawn for $z = 2, 4, 6,$ 8, 10. The intercepts ordinarily provide sufficient data to sketch any of the curves. Here it was found convenient to determine the value of y for each z when $x = 1$ (Fig. 5-7).

Before we consider the next example, a few facts should be noted about the graph of the plane curve $ax^2 + bxy + cy^2 = K$. If $b^2 - 4ac < 0$, the curve is an ellipse, and if $b^2 - 4ac > 0$, the curve is a hyperbola with oblique asymptotes. These facts are useful as a check on point-plotting. The intercepts may be found by setting $x = 0$ and solving for y, and by setting $y = 0$ and solving for x. Other points may be

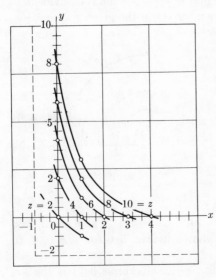

FIGURE 5-7

found by setting $y = x$ and solving for the coordinates of the points where this line cuts the curve. Similar remarks apply to the line $y = -x$.

EXAMPLE 5–5. Draw a contour map for the function

$$z = 10 - x^2 - y^2 - xy.$$

Show the contours for $z = 10, 9, 6, 1, 0$ (Fig. 5–8).

Since $b^2 - 4ac = 1 - 4 < 0$, each curve is a similar ellipse similarly placed, with size determined by $K = 10 - z$. If the first curve drawn is for $z = 0$, $x^2 + xy + y^2 = 10$, the other curves are more readily drawn. The data used to draw this curve are the intercepts and the points where the lines $x = y$ and $x = -y$ cut the curve.

x	0	$\pm\sqrt{10}$	$\pm\sqrt{10/3}$	$\pm\sqrt{10}$
y	$\pm\sqrt{10}$	0	$\pm\sqrt{10/3}$	$\mp\sqrt{10}$

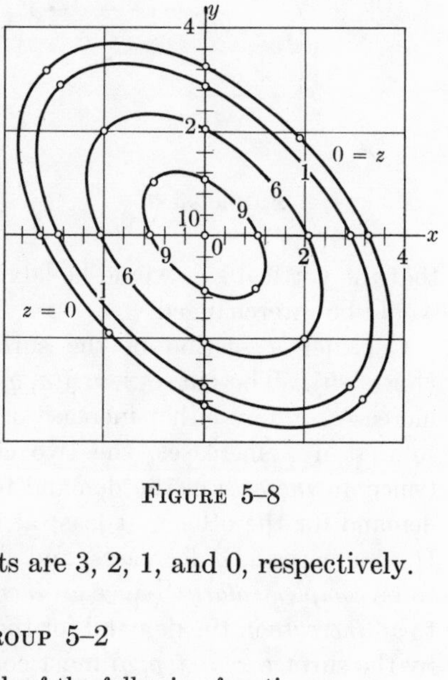

FIGURE 5–8

For $z = 1, 6, 9$, and 10, the intercepts are $3, 2, 1$, and 0, respectively.

EXERCISE GROUP 5–2

Discuss and draw a contour map for each of the following functions:

1. (a) $(x/4) + (y/3) + (z/2) = 1$.
   (b) $3z = 3x + 2y - 6$, $(-2 \leqq z \leqq 2)$.
2. (a) $z = 2x + y$. (b) $z = -2x + y$.
3. (a) $z = x^2 + y^2$. (b) $z = 25 - x^2 - y^2$.
4. (a) $x^2 + y^2 + z^2 = 4$, $(z \geqq 0)$. (b) $(x - 2)^2 + y^2 + z^2 = 4$, $(z \geqq 0)$.
5. $z = 16 - x^2 - 2y$, $(y \geqq 0, z \geqq 0)$.
6. $x^2 + y^2 - 8x + xz = 0$.
7. $z = (x + 2)(y + 1)$, $(x, y, z$ positive$)$.
8. $z = (x - 2)(y - 3)$, $(0 \leqq z \leqq 12)$.
9. $z = 12 - x^2 - y^2 + xy$. Show the contours for $z = 12, 11, 8, 3, 0, -4$.
10. $x^2 + 2xy + 2y^2 = 20 - z$. Show the contours for $z = 20, 16, 10, 4, 0$.

5–4 Demand surfaces. Let the demands for two different commodities be x and y and let the respective prices be p and q. Assume that the quantities demanded are single-valued, continuous functions of both prices; that is,

$$x = f(p, q), \qquad y = g(p, q). \tag{5–1}$$

The surfaces represented by each of these functions, with p and q considered as the independent variables, are called *demand surfaces*. Certain

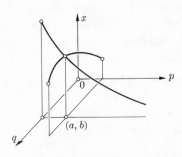

FIGURE 5–9

restrictions must be placed on the functions f and g if they are to correspond to normal economic situations. (1) All the variables are restricted to be positive. (2) If q is a fixed constant ($q = b$), then x must be a monotonically decreasing function of p (Fig. 5–9); similarly, if p is a fixed constant ($p = a$), then y must be a monotonically decreasing function of q. The diagram would be similar to that in Fig. 5–9, except that the vertical axis would be labeled y instead of x and the p- and q-axes would be interchanged.

Consider a section of the surface $x = f(p, q)$ by the plane $p = a$ (Fig. 5–9). The curve $x = f(a, q)$ in the plane $p = a$ is such that as q increases, x may either increase or decrease. As q increases, y decreases, so that if x increases, the two commodities may be called *competitive* (since an *increase* in the demand for one corresponds to a *decrease* in the demand for the other), at least at the prices a and b under consideration. If x increases as q decreases, and since y also increases, the goods are said to be *complementary** (since an *increase* in the demand for one corresponds to an *increase* in the demand for the other). Such relationships determined by the surface $x = f(p, q)$ must correspond to similar relationships on the surface $y = g(p, q)$ for the same fixed prices $p = a$, $q = b$.

(3) One further restriction is placed upon the general demand functions. The functions f and g and the pq-region for which they are defined must be such that it is possible to solve equations (5–1) for p and q in terms of x and y:

$$p = F(x, y), \qquad q = G(x, y), \tag{5–2}$$

where F and G are single-valued functions of x and y for some xy-region.

---

* The terms "competitive" and "complementary" will hereafter be used in this special restrictive sense.

Conversely, if the prices are given by equations (5–2), it must be possible to determine the demand functions in the form of (5–1).

The simplest demand surfaces are those for which f and g are linear functions of p and q, subject to the restrictions mentioned above and more explicitly stated in Section 1–3. Each demand surface is that part of a plane in the first octant corresponding to values of p and q which make both x and y positive (or zero). The indifference curves in the pq-plane are parts of a set of parallel lines. If the demand equations are written in the form

$$x = x_0 - mp + cq, \qquad y = y_0 + dp - nq,$$

the constants x_0, y_0, m, and n are positive. The constants c and d may be of either sign; the goods are competitive if c and d are both positive. If p is fixed, then an increase in q causes an increase in x but a decrease in y. Likewise, if q is fixed, an increase in p causes an increase in y but a decrease in x. A similar argument shows that if c and d are both negative, the goods are complementary for all permissible values of p and q.

EXAMPLE 5–6. If the demand functions are

$$x = 12 - 2p - q, \qquad y = 8 - p - q,$$

the commodities are complementary. The demand surfaces are planes which can be sketched from their intercepts on the coordinate axes. Since both x and y must be positive, the values of p and q are restricted to be in

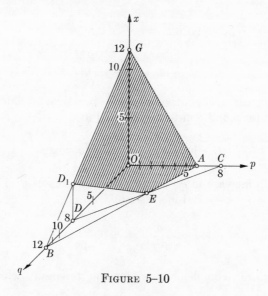

FIGURE 5–10

the two triangles formed by the p-axis, the q-axis, and by the lines $2p + q = 12$, $p + q = 8$, respectively. The common pq-region is the quadrilateral $DEAO$ of Fig. 5–10, and the corresponding x-demand surface is the quadrilateral D_1EAG shown shaded in this diagram. A similar diagram can be constructed for the y-demand surface.

EXAMPLE 5–7.   If the demand functions are

$$x = 10 - 2p + q,$$
$$y = 6 + p - q,$$

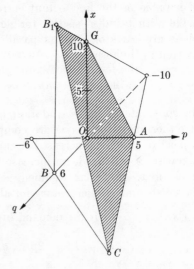

FIGURE 5–11

the commodities are competitive. The demand surfaces are planes which can be constructed as in Example 5–6. Since x, y, p, and q are positive, the values of p and q are restricted to the quadrilateral $AOBC$, bounded by the lines $p = 0$, $q = 0$, $2p - q = 10$, and $q - p = 6$ (Fig. 5–11). If the plane $x = 10 - 2p + q$ is added to this diagram, the x-demand surface is the quadrilateral AGB_1C, shown shaded. A similar diagram can be constructed for the y-demand surface.

EXAMPLE 5–8. The equations

$$x = \frac{q}{p}, \qquad y = \frac{p^2}{q}$$

represent nonlinear competitive demand functions.   These equations may be solved for p and q in terms of x and y:

$$p = xy, \qquad q = x^2y.$$

If p is fixed, an increase in q increases x and decreases y; if q is fixed, an increase in p decreases x and increases y.

The equations

$$x = \frac{a}{p^2q}, \qquad y = \frac{a}{pq}$$

represent nonlinear complementary demand functions which may also be solved for p and q in terms of x and y:

$$p = y/x, \qquad q = ax/y^2.$$

An increase in either p or q causes both x and y to decrease.

The demand functions of this example are more conveniently represented by indifference maps than by surfaces. The indifference map for $y = a/(pq)$, which represents a family of equilateral hyperbolas that approach the lines $p = 0$, $q = 0$ as y increases, is shown in Fig. 5–12.

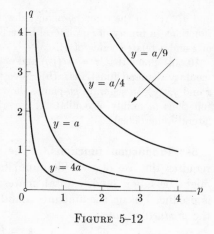

FIGURE 5–12

EXERCISE GROUP 5–3

1. Show that $x = 17 - 2p - q$ and $y = 14 - p - 2q$ are demand functions for complementary goods. Draw the corresponding x- and y-demand surfaces (planes) and indicate the parts that correspond to x and y both positive.

2. Show that $x = 11 - 2p - q$ and $y = 13 - p - 3q$ are demand functions for complementary goods. Draw the corresponding x- and y-demand surfaces (planes) and indicate the parts that correspond to x and y both positive.

3. Show that $x = 5 - 2p + q$ and $y = 6 + p - q$ are demand functions for competitive goods. Draw the x-demand plane, showing the part that corresponds to x and y both positive.

4. Show that $x = 18 - 3p + 2q$ and $y = 3 + p - q$ are demand functions for competitive goods. Draw the x-demand plane, showing the part that corresponds to x and y both positive.

5. Show that $x = 2 - 2p + q$ and $y = 6 - 2p - 3q$ are demand functions for goods that are neither complementary nor competitive. Draw the corresponding x- and y-demand surfaces (planes) and indicate the parts that correspond to x and y both positive.

6. Show that $x = 6 - 3p - 2q$ and $y = 2 + p - 2q$ are demand functions for goods that are neither complementary nor competitive. Draw the corresponding x- and y-demand surfaces (planes) and indicate the parts that correspond to x and y both positive.

7. In the same pq-plane show the indifference maps for the demand functions of Example 5–8: $x = q/p$, $y = p^2/q$ (a family of lines and a family of parabolas).

8. (a) Show that $x = q^2/p$ and $y = p^2/q$ represent nonlinear competitive demand functions. (b) Solve these equations for p and q in terms of x and y. (c) In the same pq-plane show the indifference maps for these demand functions (families of parabolas).

9. (a) Show that $x = 4/(pq)$ and $y = 16/(pq)$ represent nonlinear complementary demand functions. (b) These equations cannot be solved for p and q in terms of x and y. What relation exists between x and y for all values of p

and q? (c) In the same pq-plane show the indifference maps for these demand functions (a family of equilateral hyperbolas; each curve corresponds to a value of x and a related value of y).

10. (a) Show that $x = 4/(pq)$ and $y = 16/(p^2q)$ represent nonlinear complementary demand functions. (b) Solve these equations for p and q in terms of x and y. (c) In separate pq-planes show the indifference maps for these demand functions (a family of equilateral hyperbolas and a family of generalized equilateral hyperbolas).

5–5 Production functions.   The production of certain commodities requires the use of two (or more) factors of production. These factors might be labor, land, capital, materials, or machines. If the quantity z is produced using the amounts u and v of two factors of production, then the *production function*

$$z = f(u, v)$$

shows the amount of the *output z* when the amounts of the *inputs u* and v are used simultaneously. (We assume the single-valuedness and continuity of the function and the continuous divisibility of the inputs.) The production function is studied by using the indifference curves $f(u, v) = $ const, in the uv-plane. These curves, no two of which intersect, are also called *constant product curves*. In the simplest "normal" case, the constant product curves are such that a *decrease* in the input of one is compensated by an *increase* in the input of the other. The functions

$$z = au^n v^m, \qquad (n, m \text{ positive}), \tag{5-3}$$

with or without the restriction that $n + m = 1$, have been found to be useful production functions. The constant product curves are generalized hyperbolas. For any fixed z, v is a monotonically decreasing function of u. In logarithmic form, Eq. (5–3) becomes $\ln z = \ln a + n \ln u + m \ln v$, or

$$Z = A + nU + mV, \tag{5-4}$$

where capital letters correspond to the logarithms* of the lower-case letters. The indifference map of this function (Eq. 5–4) in the UV-plane is a set of parallel lines.

A numerical example of another type of production function for which the constant product curves are also equilateral hyperbolas now follows.

EXAMPLE 5–9.   Construct the indifference map for the production function $z = 8 - (1/u) - (1/v)$, using the values $z = 0, 4, 6, 7$.

---

* Either common or natural logarithms may be used.

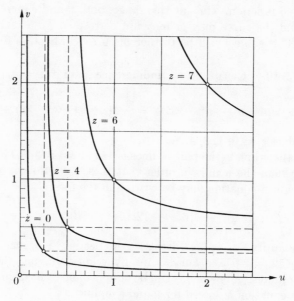

FIGURE 5–13

The given equation can be reduced to the form

$$\left(u - \frac{1}{8-z}\right)\left(v - \frac{1}{8-z}\right) = \frac{1}{(8-z)^2}$$

by the method used in Section 1–8, and the graph for each z is then obtained. For $z = 4$, the equation is then $(u - \frac{1}{4})(v - \frac{1}{4}) = (\frac{1}{4})^2$, which is an equilateral hyperbola with asymptotes $u = \frac{1}{4}$, $v = \frac{1}{4}$. One branch of the hyperbola passes through the origin but has no economic significance, since u and v are negative. The other branch passes through the point $(\frac{1}{2}, \frac{1}{2})$ and is readily drawn. Figure 5–13 shows the branches corresponding to the indicated values of z.

There exists a more general type of normal production function for which the compensation of the decrease in one input by an increase in the other input is restricted to a finite range. A typical constant product curve (Fig. 5–14) is such that between the point B, where the slope is infinite, and the point A, where the slope is zero (see Section 5–8), the curve may be used for

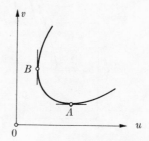

FIGURE 5–14

the production function. Outside this range, both u and v increase simultaneously, and the curve may or may not correspond to a real economic situation. (This subject will be further discussed in Section 6–4).

EXAMPLE 5–10.   Construct an indifference map for the production function

$$z = 4(4uv - u^2 - 3v^2) = -4(u - v)(u - 3v),$$

using the values $z = 0, 1, 2, 4, 8$.

If $z = 0$, the graph is the pair of lines $v = u$, $v = u/3$. (The v unit is taken larger than the u unit in order that these lines do not appear too close.) The given equation may be written in the form

$$4u^2 - 16uv + 12v^2 + z = 0.$$

Since the quantity $b^2 - 4ac$ (discussed in Section 5–3) has the value $16^2 - 4 \cdot 4 \cdot 12 = 64$, the curves are hyperbolas having the lines as oblique asymptotes. A few points can be obtained on each curve as follows. If the above equation is solved for u and simplified,

$$u = \frac{4v \pm \sqrt{4v^2 - z}}{2}.$$

After the value of z is selected (here, $z = 8$), values may be assigned to v

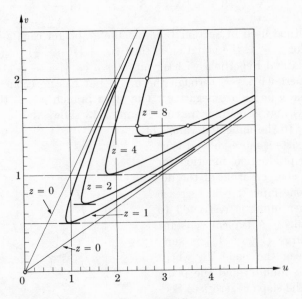

FIGURE 5–15

and the two corresponding values of u computed:

$$u = 2v \pm \sqrt{v^2 - 2}.$$

For real values of $u, v \geqq \sqrt{2}$, the curve may be sketched from

v	$\sqrt{2}$	2	3/2
u	$2\sqrt{2}$	$4 \pm \sqrt{2}$	$3 \pm 1/2$

The other curves in Fig. 5-15 are found with $z = 1, 2$, and 4.

EXERCISE GROUP 5-4

1. Discuss the indifference maps for the production function $z = 10uv$, in the uv-plane and in the UV-plane, where the capital letters represent the common logarithms of the lower-case letters.

2. Discuss the indifference maps for the production function $z = 4u^2v$, in the uv-plane and in the UV-plane, where the capital letters represent the natural logarithms of the lower-case letters.

3. Discuss the indifference maps for the following production functions in the given forms and in their corresponding logarithmic forms:

(a) $z = 4u^{1/2}v^{1/2}$; (b) $z = 2u^{3/4}v^{3/4}$.

4. If Z represents an index number for the amount of goods produced by labor L and capital C, discuss the indifference map for the following production functions: (a) $Z = L^{0.75}C^{0.25}$; (b) $Z = L^{0.4}C^{0.3}$.

5. Construct an indifference map for the production function

$$z = 5 - (1/u) - (1/v),$$

using the values $z = 0, 2, 4$.

6. Construct an indifference map for the production function

$$z = 5 - (1/u) - (2/v),$$

using the values $z = 0, 2, 4$.

7. Construct an indifference map for the production function

$$z = -(2u^2 - 5uv + 2v^2) = -(u - 2v)(2u - v).$$

Show the curves which pass through the points $(0, 0)$, $(1, 1)$, $(3, 3)$, $(5, 5)$.

8. Construct an indifference map for the production function

$$z = -(3u^2 - 7uv + 2v^2) = -(3u - v)(u - 2v).$$

Use the values $z = 0, 2, 8, 18$.

5–6 Partial derivatives. If $z = f(x, y)$ is a single-valued function of two independent variables, the *partial derivative of z with respect to x is* the function of x and y obtained by differentiating z with respect to x while considering y as a constant. This derivative is represented by

$$\frac{\partial z}{\partial x}, \quad z_x, \quad \text{or} \quad f_x(x, y).$$

In terms of the Δ-process,

$$\frac{\partial z}{\partial x}\bigg|_{x=x_0} = \lim_{\Delta x \to 0} \frac{f(x_0 + \Delta x, y) - f(x_0, y)}{\Delta x} = f_x(x_0, y).$$

If this limit exists for every x_0 in the interval $a \leqq x_0 \leqq b$, the subscript is dropped:

$$\frac{\partial z}{\partial x} = \lim_{\Delta x \to 0} \frac{f(x + \Delta x, y) - f(x, y)}{\Delta x} = f_x(x, y).$$

Geometrically, this derivative represents the slope of the curve that is the intersection of the surface $z = f(x, y)$ by the plane $y = $ const.

The partial derivative of z with respect to y,

$$\frac{\partial z}{\partial y}, \quad z_y, \quad \text{or} \quad f_y(x, y),$$

is the derivative of z taken with respect to y while considering x as a constant. It corresponds to the slope of the curve $z = f(x, y)$, $x = $ const.

EXAMPLE 5–11. If $z = 12xy - 5x^2 - 4y^2$, then

$$\frac{\partial z}{\partial x} = 12y - 10x, \quad \frac{\partial z}{\partial y} = 12x - 8y.$$

The point $(1, 1, 3)$ is on this surface; the plane $y = 1$ cuts the surface in a parabola $z = 12x - 5x^2 - 4$, $y = 1$, whose slope at the given point is $12 - 10 = 2$; the plane $x = 1$ cuts the surface in a parabola whose slope at the given point is 4.

Marginal demands. If the demand functions for two related commodities are given in the form

$$x = f(p, q), \quad y = g(p, q),$$

then

$\partial x / \partial p$ is the (partial) marginal demand of x with respect to p,

$\partial x / \partial q$ is the (partial) marginal demand of x with respect to q,

$\partial y / \partial p$ is the (partial) marginal demand of y with respect to p,

$\partial y / \partial q$ is the (partial) marginal demand of y with respect to q.

The statements given in Section 5–4 concerning demand surfaces are now restated here:

$\partial x/\partial p$ and $\partial y/\partial q$ are negative for all permissible p and q, since x must increase if its corresponding price p decreases, and y must increase if its corresponding price q decreases (for normal demand functions).

If $\partial x/\partial q$ and $\partial y/\partial p$ are both negative for a given (p, q), the goods are complementary, since then a decrease in q will cause x as well as y to increase, and a decrease in p will cause y as well as x to increase. That is, a decrease in either price will cause both demands to increase. An analogous argument shows that if $\partial x/\partial q$ and $\partial y/\partial p$ are both positive, the goods are competitive at these prices, since, for example, $\partial x/\partial q$ and $\partial y/\partial q$ will now have opposite signs. For the linear demand functions

$$x = x_0 - mp + cq, \qquad y = y_0 + dp - nq,$$

these statements are consistent with the following data:

$$\frac{\partial x}{\partial p} = -m < 0, \qquad \frac{\partial y}{\partial q} = -n < 0,$$

$$\frac{\partial x}{\partial q} = c, \qquad \frac{\partial y}{\partial p} = d.$$

Marginal cost. If the joint-cost function of producing the quantities x and y of two commodities is given by $Q = Q(x, y)$, then the partial derivatives of Q are called the *marginal cost functions.*

EXAMPLE 5–12. If $Q = 10 + x^2 + 2xy + 4y^2$, the marginal cost with respect to x is $\partial Q/\partial x = 2x + 2y$, and the marginal cost with respect to y is $\partial Q/\partial y = 2x + 8y$. In the normal case these marginal costs must be positive. Thus, if

$$Q = x \ln (2 + y),$$

then

$$Q_x = \ln (2 + y), \qquad Q_y = \frac{x}{2 + y},$$

which are positive functions for all positive x and y.

Marginal productivity. If a production function is given in the form $z = f(u, v)$, then $\partial z/\partial u$ and $\partial z/\partial v$ are called the *marginal productivities.* If the production function is represented by its system of indifference (equal product) curves, each labeled according to its value of z, then $\partial z/\partial u$ represents the rate at which z changes by moving parallel to the u-axis, and $\partial z/\partial v$ represents the rate at which z changes by moving parallel

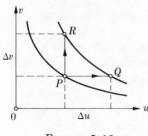

FIGURE 5–16

to the v-axis. If the curves are drawn for small changes in z, these derivatives can be approximated by

$$\frac{\partial z}{\partial u} \doteq \frac{z_2 - z_1}{\Delta u} = \frac{z_2 - z_1}{PQ},$$

$$\frac{\partial z}{\partial v} \doteq \frac{z_2 - z_1}{PR},$$

as shown in Fig. 5–16.

Partial elasticity of demand. If the demand x is a function of two prices p and q, the *partial elasticity of demand with respect to p* is defined as the limit of the ratio of the *relative* change in demand $(\Delta x/x)$ to the *relative* change in price $(\Delta p/p)$, as $\Delta p \to 0$ and q remains fixed:

$$\left(\frac{Ex}{Ep}\right)_{q=c} = \lim_{\Delta p \to 0} \frac{\Delta x/x}{\Delta p/p} = \left(\frac{p}{x}\right)\left(\frac{\partial x}{\partial p}\right) = \frac{\partial (\ln x)}{\partial (\ln p)} = \frac{\partial X}{\partial P},$$

where $X = \ln x$ and $P = \ln p$.

The partial elasticity of demand with respect to q is

$$\left(\frac{Ex}{Eq}\right)_{p=c} = \left(\frac{q}{x}\right)\left(\frac{\partial x}{\partial q}\right) = \frac{\partial (\ln x)}{\partial (\ln q)} = \frac{\partial X}{\partial Q},$$

where, similarly, $Q = \ln q$.

EXAMPLE 5–13. If x and p represent the demand and price for margarine, and y and q represent the demand and price for butter, it was found that, approximately,

$$x = p^{-1.3}q^{0.4}, \qquad y = p^{0.3}q^{-0.1}.$$

We are to show that the commodities are competitive, and find the four partial elasticities of demand:

$$\frac{\partial x}{\partial p} = -1.3p^{-2.3}q^{0.4} < 0, \qquad \frac{\partial x}{\partial q} = 0.4p^{-1.3}q^{-0.6} > 0,$$

$$\frac{\partial y}{\partial q} = -0.1p^{0.3}q^{-1.1} < 0, \qquad \frac{\partial y}{\partial p} = 0.3p^{-0.7}q^{-0.1} > 0.$$

The conditions for demand functions and competitive goods are satisfied for all positive p and q.

$$\left(\frac{Ex}{Ep}\right)_{q=c} = -1.3p^{-2.3}q^{0.4} \cdot \frac{p}{p^{-1.3}q^{0.4}} = -1.3 \qquad \text{(a constant)}.$$

(Cf. Section 3–2.)   The other required elasticities of demand could be found similarly, but it is simpler to use the demand laws in logarithmic form.   In the usual notation,

$$X = -1.3P + 0.4Q, \qquad Y = 0.3P - 0.1Q,$$

$$\left(\frac{Ex}{Ep}\right)_{q=c} = \frac{\partial X}{\partial P} = -1.3, \qquad \left(\frac{Ex}{Eq}\right)_{p=c} = \frac{\partial X}{\partial Q} = 0.4,$$

$$\left(\frac{Ey}{Ep}\right)_{q=c} = \frac{\partial Y}{\partial P} = 0.3, \qquad \left(\frac{Ey}{Eq}\right)_{p=c} = \frac{\partial Y}{\partial Q} = -0.1.$$

If z is a function of more than two independent variables, then $\partial z/\partial x$ is found by holding constant all the independent variables except x.

EXERCISE GROUP 5–5

1. For each of the following functions find $\partial z/\partial x$ and $\partial z/\partial y$.   Evaluate these for the given values of x and y and interpret the result geometrically.

   (a) $z = 12 - x^2 - y^2 + xy$, $(x = 2, y = 3)$.
   (b) $z = x^2 + 2xy + 4y^2 - 2x + 4y + 4$, $(x = 2, y = -1)$.
   (c) $z = e^{x^2 + y^2}$, $(x = 1, y = 0)$.
   (d) $z = xy/(x + y)$, $(x = 2, y = 2)$.
   (e) $x^2 + y^2 - 8x + xz = 0$, $(x = 1, y = 2)$.   (Solve for z.)

2. Proceed as in problem 1 for the following functions:

   (a) $z = 20 - x^2 + 2xy - 2y^2$, $(x = 2, y = 3)$.
   (b) $z = x^2 - 2xy + 2y^2 + 6x - 8y + 10$, $(x = -2, y = 1)$.
   (c) $z = \ln(x^2 + y^2)$, $(x = 1, y = 0)$.
   (d) $z = xy/(x + 2)$, $(x = 2, y = 2)$.
   (e) $y = 10x - 5x^2 - xz$, $(x = 1, y = 2)$.   (Solve for z.)

3. For each of the following pairs of linear functions, determine the four partial marginal demands and discuss the nature of the relation between the two commodities:

   (a) $x = 17 - 2p - q$, $y = 14 - p - 2q$.
   (b) $x = 5 - 2p + q$, $y = 6 + p - q$.
   (c) $x = 2 - 2p + q$, $y = 6 - 2p - 3q$.

4. Determine the four partial elasticities of demand for each part of problem 3.

5. Determine the four partial elasticities of demand for each of the following pairs of demand functions:

   (a) $x = q/p$, $\qquad y = p^2/q$.
   (b) $x = 1/(p^2q)$, $\quad y = 1/(pq)$.

6. The demand functions for two related commodities are given.   Determine whether the commodities are complementary or competitive and find the four partial elasticities of demand.

   (a) $x = p^{-1.7}q^{0.8}$, $\qquad y = p^{0.5}q^{-0.2}$.
   (b) $x = p^{-1.5}q^{-0.4}$, $\quad y = p^{-0.5}q^{-0.4}$.

7. Find the marginal productivities for each of the following production functions:

(a) $z = 5 - (1/u) - (1/v)$ at $(u = 1, v = 1)$.
(b) $z = 4(4uv - u^2 - 3v^2)$ at $(u = 1, v = \frac{1}{2})$.

8. Find the marginal productivities for each of the following production functions:

(a) $z = 5 - (1/u) - (2/v)$ at $(u = 1, v = 1)$.
(b) $z = 5uv - 2u^2 - 2v^2$ at $(u = 1, v = 1)$.

5–7 Partial derivatives of higher order. If $z = f(x, y)$, then f_x and f_y are also functions of x and y. Hence, under suitable restrictions, they also have derivatives which are second-order derivatives of z:

$$\frac{\partial}{\partial x}\left(\frac{\partial z}{\partial x}\right) \equiv \frac{\partial^2 z}{\partial x^2} \equiv f_{xx},$$

the second partial derivative of z with respect to x;

$$\frac{\partial}{\partial y}\left(\frac{\partial z}{\partial x}\right) = \frac{\partial^2 z}{\partial y \, \partial x} \equiv f_{xy},$$

the second partial derivative of z with respect to x and y;

$$\frac{\partial}{\partial x}\left(\frac{\partial z}{\partial y}\right) = \frac{\partial^2 z}{\partial x \, \partial y} \equiv f_{yx},$$

the second partial derivative of z with respect to y and x;

$$\frac{\partial}{\partial y}\left(\frac{\partial z}{\partial y}\right) = \frac{\partial^2 z}{\partial y^2} \equiv f_{yy},$$

the second partial derivative of z with respect to y.

For the types of functions considered in this text, the mixed derivatives f_{xy} and f_{yx} are equal, that is, the order of differentiation with respect to x and y does not affect the result.

EXAMPLE 5–14. If $z = x^2 \ln y$, $(y > 0)$, then

$$\frac{\partial z}{\partial x} = 2x \ln y, \qquad \frac{\partial^2 z}{\partial x^2} = 2 \ln y, \qquad \frac{\partial z}{\partial y} = \frac{x^2}{y}, \qquad \frac{\partial^2 z}{\partial y^2} = -\frac{x^2}{y^2},$$

and

$$\frac{\partial}{\partial y}\left(\frac{\partial z}{\partial x}\right) = \frac{2x}{y}, \qquad \text{and also} \qquad \frac{\partial}{\partial x}\left(\frac{\partial z}{\partial y}\right) = \frac{2x}{y}.$$

The extension of these definitions and concepts to derivatives of higher orders and to functions of more than two variables is quite simple.

5–8 Implicit differentiation.

(A) When the relation between two variables is given in implicit form, say $F(x, y) = 0$, it may not be convenient or possible to solve the equation for y in terms of x. It is assumed that there exists at least one solution $y = f(x)$ which, for some interval $a \leqq x \leqq b$, is single-valued and continuous. However, it is often desirable to determine dy/dx without solving for y. One procedure for finding dy/dx was discussed in Section 2–8; it is now possible to find an explicit formula for dy/dx which extends easily to the case of an implicit function of three variables.

The equation $F(x, y) = 0$, or the implied relation $y = f(x)$, yields a curve in the xy-plane. Let $P(x_0, y_0)$ and $Q(x_0 + \Delta x, y_0 + \Delta y)$ be two points on the curve, so that $F(x_0, y_0) = 0$ and $F(x_0 + \Delta x, y_0 + \Delta y) = 0$. We form the difference quotient given below, subtract and add the quantity $F(x_0, y_0 + \Delta y)$ and make the indicated changes:

$$0 = \frac{F(x_0 + \Delta x, y_0 + \Delta y) - F(x_0, y_0)}{\Delta x}$$

$$= \left[\frac{F(x_0 + \Delta x, y_0 + \Delta y) - F(x_0, y_0 + \Delta y)}{\Delta x} \right]$$

$$+ \left[\frac{F(x_0, y_0 + \Delta y) - F(x_0, y_0)}{\Delta y} \right] \frac{\Delta y}{\Delta x} .$$

If $\Delta x \to 0$, then $\Delta y \to 0$ (continuity). The term in the first bracket becomes

$$\frac{\partial F(x_0, y_0)}{\partial x}$$

and the term in the second bracket and its factor become

$$\left[\frac{\partial F(x_0, y_0)}{\partial y} \right] \frac{dy}{dx} .$$

Hence, in simplified notation (after the subscripts are **dropped**),

$$0 = F_x + F_y \left(\frac{dy}{dx} \right), \quad \text{or} \quad \frac{dy}{dx} = -\frac{F_x}{F_y} \quad (\text{when } F_y \neq 0). \quad (5\text{–}5)$$

Note that $F_x = \partial F/\partial x$ is a *single* function of x and y, and is not ordinarily a quotient.

EXAMPLE 5–15. If $4x^2 + 2xy + y^2 - 16 = 0$, then

$$\frac{dy}{dx} = -\frac{F_x}{F_y} = -\frac{8x + 2y}{2x + 2y} = -\frac{4x + y}{x + y}.$$

The points on the curve where $dy/dx = 0$ are found by solving $4x + y = 0$ simultaneously with the equation of the curve. The points where $dy/dx = \infty$ are found by solving $x + y = 0$ with the equation of the curve.

(B) Let z be given implicitly as a function of the independent variables x and y. From $F(x, y, z) = 0$, we have

$$F_x + F_z \left(\frac{\partial z}{\partial x}\right) = 0, \qquad F_y + F_z \left(\frac{\partial z}{\partial y}\right) = 0. \qquad (5\text{--}6)$$

For the first of these formulas, y is considered a constant and z replaces y in the above proof. For the second formula, x is considered a constant, and x and y of the above proof are replaced by y and z, respectively. The difference quotient is

$$0 = \left[\frac{F(x, y_0 + \Delta y, z_0 + \Delta z) - F(x, y_0, z_0 + \Delta z)}{\Delta y}\right]$$

$$+ \left[\frac{F(x, y_0, z_0 + \Delta z) - F(x, y_0, z_0)}{\Delta z}\right]\frac{\Delta z}{\Delta y}.$$

The required formula is obtained by passing to the limit. In using formulas (5–6) or the equivalent formulas

$$\frac{\partial z}{\partial x} = -\frac{F_x}{F_z}, \qquad \frac{\partial z}{\partial y} = -\frac{F_y}{F_z}, \qquad (F_z \neq 0), \qquad (5\text{--}7)$$

it is understood that F_x is a derivative taken with respect to x while y and z are constant, that F_y is a derivative taken with respect to y while x and z are constant, and that F_z is a derivative taken with respect to z while x and y are constant.

EXAMPLE 5–16. A production function is given in the form

$$z^2 + 4u^2 + 5v^2 - 12uv = 0,$$

where z is the amount of the output, and u and v are the amounts of the inputs. Find the marginal productivities.

If the given function is called $F(u, v, z)$, then the marginal productivities are $\partial z/\partial u$ and $\partial z/\partial v$.

$$\frac{\partial F}{\partial u} = 8u - 12v, \qquad \frac{\partial F}{\partial v} = -12u + 10v, \qquad \frac{\partial F}{\partial z} = 2z.$$

Hence

$$\frac{\partial z}{\partial u} = -\frac{4u - 6v}{z} \quad \text{and} \quad \frac{\partial z}{\partial v} = -\frac{-6u + 5v}{z}.$$

(C) Let the dependent variable u be given in terms of a function of a function, say $u = F(x, y)$, where the variables x and y are related by an equation of the form $G(x, y) = 0$ or $y = g(x)$. Under these conditions, u is a function of x alone and it may be desirable to find the derivative of u without eliminating the auxiliary variable y.

An analysis similar to that just used shows that

$$\frac{\Delta u}{\Delta x} = \frac{F(x + \Delta x, y + \Delta y) - F(x, y)}{\Delta x}$$

$$= \left[\frac{F(x + \Delta x, y + \Delta y) - F(x, y + \Delta y)}{\Delta x} \right]$$

$$+ \left[\frac{F(x, y + \Delta y) - F(x, y)}{\Delta y} \right] \frac{\Delta y}{\Delta x}.$$

If $\Delta x \to 0$, then $\Delta y \to 0$, which leads to the result

$$\frac{du}{dx} = \frac{\partial F}{\partial x} + \left(\frac{\partial F}{\partial y} \right) \left(\frac{dy}{dx} \right), \tag{5–8}$$

where

$$\frac{\partial F}{\partial x} \equiv \frac{\partial u}{\partial x}, \qquad \frac{\partial F}{\partial y} \equiv \frac{\partial u}{\partial y}, \qquad \text{and} \quad \frac{dy}{dx} = g'(x) \quad \text{or} \quad -\frac{G_x}{G_y},$$

depending on the manner in which the relationship between x and y is given. (Formula (5–5) is the special case of formula (5–8) where $u \equiv 0$.)

The derivative du/dx is itself a function of x, given implicitly in the form

$$\frac{du}{dx} = F_1(x, y), \quad \text{where} \quad y = g(x).$$

Hence d^2u/dx^2 can be found from F_1 in the same manner that du/dx was found from F.

EXAMPLE 5–17.   If $u = xy$, where $2x + y^2 = a^2$, find du/dx and d^2u/dx^2 by using implicit differentiation.

$$2 + 2y\left(\frac{dy}{dx}\right) = 0, \quad \text{or} \quad \frac{dy}{dx} = -\frac{1}{y};$$

$$\frac{du}{dx} = \frac{\partial u}{\partial x} + \left(\frac{\partial u}{\partial y}\right)\left(\frac{dy}{dx}\right) = y + x\left(-\frac{1}{y}\right) = u_1(x, y);$$

$$\frac{d^2u}{dx^2} = \frac{du_1}{dx} = \frac{\partial u_1}{\partial x} + \left(\frac{\partial u_1}{\partial y}\right)\left(\frac{dy}{dx}\right)$$

$$= -\frac{1}{y} + \left(1 + \frac{x}{y^2}\right)\left(-\frac{1}{y}\right)$$

$$= -\frac{2}{y} - \frac{x}{y^3} = \cdots = \frac{3x - 2a^2}{(a^2 - 2x)^{3/2}}.$$

This result may be verified by explicit differentiation of $u = x(a^2 - 2x)^{1/2}$

EXERCISE GROUP 5–6

1. Evaluate the three second partial derivatives of z at the given point:
   (a) $z = 12 - x^2 - y^2 + xy$, $(2, 3)$.
   (b) $z = 5uv - 2u^2 - 2v^2$, $(1, 1)$.

2. Evaluate the three second partial derivatives of z at the given point:
   (a) $z = 20 - x^2 + 2xy - 2y^2$, $(2, 3)$.
   (b) $z = 4(4uv - u^2 - 3v^2)$, $(1, \frac{1}{2})$.

3. Find the three second partial derivatives of z:
   (a) $z = xy/(x + y)$, (b) $z = e^{x^2 + v^2}$.

4. If $z = \ln(x^2 + y^2)$, show that $f_{xx} + f_{yy} = 0$ and find f_{xy}. Discuss the nature of the surface for the given function and discuss the nature of the equilevel curves.

5. If $z = \ln(1 + x^2 + y^2)$, find $(f_{xx} + f_{yy})$ and f_{xy}. Discuss the nature of the surface for this function and discuss the nature of the equilevel curves.

6. (a) Find the points where dy/dx is zero or infinite for the ellipse

$$x^2 - xy + y^2 = 3.$$

Use these points and the intercepts to sketch the curve. (b) Repeat part (a) for the ellipse of Example 5–15: $4x^2 + 2xy + y^2 = 16$.

7. Find the points where dy/dx is zero or infinite for the hyperbola

$$5xy - 2x^2 - 2y^2 - 18 = 0.$$

Use these points and the asymptotes

$$2x^2 - 5xy + 2y^2 \equiv (x - 2y)(2x - y) = 0$$

to sketch the curve.

8. Find $\partial z/\partial x$ and $\partial z/\partial y$ without solving for z: (a) $x^2 + y^2 - 8x + xz = 0$. (b) $y - 10x + 5x^2 + xz = 0$.

9. Find the first and second derivative of u with respect to x, using implicit differentiation:

(a) $u = x^2 + y^2$, $x + y = C$.
(b) $u = x + y$, $x^2 + y^2 = a^2$.

10. Find the first and second derivative of u with respect to x, by (a) eliminating y and using explicit differentiation, and (b) using implicit differentiation:

(a) $u = 12 - x^2 - xy - y^2$, $2x + y = 6$.
(b) $u = 12 - x^2 - xy - y^2$, $xy = 4$.

CHAPTER 6

MAXIMA AND MINIMA PROBLEMS

6–1 Maxima and minima of a function of two variables. A highly important application of partial differentiation to problems of economics involves the maximum and minimum values of a function of several variables. We shall consider the case of two independent variables, noting that extensions to more variables can often be made without difficulty. It is assumed that the function $z = f(x, y)$ is single-valued, continuous, and has such partial derivatives as are needed.

The function $z = f(x, y)$ has a *relative maximum* at (x_0, y_0) provided that $f(x_0, y_0) \geqq f(x, y)$ for every point (x, y) in the neighborhood of (x_0, y_0). If this same inequality is valid for every (x, y) in the region of the xy-plane being considered, then z has an *absolute maximum* at (x_0, y_0). The definitions of *relative* and *absolute minimum* are obtained by reversing the sign in the foregoing inequality so that $f(x_0, y_0) \leqq f(x, y)$. Maximum and minimum values are referred to as *extremal values* or *extrema*.

It may be possible to determine the maximum and minimum values of a simple function by a study of the function and its indifference map in the xy-plane. This is illustrated by several examples.

EXAMPLE 6–1. $z = x^2 + y^2$.

We see that if $x = 0$ and $y = 0$, then $z = 0$; for any other values of x and y, $z > 0$. Hence this function has an absolute minimum at the origin.

EXAMPLE 6–2. $z = x^2 - y^2$.

If $x = 0$ and $y = 0$, then $z = 0$, but this function has neither a maximum nor a minimum at the origin. If $x = 0$, then z is negative for every $y \neq 0$, while if $y = 0$, z is positive for every $x \neq 0$. The indifference map consists of two families of equilateral hyperbolas which have the lines $y = \pm x$ as asymptotes. Along these lines, $z = 0$. One family of the hyperbolas corresponds to $z > 0$ (shaded area in Fig. 6–1) and the other family to $z < 0$.

EXAMPLE 6–3. $z = 6 - 2(x - 1)^2 - 3(y - 2)^2$.

This function has an absolute maximum of 6 at $x = 1$, $y = 2$. For any other values of x and y, $z < 6$. If the function were given in the expanded form $z = -2x^2 - 3y^2 + 4x + 12y - 8$, it could be transformed to the original form by a process of "completing the square." The indifference map is a family of ellipses with center $(1, 2)$. If new axes parallel to the

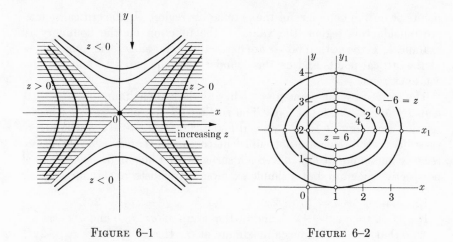

FIGURE 6–1   FIGURE 6–2

old axes are taken through the center, the equation can be written as

$$\frac{x_1^2}{(6-z)/2} + \frac{y_1^2}{(6-z)/3} = 1.$$

For any given $z \leqq 6$, the oval can be constructed from its intercepts on the new axes. If $z = 6$, the oval is a single point; if $z > 6$, there is no locus; and if $z < 6$, the ovals expand as z decreases (Fig. 6–2). Such behavior is typical of a maximum point on a contour map.

6–2 Necessary and sufficient conditions for an extremum. For most functions the algebraic (or geometric) procedures illustrated in the preceding section are difficult to apply. If the surface $z = f(x, y)$ has a relative maximum at (x_0, y_0) inside the region under consideration, then the plane $y = y_0$ cuts the surface in a curve which has a relative maximum at the same point (Fig. 6–3). This also holds for the section of the surface by the plane $x = x_0$. Analogous statements hold if "maximum" is replaced by "minimum," and these properties can hold only if

$$\frac{\partial f}{\partial x} = 0, \quad \frac{\partial f}{\partial y} = 0, \quad \text{at} \quad (x_0, y_0).$$

$$(6\text{–}1)$$

A point where $\partial f/\partial x = 0$ and $\partial f/\partial y = 0$ is called a *critical point*. The maximum and minimum values of the function occur at these critical

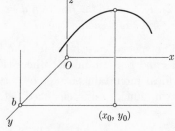

FIGURE 6–3

points or on the boundary of the permissible region. If the critical points are outside this region, the value of the function on the boundary is examined. If the critical points are inside the permissible region, the values at the critical points and on the boundary are compared to find the absolute extrema.

The section by the plane $y = y_0$ has a relative maximum if $\partial f/\partial x = 0$ and $\partial^2 f/\partial x^2 < 0$, at (x_0, y_0). The section by the plane $x = x_0$ has a relative maximum if $f_y(x_0, y_0) = 0$ and $f_{yy}(x_0, y_0) < 0$. Unfortunately, these four conditions are not sufficient to ensure that $z = f(x, y)$ has a relative maximum at (x_0, y_0). Such surfaces are difficult to visualize in a perspective diagram, but a simple example may illustrate this situation.

EXAMPLE 6–4. $z = (y - 2x)(x - 2y) = 5xy - 2x^2 - 2y^2$.

If $y = 0$, then $z = -2x^2$, and at the origin $\partial z/\partial x = 0$ and $\partial^2 z/\partial x^2 = -4$, so that this section has a maximum at O. If $x = 0$, then $z = -2y^2$, and similarly, this section has a maximum at O. But, if $y = x$, then $z = x^2$, and it is quite obvious that this section has a minimum at O. Hence this surface has neither a maximum nor a minimum at O.

The geometry of surfaces is intrinsically more difficult than that of curves. If the surface has a relative maximum, the above four conditions are satisfied, but the converse is not true. One further condition (which we are not in a position to prove) must be added to provide *sufficient* conditions for a maximum. The sufficient conditions may be stated as follows:

(1) *If the determinant*

$$\Delta \equiv \begin{vmatrix} f_{xx}(x_0, y_0) & f_{xy}(x_0, y_0) \\ f_{xy}(x_0, y_0) & f_{yy}(x_0, y_0) \end{vmatrix} = f_{xx}f_{yy} - (f_{xy})^2 > 0$$

at a critical point (x_0, y_0), *then the function has a relative extremum at* (x_0, y_0). The value of z is a relative maximum if $f_{xx} < 0$ and a relative minimum if $f_{xx} > 0$. (The condition on f_{yy} is not needed, since it is not independent of those stated for Δ and f_{xx}.)

(2) *If* $\Delta < 0$, *the function does not have a relative extremum at the critical point but has a saddle** point.*

The special case in which the function has a maximum in some directions and a minimum in others (Fig. 6–4) may be visualized by imagining an ideal mountain pass or by examining the surface in the neighborhood of two knuckles of a clenched fist.

---

* See A. E. Taylor, *Advanced Calculus*, pp. 232–234, Ginn, 1956, or T. M. Apostol, *Mathematical Analysis*, p. 149, Addison-Wesley, 1957.

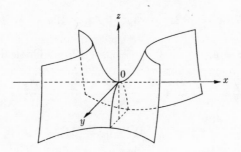

FIGURE 6–4

(3) *If* $\Delta = 0$, *the test fails* and further study of the function is required.

These three criteria are now applied to the Examples of the preceding section.

EXAMPLE 6–5. $z = x^2 + y^2$.

$$\frac{\partial z}{\partial x} = 2x, \qquad \frac{\partial z}{\partial y} = 2y, \qquad \frac{\partial^2 z}{\partial x^2} = 2, \qquad \frac{\partial^2 z}{\partial y^2} = 2, \qquad \frac{\partial^2 z}{\partial x\, \partial y} = 0.$$

The only critical point is $(0, 0)$ and the second derivatives are constants.

$$\Delta = \begin{vmatrix} 2 & 0 \\ 0 & 2 \end{vmatrix} = 4 > 0 \qquad \text{and} \qquad \frac{\partial^2 z}{\partial x^2} > 0.$$

Therefore the critical point gives a relative minimum value of z, which is also the absolute minimum, since there is only one critical point for all x and y.

EXAMPLE 6–6. $z = x^2 - y^2$. (See Fig. 6–4.)

$$\frac{\partial z}{\partial x} = 2x, \qquad \frac{\partial z}{\partial y} = -2y, \qquad \frac{\partial^2 z}{\partial x^2} = 2, \qquad \frac{\partial^2 z}{\partial x^2} = -2, \qquad \frac{\partial^2 z}{\partial x\, \partial y} = 0.$$

The only critical point is $(0, 0)$.

$$\Delta = \begin{vmatrix} 2 & 0 \\ 0 & -2 \end{vmatrix} = -4 < 0.$$

The function has no extremal value. It is easy to see (from Section 6–1) that the section by $y = 0$ has a minimum at $x = 0$ and the section by $x = 0$ has a maximum at $y = 0$. The critical point is a saddle point on the surface. (Figure 6–1 shows the indifference map at a saddle point.)

EXAMPLE 6–7. $z = -2x^2 - 3y^2 + 4x + 12y - 8$.

$$\frac{\partial z}{\partial x} = -4x + 4, \qquad \frac{\partial z}{\partial y} = -6y + 12, \qquad \text{Critical point: } (1, 2);$$

$$\frac{\partial^2 z}{\partial x^2} = -4 < 0, \qquad \frac{\partial^2 z}{\partial x\,\partial y} = 0, \qquad \frac{\partial^2 z}{\partial y^2} = -6;$$

$$\Delta = (-4)(-6) = 24 > 0.$$

Since there is only one critical point in the entire xy-plane, the surface has an absolute maximum at $x = 1$, $y = 2$, and

$$z_{\max} = -2 - 12 + 4 + 24 - 8 = 6.$$

EXAMPLE 6–8. $z = 4uv - u^2 - 3v^2$. (This production function was considered in Section 5–5, using Fig. 5–15.)

$$\frac{\partial z}{\partial u} = 4v - 2u, \quad \frac{\partial z}{\partial v} = 4u - 6v, \qquad \text{Critical point: } u = 0, v = 0; z = 0;$$

$$\frac{\partial^2 z}{\partial u^2} = -2, \qquad \frac{\partial^2 z}{\partial u\,\partial v} = 4, \qquad \frac{\partial^2 z}{\partial v^2} = -6,$$

$$\Delta = \begin{vmatrix} -2 & 4 \\ 4 & -6 \end{vmatrix} = 12 - 16 = -4.$$

Hence there is no extremum. The section of the surface by the plane $u = 0$ has a maximum at the critical point, as does the section by the plane $v = 0$, but the surface does not have a maximum at $(0, 0)$. A study of the indifference map in the uv-plane (Fig. 5–15) shows that z is positive in one part of the plane between the lines $v = u$ and $v = u/3$, and that $z = 0$ along these lines and is negative elsewhere. The surface has a saddle point at $(0, 0, 0)$.

EXAMPLE 6–9. $z = x^2 + y^4$.

$$z_x = 2x, \qquad z_y = 4y^3, \qquad z_{xx} = 2, \qquad z_{xy} = 0, \qquad z_{yy} = 12y^2.$$

At the critical point $(0, 0)$, $z_{yy} = 0$. Hence

$$\Delta = \begin{vmatrix} 2 & 0 \\ 0 & 0 \end{vmatrix} = 0,$$

and the test fails. The method used in Section 6–1 shows that the smallest value z can have is zero, corresponding to $x = 0$, $y = 0$.

EXAMPLE 6–10.

$$z = 9 - (x + 1)^2 - (y - 2)^2,$$

$(x, y, z$ zero or positive).

The critical point is at $x = -1$, $y = 2$, a point outside the permissible xy-region. The indifference map is a set of circles (Fig. 6–5), each having $(-1, 2)$ as center. The point circle corresponds to $z = 9$. As z decreases to zero, the circle expands. The maximum value of z occurs at $(0, 2)$ when a circle is just tangent to the line $x = 0$. This may be verified by noting that on the boundary $x = 0$, $z = 8 - (y - 2)^2$, and the largest value of z ($z_{\max} = 8$) occurs when $y = 2$. The largest value z can have on the boundary $y = 0$ occurs when $x = 0$, and this value is less than 8.

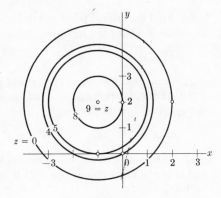

FIGURE 6–5

EXERCISE GROUP 6–1

1. If $z = 16 - x^2 - y^2$, ($z \geqq 0$), find the largest and smallest values that z may have. Discuss the corresponding surface.

2. (a) If $z = 36 - 9x^2 - 4y^2$, ($z \geqq 0$), find the largest and smallest values that z may have. (b) If the additional conditions $0 \leqq x \leqq 1$, $0 \leqq y \leqq 2$, are imposed upon the above function, what is the smallest value z can have? Discuss the corresponding surface.

3. Determine the critical points for the following functions and test these for maximum or minimum values of z:

    (a) $z = 28 + x^2 + 2xy + 4y^2$.   (b) $z = 48 - x^2 + 3xy - 3y^2$.

4. If $z = 48 - 4x^2 - 4xy - 2y^2 + 16x + 12y$, show that z has a maximum value and find this value.

5. (a) If $z = 13 - (x - 2)^2 - (y - 3)^2$, ($z \geqq 0$), determine the maximum value of z. (b) If the additional restrictions $0 \leqq x \leqq 1$, $0 \leqq y \leqq 1$, are imposed, what is the largest value z can have? Draw the corresponding indifference map.

6. If $z = 24x + 32y - x^2 - y^2$, ($z \geqq 0$), determine the maximum value of z. Draw the corresponding indifference map.

7. Show that $z = xy$ has a saddle point at $(0, 0)$ and discuss the maximum or minimum values of the sections of this surface by the planes $x = y$ and $x = -y$.

8. Show that $z = 48 - x^2 + 3xy - y^2$ has a saddle point at $(0, 0)$ and discuss the maximum or minimum values of the sections of this surface by the planes $x = y$ and $x = -y$.

9. Find the critical point and show that it is a saddle point for the following surfaces:

    (a) $z = xy - 2x - 4y$.   (b) $z = x^2 - y^2 - 2x - 4y$.

10. Find the critical point and determine whether it is a maximum, minimum, or saddle point for the following surfaces:

(a) $z = 3x - x^2 + xy - y^2$.   (b) $z = x - 4y - x^2 + 3xy - y^2$.

11. Show that the origin is a critical point for each of the following functions and that the determinant test fails in each case. Determine the nature of the critical point.

(a) $z = x^4 + y^2$.   (b) $z = x^4 + y^3$.   (c) $z = x^4 + y^4$.

12. Show that the origin is a critical point for each of the following functions and that the determinant test fails in each case. Determine the nature of the critical point.

(a) $z = x^2 + 2xy^2 + 2y^4$.   (b) $z = x^4 - 2x^2y^2 + 3y^4$.

13. If $z = 4x^2 - xy + y^2 - x^3$, show that there are two critical points and determine whether they correspond to maximum, minimum, or saddle points on the surface.

14. (a) If $z = 16 - (x + 2)^2 - (y - 2)^2$, $(z \geqq 0)$, determine the maximum value of z. Draw the indifference map. (b) If the additional restrictions $x \geqq 0$, $y \geqq 0$, are imposed upon the function, show that the maximum value of z is 12.

15. If $z = 16 - (x + 3)^2 - (y - 2)^2$, $(x \geqq 0, y \geqq 0, z \geqq 0)$, find the maximum value of z. Draw the indifference map.

16. (a) If $z = 20 - 2(x + 2)^2 - 3(y - 2)^2$, $(z \geqq 0)$, determine the maximum value of z. Draw the indifference map. (b) If the additional conditions $x \geqq 0$, $y \geqq 0$, are imposed upon the above function, show that the maximum value of z is 12.

6–3 Monopoly and the production of two commodities.

A monopolist who produces two commodities with known demand and joint-cost functions

$$x = f(p, q), \qquad y = g(p, q), \qquad Q = Q(x, y)$$

seeks to adjust the production of each commodity so as to maximize his profit. His revenue is $px + qy$ and his profit

$$\Pi = px + qy - Q(x, y).$$

If x and y are replaced by $f(p, q)$ and $g(p, q)$, respectively, Π is a function of p and q alone. The necessary conditions for maximum profit are that $\Pi_p = \Pi_q = 0$. After the critical points are obtained, one of the sufficient conditions discussed in Section 6–2 can be applied, and the quantity of each commodity and the maximum profit can then be computed. If a critical point yields the *absolute* maximum profit, there is no incentive for the monopolist to change his production schedule, and the situation is said to correspond to *economic stability.*

If the demand equations are solved for p and q in terms of x and y, the profit may be considered as a function of x and y. The necessary and sufficient conditions for maximum profit can then be applied to this function. (This corresponds to the first method used in Section 3–6.)

EXAMPLE 6–11. If the demand functions are

$$p = 36 - 3x, \qquad q = 40 - 5y,$$

and the joint-cost function is $Q = x^2 + 2xy + 3y^2$, determine the quantities and prices that maximize the profit and find the maximum profit.

$$\begin{aligned} \Pi &= px + qy - Q \\ &= 36x - 3x^2 + 40y - 5y^2 - x^2 - 2xy - 3y^2 \\ &= 36x + 40y - 4x^2 - 2xy - 8y^2, \end{aligned}$$

$$\frac{\partial \Pi}{\partial x} = 36 - 8x - 2y = 0, \qquad 4x + y = 18 \Big| -1$$

$$\frac{\partial \Pi}{\partial y} = 40 - 2x - 16y = 0, \qquad \underline{x + 8y = 20 \Big| \; 4}$$

$$31y = 62$$

Critical point: $y = 2$, $x = 4$;

$$\frac{\partial^2 \Pi}{\partial x^2} = -8, \qquad \frac{\partial^2 \Pi}{\partial x \, \partial y} = -2, \qquad \frac{\partial^2 \Pi}{\partial y^2} = -16,$$

$$\Delta = \begin{vmatrix} -8 & -2 \\ -2 & -16 \end{vmatrix} = 124 > 0.$$

Hence there is a relative maximum where $x = 4$, $y = 2$. Since there is only one critical point in the entire plane, and since $\Pi(x, y)$ is numerically large and negative for large x and y, the relative maximum is an absolute maximum. This situation corresponds to economic stability.

$$p = 36 - 12 = 24, \qquad q = 40 - 10 = 30,$$

$$\Pi_{\max} = 24 \cdot 4 + 30 \cdot 2 - (16 + 16 + 12) = 112.$$

EXAMPLE 6–12. The demand functions for two competitive commodities are

$$x = 7 - p + q, \qquad y = 6 + p - 2q,$$

and the average costs of production of the commodities are the constants 3 and 2, respectively. Determine the prices and quantities that maximize the profit.

The revenue is $R = px + qy$ and the total cost function is $Q = 3x + 2y$. Thus the profit can be written as

$$
\begin{aligned}
\Pi &= px + qy - 3x - 2y \\
&= (p - 3)x + (q - 2)y \\
&= (p - 3)(7 - p + q) + (q - 2)(6 + p - 2q) \\
&= -p^2 + 2pq - 2q^2 + 8p + 7q - 33,
\end{aligned}
$$

$$\frac{\partial \Pi}{\partial p} = -2p + 2q + 8, \qquad \frac{\partial \Pi}{\partial q} = 2p - 4q + 7.$$

The critical point is found to be $p = 23/2$, $q = 15/2$.

$$\frac{\partial^2 \Pi}{\partial p^2} = -2, \qquad \frac{\partial^2 \Pi}{\partial p\,\partial q} = 2, \qquad \frac{\partial^2 \Pi}{\partial q^2} = -4,$$

$$\Delta = \begin{vmatrix} -2 & 2 \\ 2 & -4 \end{vmatrix} = 4 > 0.$$

As in Example 6–11, the critical point corresponds to an absolute maximum:

$$x = 3, \qquad y = \tfrac{5}{2}, \qquad \Pi_{\max} = 39\tfrac{1}{4}.$$

The indifference diagram in the pq-plane consists of a family of concentric ellipses. The point $(23/2, 15/2)$ corresponds to the maximum profit; as the profit decreases, the ellipse expands. Figure 6–6 shows the ellipse through the origin, corresponding to $\Pi = -33$.

The same problem may be solved by considering x and y as the independent variables. Then

$$p = 20 - 2x - y, \qquad q = 13 - x - y,$$
$$\Pi = 17x + 11y - 2x^2 - 2xy - y^2.$$

The details and the completion of the solution are left as an exercise.

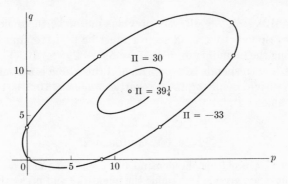

FIGURE 6–6

EXAMPLE 6–13. Suppose that a company produces the quantities x and y of two essentially independent goods whose demand functions are $p = 16 - x^2$ and $q = 8 - 2y$, respectively. Let the joint-cost function be $Q = 10 + 4x + 2y$. Determine the quantities and the prices that maximize the company's profit.

$$\Pi = px + qy - Q$$
$$= 16x - x^3 + 8y - 2y^2 - (10 + 4x + 2y)$$
$$= 12x - x^3 + 6y - 2y^2 - 10,$$

$$\frac{\partial \Pi}{\partial x} = 16 - 3x^2 - 4 = 0, \qquad \frac{\partial \Pi}{\partial y} = 6 - 4y = 0;$$

$$x = \pm 2, \ y = \frac{3}{2}, \qquad \text{so that} \quad p = 12, \ q = 5.$$

There are two critical points but only the point $(x = 2, y = 3/2)$ is in the permissible region.

$$\frac{\partial^2 \Pi}{\partial x^2} = -6x, \qquad \frac{\partial^2 \Pi}{\partial x \, \partial y} = 0, \qquad \frac{\partial^2 \Pi}{\partial y^2} = -4.$$

At this critical point,

$$\Delta = \begin{vmatrix} -12 & 0 \\ 0 & -4 \end{vmatrix} > 0,$$

and hence $(2, 3/2)$ corresponds to a relative maximum value of Π, which is $\Pi_{\max} = 10.5$. It can be shown that this value is also the absolute maximum (corresponding to economic stability). Along the boundary

$y = 0$, $\Pi = 12x - x^3 - 10$. By previous methods, the maximum value of this Π corresponds to $x = 2$, since x must be positive, and this value is $\Pi = 6$. Along the boundary $x = 0$, $\Pi = 6y - 2y^2 - 10$. The maximum value of this Π corresponds to $y = 3/2$, and this value is actually negative. For large positive x and y, Π is negative. Hence 10.5 is the absolute maximum value of Π.

Exercise Group 6–2*

In the following problems the demand functions and joint-cost function for two commodities are given. Determine the quantities and prices that maximize the profit and find the maximum profit. Justify your conclusions.

1. $p = 36 - 3x$, $\quad q = 40 - 5y$, $\quad Q = 12x + 20y$.

Discuss the nature of the indifference diagram without drawing it.

2. $p = 12 - x$, $\quad q = 15 - y$, $\quad Q = 4x + 5y$.

Draw the indifference diagram.

3. $p = 40 - 5x$, $\quad q = 30 - 3y$, $\quad Q = x^2 + 2xy + 3y^2$.
4. $p = 12 - x$, $\quad q = 15 - y$, $\quad Q = xy$.
5. $p = 12 - x$, $\quad q = 13 - y$, $\quad Q = 3xy$.

Show that the critical point does not correspond to maximum profit. The maximum profit corresponds to some point on the boundary ($x = 0, y \geqq 0$; $y = 0, x \geqq 0$).

6. Complete the second solution of Example 6–12 suggested in the text:

$$x = 7 - p + q, \qquad y = 6 + p - 2q, \qquad Q = 3x + 2y.$$

Consider x and y as the independent variables.

7. $x = 1 - p + 2q$, $\quad y = 11 + p - 3q$, $\quad Q = 4x + y$.

Solve the problem in the two ways suggested under Example 6–12.

8. The demand functions for two complementary goods are

$$x = 11 - 2p - 2q, \qquad y = 16 - 2p - 3q.$$

The joint-cost function is $Q = 3x + y$.

9. The demand functions are

$$p = 20 - 2x - y, \qquad q = 12 - x - y,$$

and the joint-cost function is $Q = x^2 + 2y^2$.

10. $p = 8 - 2x$, $\quad q = 14 - y^2$, $\quad Q = 10 + 4x + 2y$.
11. $p = 40 - 2x^2$, $\quad q = 12 - 3y$, $\quad Q = 8 + 4x + 3y$.
12. $p = 16 - x^2$, $\quad q = 9 - y^2$, $\quad Q = x + 3y$.
13. $p = 16 - x^2$, $\quad q = 9 - y^2$, $\quad Q = x^2 + 3y^2$.

---

* It is expected that this Exercise Group will require two assignments, even with a selection of problems.

6–4 Production under pure competition with two inputs. Consider now a company whose product involves two factors of production. Let the amounts of the inputs be u and v, the amount of the output be z, and let the given production function be $z = f(u, v)$. Under pure competition the company cannot determine the prices; they are constants determined by the general economy. Let the prices of the inputs be a and b, respectively, and the price of the output be c. The profit is the revenue less the total cost, or

$$\Pi = cz - au - bv = cf(u, v) - au - bv.$$

Assuming that its production is independent of that of any other firm, the company seeks to maximize its profit.

The second derivatives of the profit Π are (except for the positive numerical factor c) the same as the second derivatives of the production function f. Hence (1) there is a stable maximum profit if and only if the production function has a maximum at a critical point. (2) If the production function has saddle points at its critical points, there is no maximum profit, in the sense that by increasing the amounts of the inputs the profit is decreased. If, however, a restriction is placed on the amounts of the inputs, the problem reduces to one of maximizing a function of one variable, and there will be, in general, an unstable maximum profit. Both the above situations are illustrated by examples which follow.

EXAMPLE 6–14. Let the production function be

$$16z = 60 - 2(u - 5)^2 - 4(v - 4)^2,$$

and the prices be $a = 8$, $b = 4$, $c = 16$. Determine the maximum profit.
  The equation for the profit is

$$\Pi = 16z - 8u - 4v$$
$$= 60 - 2(u - 5)^2 - 4(v - 4)^2 - 8u - 4v;$$
$$\Pi_u = -4(u - 5) - 8, \qquad \Pi_v = -8(v - 4) - 4,$$
$$\Pi_{uu} = -4, \qquad \Pi_{uv} = 0, \qquad \Pi_{vv} = -8.$$

The only critical point is at $u = 3$, $v = 7/2$, and since $\Delta = 32 > 0$, the profit has an absolute (economically stable) maximum value:

$$\Pi_{\max} = 60 - 2(-2)^2 - 4\left(-\tfrac{1}{2}\right)^2 - 24 - 14 = 13.$$

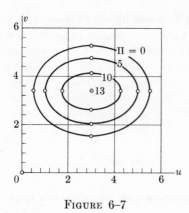

FIGURE 6–7

The critical values of u, v, and Π indicate that the equation for the profit could be written in the form

$$\Pi = 13 - 2(u - 3)^2 - 4(v - \tfrac{7}{2})^2,$$

which may be verified by direct comparison of the two forms of Π. The form

$$\frac{(u - 3)^2}{(13 - \Pi)/2} + \frac{(v - \tfrac{7}{2})^2}{(13 - \Pi)/4} = 1$$

shows that the indifference map is a family of concentric ellipses (Fig. 6–7) with center $u = 3$, $v = 7/2$ corresponding to the maximum profit 13.

EXAMPLE 6–15. The production function is $z = 12 - (2/u) - (4/v)$, and the prices corresponding to u, v, z are 2, 4, 9, respectively. Find the maximum profit.

$$\Pi = 9z - 2u - 4v$$

$$= 108 - \frac{18}{u} - \frac{36}{v} - 2u - 4v,$$

$$\frac{\partial \Pi}{\partial u} = \frac{18}{u^2} - 2, \qquad \frac{\partial \Pi}{\partial v} = \frac{36}{v^2} - 4.$$

The critical point is $(3, 3)$, since u and v must be positive.

$$\frac{\partial^2 \Pi}{\partial u^2} = -\frac{36}{u^3}, \qquad \frac{\partial^2 \Pi}{\partial u \, \partial v} = 0, \qquad \frac{\partial^2 \Pi}{\partial v^2} = -\frac{72}{v^3}.$$

Hence

$$\Delta = \frac{36 \cdot 72}{u^3 v^3} > 0,$$

and the critical point corresponds to maximum profit. The corresponding value of z and the maximum profit are

$$z = 12 - \tfrac{2}{3} - \tfrac{4}{3} = 10, \qquad \Pi_{max} = 90 - 6 - 12 = 72.$$

EXAMPLE 6–16. Let the production function be $z = uv$, the prices corresponding to u, v, z be $a = 4$, $b = 8$, $c = 8$, respectively, and impose the restrictions that $0 \leqq u \leqq 2$, $0 \leqq v \leqq 2$. Some restrictions on u and v are necessary; otherwise z, and hence Π, could be increased indefinitely by increasing u and v. The equation for profit is

$$\Pi = 8uv - 4u - 8v;$$

$$\frac{\partial \Pi}{\partial u} = 8v - 4, \qquad \frac{\partial \Pi}{\partial v} = 8u - 8.$$

Hence there is a critical point at $u = 1$, $v = \frac{1}{2}$.

$$\frac{\partial^2 \Pi}{\partial u^2} = 0, \qquad \frac{\partial^2 \Pi}{\partial u \, \partial v} = 8, \qquad \frac{\partial^2 \Pi}{\partial v^2} = 0,$$

$$\Delta = -64.$$

There is a saddle point on the surface at the critical point. If there is a maximum value of Π it will occur on the boundary $u = 2$, $v \geqq 0$, or $v = 2$, $u \geqq 0$.

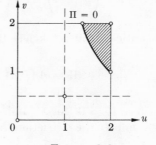

The profit equation may be reduced to the form

$$\Pi = 8(u - 1)(v - \tfrac{1}{2}) - 4,$$

from which we see that the maximum value of Π occurs when both u and v are made as large as is permissible, that is, $u = 2$, $v = 2$. Hence

$$\Pi_{\max} = 8 \cdot 1 \cdot \tfrac{3}{2} - 4 = 8.$$

FIGURE 6–8

Figure 6–8 shows the indifference curve corresponding to $\Pi = 0$, and a shaded region; if the point (u, v) is inside this region, Π is positive. The maximum profit $\Pi_{\max} = 8$ occurs at the corner $u = 2$, $v = 2$ of this region.

EXAMPLE 6–17. Let the production function be $z = 4uv - u^2 - 3v^2$ (cf. Example 5–10) and let the prices be $a = 2$, $b = 4$, $c = 4$. Determine the maximum profit.

$$\Pi = 4 \left(-u^2 + 4uv - 3v^2\right) - 2u - 4v,$$

$$\Pi_u = -8u + 16v - 2, \qquad \Pi_v = 16u - 24v - 4.$$

The critical point is found by solving the simultaneous equations

$$-4u + 8v = 1$$

$$\frac{4u - 6v = 1}{2v = 2}, \quad v = 1,\; u = \frac{7}{4};$$

$$\Pi_{uu} = -8, \quad \Pi_{uv} = 16, \quad \Pi_{vv} = -24,$$

$$\Delta = \begin{vmatrix} -8 & 16 \\ 16 & -24 \end{vmatrix} = 192 - 256 < 0.$$

There is a saddle point at the only critical point, and there is no absolute maximum value of Π. The value of Π at the critical point is

$$\Pi_s = 4\left(-\frac{49}{16} + 7 - 3\right)\left(\frac{7}{2} - 4\right) = -\frac{15}{4},$$

which indicates that Π can be written in the form

$$\Pi = 4\left[-\left(u - \frac{7}{4}\right)^2 + 4\left(u - \frac{7}{4}\right)(v - 1) - 3(v - 1)^2\right] - \frac{15}{4}.$$

If the critical point is taken as the new origin, the above equation becomes

$$\Pi = 4\left(-u_1^2 + 4u_1 v_1 - 3v_1^2\right) - \frac{15}{4}.$$

The curve $\Pi = 0$ (for u_1 and v_1 positive) is a hyperbola (Fig. 6–9). If we now impose the restriction that $u \leq 4$, the maximum profit then occurs

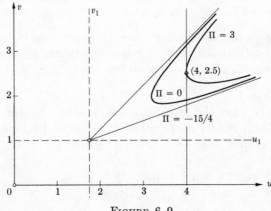

FIGURE 6–9

on the boundary line $u = 4$ between the points where it cuts this hyperbola. If $u = 4$, call the profit Π_1, where Π_1 is a function of v alone:

$$\Pi_1 = 4\,(-16 + 16v - 3v^2) - 8 - 4v$$

$$= -72 + 60v - 12v^2,$$

$$\frac{d\Pi_1}{dv} = 60 - 24v, \qquad \frac{d^2\Pi_1}{dv^2} = -24.$$

Therefore Π_1 has a relative maximum which is also an absolute maximum at $v = 5/2$.

$$\Pi_{1,\,\mathrm{max}} = -72 + 150 - 12 \cdot \frac{25}{4} = 3.$$

Hence the maximum profit under the given restriction occurs when $u = 4$, $v = 5/2$, and $\Pi_{\mathrm{max}} = 3$.

EXERCISE GROUP 6–3

1. If the production function for a commodity which uses two inputs is $8z = 50 - (u - 4)^2 - (v - 5)^2$, and if the prices of u, v, and z are 2, 6, and 8, respectively, determine the maximum profit. Draw the indifference map in the uv-plane.

2. If the production function for a commodity which uses two inputs is $16z = 60 - 4(u - 5)^2 - 2(v - 4)^2$, and if the prices corresponding to u, v, and z are 8, 4, and 16, determine the maximum profit. Draw the indifference map in the uv-plane.

3. If the production function for a commodity which uses two inputs is $5z = 6u + 24v - u^2 - 4v^2 - 25$ and the corresponding prices are $a = 8$, $b = 16$, and $c = 20$, determine the maximum profit. Draw the indifference map in the uv-plane. (After the critical point and Π_{max} are found, express Π in a form that shows these three values.)

4. If the production function is $z = 5 - u^{-1} - v^{-1}$ and the corresponding prices are $a = 1$, $b = 4$, and $c = 9$, determine the maximum profit.

5. If the production function is $z = 5 - u^{-1} - 2v^{-1}$ and the corresponding prices are $a = 1$, $b = 4$, and $c = 9$, determine the maximum profit.

6. If the production function is $z = 5 - (1/u) - (1/v^2)$ and the corresponding prices are $a = 1$, $b = 4$, and $c = 9$, determine the maximum profit.

7. If the production function is $z = 4 - (8/uv)$ and the prices corresponding to u, v, and z are 10, 5, and 20, determine the maximum profit. Justify your conclusions.

8. If the production function is $z = 4 - (2/u^2v)$ and the prices corresponding to u, v, and z are 5, 5, and 10, determine the maximum profit. Justify your conclusions.

9. If the production function is $z = uv - 2v$, $(0 \leq u \leq 4, 0 \leq v \leq 2)$, and the corresponding prices are $a = 4$, $b = 4$, and $c = 8$, show that the maximum profit occurs on the boundary. Find the maximum profit.

10. If the production function is $z = \frac{1}{2}u^2v$, $(0 \leq u \leq 3, 0 \leq v \leq 2)$, and the corresponding prices are $a = 6$, $b = 3$, and $c = 6$, show that the maximum profit occurs on the boundary and has the value 30. Show that part of the indifference map which corresponds to $u \geq 1$, $v \geq 0$, and $\Pi = 0, 6, 15, 24$.

11. Reconsider Example 6–17: $z = 4uv - u^2 - 3v^2$, $a = 2$, $b = 4$, $c = 4$, with the limitation replaced by (a) $u = 6$, and (b) $v = 4$.

12. If the production function is $z = 5uv - 2u^2 - 2v^2$ and the prices corresponding to u, v, and z are 4, 4, and 6, respectively, show that the critical point for the profit function corresponds to a saddle point and that the value of the profit is $-8/3$ at this point. If the condition $u \leq 3$ is imposed upon the production function, determine the maximum profit.

6–5 Maxima and minima under constraint. It is frequently required to maximize or minimize a function of several variables under restrictions (constraints) on the variables. One such problem was considered in Section 6–4 where it was required to maximize a function of three variables, $\Pi = cz - au - bv$, subject to the constraint $z = f(u, v)$. The method used in Section 6–4 is known as the *explicit* method. By eliminating z, Π was expressed in terms of u and v, and the necessary and sufficient conditions given in Section 6–2 were applied. This problem will be considered further after the corresponding problem for a function of two variables has been discussed.

To find the extremal values of a function of two variables subject to a condition of constraint, four different but related solutions are suggested.

(A) *Explicit method.* If $u = f(x, y)$ and $y = g(x)$, then by eliminating y,

$$u = f[x, g(x)] = F(x).$$

The necessary and sufficient conditions that u have a maximum are

$$\frac{du}{dx} = \frac{dF(x)}{dx} = 0 \quad \text{and} \quad \frac{d^2u}{dx^2} < 0,$$

and for a minimum, the second condition is

$$\frac{d^2u}{dx^2} > 0.$$

(B) *Implicit method.* If the condition of constraint is given in the implicit form $G(x, y) = 0$, it may not be convenient to solve for y. In that case, du/dx and dy/dx may be found by implicit differentiation (see

Sections 2–8 and 5–8):

$$\frac{du}{dx} = \frac{\partial u}{\partial x} + \frac{\partial u}{\partial y} \cdot \frac{dy}{dx}, \qquad \frac{dy}{dx} = -\frac{\partial G/\partial x}{\partial G/\partial y}.$$

However, the differentiation may be accomplished without using these formulas. If dy/dx is eliminated from the two equations above, then

$$\frac{du}{dx} = f_1(x, y).$$

A similar procedure can then be used to find

$$\frac{d^2 u}{dx^2} = \frac{df_1(x, y)}{dx}.$$

The critical points are found from the simultaneous solution of

$$\frac{du}{dx} = f_1(x, y) = 0, \qquad G(x, y) = 0,$$

and the second derivative is then examined at each critical point in the region under consideration.

EXAMPLE 6–18. Determine the extremal values of $u = 16 - x^2 - 2y^2$ subject to the condition $x + y = 2$.

Explicit solution.

$$u = 16 - x^2 - 2y^2 = 16 - x^2 - 2(2 - x)^2$$
$$= 8 + 8x - 3x^2,$$
$$\frac{du}{dx} = 8 - 6x, \qquad \frac{d^2 u}{dx^2} = -6.$$

The critical point $x = 4/3$, $y = 2/3$ gives a relative and absolute maximum value of u:

$$u_{\max} = 8 + \frac{32}{3} - \frac{16}{3} = \frac{40}{3}.$$

Implicit solution.

$$\frac{du}{dx} = -2x - 4y\frac{dy}{dx}, \qquad 1 + \frac{dy}{dx} = 0, \quad \text{or} \quad \frac{dy}{dx} = -1,$$

so that

$$\frac{du}{dx} = -2x + 4y, \qquad \frac{d^2 u}{dx^2} = -2 + 4\frac{dy}{dx} = -6.$$

The critical point, found by solving simultaneously $x + y = 2$ and $-2x + 4y = 0$, is $x = 4/3$, $y = 2/3$, which gives a relative and absolute maximum value of $u_{max} = 40/3$.

(C) *Lagrange multiplier method.* This third method for finding extremal values uses the notation of method (B). We define a new function $L(x, y)$ as

$$L(x, y) \equiv f(x, y) - \lambda G(x, y),$$

where the constant multiplier λ is to be determined. Necessary conditions that f shall have an extremal value are

$$\frac{\partial L}{\partial x} = 0 \quad \text{and} \quad \frac{\partial L}{\partial y} = 0.$$

These two equations together with $G(x, y) = 0$ are, in general, sufficient to determine λ, x, and y, for the critical points.

A disadvantage of this method is that there is, in general, no simple way to find the second derivative of u, as is necessary to apply the sufficient condition. (However, see Section 6–7 for an important special case.) A combination of methods (B) and (C) sometimes has the advantage of algebraic simplicity. Another advantage, especially for functions of several variables arising from problems of economics, lies in the fact that λ can be given an interpretation related to such concepts as marginal cost or marginal utility of money.*

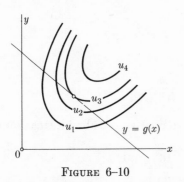

FIGURE 6–10

(D) *Geometric solution.* Draw the indifference map to represent the function $u = f(x, y)$, and in the same diagram draw the curve of constraint $y = g(x)$ or $G(x, y) = 0$. If this curve is tangent to an indifference curve for some particular u, a point of contact corresponds to critical values of x and y, and the value of u corresponds to the extremal value of u. Let a u-curve near the critical u-curve cut the curve of constraint. If this value of u is less than the critical value of u, then the critical value of u is a relative maximum; if this value of u is greater than the critical value of u, then the critical value of u is a relative minimum. The absolute maximum and minimum are found as in previous situations.

---

* See P. A. Samuelson, *Foundations of Economic Analysis*, pp. 65, 100, and R. D. G. Allen, *Mathematical Analysis for Economists*, p. 512.

Methods (C) and (D) are now illustrated by a further discussion of Example 6–18.

EXAMPLE 6–19. Determine the extremal values of $u = 16 - x^2 - 2y^2$ subject to the condition $x + y = 2$.

Solution using the Lagrange multiplier.

$$L(x, y) = 16 - x^2 - 2y^2 - \lambda(x + y - 2),$$

$$\frac{\partial L}{\partial x} = -2x - \lambda = 0, \qquad \frac{\partial L}{\partial y} = -4y - \lambda = 0.$$

The two equations above imply that $x = 2y$, and this together with $x + y = 2$ yields the critical values $x = 4/3$, $y = 2/3$, $u = 40/3$. To show that the critical point $(4/3, 2/3)$ corresponds to maximum u, consider the indifference map (Fig. 6–11), where the indifference curves are ellipses $x^2 + 2y^2 = 16 - u$, $(0 \leq u \leq 16)$. (For simplicity, only that part of the indifference map in the first quadrant is shown.) The curve of constraint is a straight line, and the ellipse that is tangent to this line at $(4/3, 2/3)$ corresponds to the value $u = 40/3$. To find an ellipse that cuts this line, it is necessary to decrease the value of u. Hence $40/3$ is the maximum value of u. It is not necessary to draw the

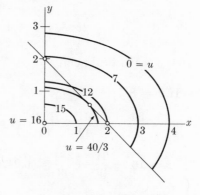

FIGURE 6–11

entire indifference map. Since there is only one critical point, the value of u at this critical point, $u_c = 40/3$, is compared with the values of u at points on the line of constraint, one on each side of the critical point. Since $u(2, 0) = 12$ and $u(0, 2) = 8$ are both less than $u(4/3, 2/3)$, the absolute maximum value of u is $40/3$.

EXAMPLE 6–20. Determine the extremal values of $u = 16 - x^2 - 2y^2$ subject to the condition $4x^2 - 8x + y^2 = 0$.

The solution by the implicit method, and its geometric interpretation, will be given. The indifference curves form the same family (Fig. 6–11) discussed in Example 6–19. The curve of constraint is the ellipse

$$\frac{(x - 1)^2}{1} + \frac{y^2}{4} = 1.$$

Since this curve is such that $0 \leq x \leq 2$, and since the absolute extremal values are sought, it is necessary to consider the values of u at the end points of this interval together with those at the critical values of x.

$$\text{If } x = 0, \quad \text{then} \quad y = 0 \text{ and} \quad u = 16,$$
$$\text{If } x = 2, \quad \text{then} \quad y = 0 \text{ and} \quad u = 12.$$

Note that the point ellipse $u = 16$ and the ellipse corresponding to $u = 12$ are tangent to the curve of constraint (Fig. 6–12). To find the critical point we use implicit differentiation:

$$\frac{du}{dx} = -2x - 4y \frac{dy}{dx},$$

$$8x - 8 + 2y \frac{dy}{dx} = 0, \quad \text{or} \quad y \frac{dy}{dx} = 4 - 4x,$$

$$\frac{du}{dx} = -2x - 4(4 - 4x) = 14x - 16, \quad \frac{d^2u}{dx^2} = 14.$$

Hence the critical point $x = 8/7$ gives a relative minimum value of u.

If $x = 8/7$,

$$y^2 = \frac{64}{7} - 4 \cdot \frac{64}{49} = \frac{192}{49},$$

$$z = 16 - \frac{64}{49} - \frac{384}{49} = 6.94,$$

or approximately 7.

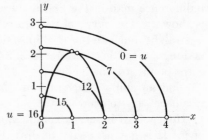

FIGURE 6–12

This result agrees with the geometric diagram (Fig. 6–12), which shows that in order for an indifference curve to intersect the ellipse of constraint, the value of u must be increased, and hence the value of u at the critical point is a relative minimum. Since this value (7) is less than that at either end point, it is the absolute minimum value of u. The absolute maximum value of u is 16.

The implicit method and the Lagrange multiplier method can also be used to find the maximum of a function of three (or more) variables subject to a condition of constraint. These methods are now used to solve Example 6–15.

The critical point is found by the Lagrange multiplier method and the second derivatives are found by implicit differentiation. The problem is to maximize the profit

$$\Pi = 9z - 2u - 4v, \quad \text{subject to } z = 12 - \frac{2}{u} - \frac{4}{v}.$$

We form the function

$$L(u, v, z) = (9z - 2u - 4v) - \lambda \left(z + \frac{2}{u} + \frac{4}{v} - 12 \right),$$

and determine the values of u, v, z, and λ that satisfy the equation of constraint and make the partial derivatives of L with respect to u, v, and z vanish.

$$\frac{\partial L}{\partial u} = -2 - \lambda \left(-\frac{2}{u^2} \right) = 0,$$

$$\frac{\partial L}{\partial v} = -4 - \lambda \left(-\frac{4}{v^2} \right) = 0,$$

$$\frac{\partial L}{\partial z} = 9 - \lambda = 0.$$

Hence $\lambda = 9$, $u^2 = 9$, $v^2 = 9$, and since u and v are positive, the critical conditions are $u = 3$, $v = 3$, $z = 10$, $\Pi = 72$. It is possible to show that this is the maximum profit by considering the second derivatives of Π:

$$\frac{\partial \Pi}{\partial u} = 9\frac{\partial z}{\partial u} - 2 = \frac{18}{u^2} - 2, \qquad \frac{\partial \Pi}{\partial v} = 9\frac{\partial z}{\partial v} - 4 = \frac{36}{v^2} - 4,$$

$$\frac{\partial^2 \Pi}{\partial u^2} = -\frac{36}{u^3}, \qquad \frac{\partial^2 \Pi}{\partial u\, \partial v} = 0, \qquad \frac{\partial^2 \Pi}{\partial v^2} = -\frac{72}{v^3}.$$

Hence $\Delta > 0$, so that $\Pi = 72$ is the maximum profit.

EXERCISE GROUP 6–4*

1. Determine the maximum value of z, if $z = 16 - x^2 - y^2$ and $x + 2y = 3$. Discuss the corresponding geometric problem with respect to a space diagram and also with respect to the indifference map.

2. Determine the extremal value of z, if $z = (x - 8)^2 + (y - 2)^2$ subject to the constraint $x + 3y = 14$. Solve the problem by two methods.

3. Determine the extremal value of $z = 2x^2 + 4y^2 + 5$, where $x + y = 3$. Justify your conclusions algebraically and geometrically.

4. Determine the extremal values of $z = 2x^2 + 4y^2 + 5$, where $x^2 + y^2 = 2x$. Justify your conclusions algebraically and geometrically.

5. Determine the extremal values of $z = 25 - x^2 - y^2$ subject to the condition $x^2 - 4x + y^2 = 0$. Justify your conclusions.

---

* This set would normally require more than one assignment. It is suggested that the first assignment be selected from problems 1 through 7 above, a second assignment be selected from problems 8 through 10 above and 1 through 6 of Exercise Group 6–5, and a third assignment be selected from problems 7 through 16 of Exercise Group 6–5.

6. Determine the extremal values of $z = y^2 - 4xy + 27$ subject to the condition $y = x^2$. Use the explicit, implicit, and Lagrange multiplier methods to obtain the critical points. Apply the appropriate test for each critical point.

7. Determine the extremal values of $z = 3x^2 + 4y^2 + 2y + 3$ subject to the constraint $x^2 + 2y = 5$. (a) Use y as the independent variable and solve the problem using the explicit method. (b) Solve the problem by obtaining the critical point through use of the Lagrange multiplier method. Find the second derivative by implicit differentiation.

In problems 8, 9, 10 a production function is given, and the prices corresponding to u, v, and z are a, b, and c, respectively. Determine the maximum profit, and justify your conclusions. Use the Lagrange multiplier method to find the critical points and the implicit differentiation method to find the second derivatives of Π. (These problems are taken from Exercise Group 6–3.)

8. (a) $8z = 50 - (u - 4)^2 - (v - 5)^2$, $a = 2$, $b = 6$, $c = 8$.

(b) $5z = 6u + 24v - u^2 - 4v^2 - 25$, $a = 8$, $b = 16$, $c = 20$.

(Problems 1 and 3, Exercise Group 6–3.)

9. (a) $z = 5 - (1/u) - (2/v)$, $a = 1$, $b = 4$, $c = 9$.

(b) $z = 5 - (1/u) - (1/v^2)$, $a = 1$, $b = 4$, $c = 9$.

(Problems 5 and 6, Exercise Group 6–3.)

10. (a) $z = 4 - (8/uv)$, $a = 10$, $b = 5$, $c = 20$.

(b) $z = 4 - (2/u^2v)$, $a = 5$, $b = 5$, $c = 10$.

(Problems 7 and 8, Exercise Group 6–3.)

6–6 Utility index and the budget equation. *Utility* (as the term is used in economics) refers to the satisfaction derived by the individual or group from the possession or use of varying amounts of different commodities. Because it indicates the *relative preferences* for the commodities, it is related to the concept of ordered rather than measurable magnitudes. Since there does not exist a natural unit by which this elusive satisfaction or preference can be measured, we use the term *utility index* and introduce arbitrary units for the statistical measurement of the degree of these preferences.

Our attention is confined to the case of two commodities, but the ideas may be extended to more. Suppose that the utility index U is given by some positive function of the variable amounts of the two commodities x and y, that is, $U = f(x, y)$, $(x, y, U$ positive). There are natural limitations on the nature of the utility index function, and it is assumed that the following conditions hold. (1) For any given value of U, an increase of x is accompanied by a decrease of y; that is, the slope of each curve in the indifference map is negative and the curve is convex toward the origin.

(2) If either x or y is fixed, and the other variable increases, the consumer increases his satisfaction, and hence the values of U increase from one indifference curve to the other in the direction away from the origin (Fig. 6–13). Various types of generalized hyperbolas and closed ovals with centers at a point distinct from the origin have been found useful for the study of the utility concept. In either case only that part of each curve which satisfies conditions (1) and (2) is used.

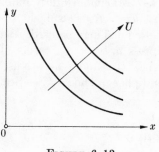

FIGURE 6–13

Let the prices of the two commodities be the positive constants a and b. These prices are established independently of any action of the individual or group in question. If the amount of income which is expendable upon these commodities is the constant k, then x and y are restricted by the *budget equation*,

$$ax + by = k.$$

The fundamental problem is to determine those values of x and y that maximize the utility index, subject to the budget equation, rather than to measure the maximum utility. The utility index U, under the given constraint, may be considered as a function of x alone; that is, $U = f(x, y) = F(x)$. Suppose that $Z = \phi(U)$ is any positive monotonically increasing function of U, so that Z and the corresponding slope $\phi'(U)$ are always positive for all U under consideration. (Simple examples of such functions are U^2, $\ln (1 + U)$, and e^U.) Then

$$\frac{dZ}{dx} = \frac{dZ}{dU} \cdot \frac{dU}{dx} = \phi'(U) \frac{dU}{dx}.$$

It follows that $dZ/dx = 0$ if and only if $dU/dx = 0$. Hence the functions Z and U have the same critical points.

$$\frac{d^2Z}{dx^2} = \phi''(U) \left(\frac{dU}{dx}\right)^2 + \phi'(U) \frac{d^2U}{dx^2}.$$

At the critical points, $dU/dx = 0$, and hence d^2Z/dx^2 and d^2U/dx^2 always have the same sign. It follows that for the fundamental problem either U or Z may be used as the utility index. This property compensates for the lack of a natural unit of measurement and justifies the introduction of an arbitrary unit for statistical purposes. (See Example 6–23.)

6-7 Maximum utility index subject to the budget equation. To maximize $U = f(x, y)$ subject to $ax + by = k$, any of the four methods of Section 6-5 may be used. Because the constraint is linear, it is possible to express d^2U/dx^2 in terms of the second partial derivatives of U with respect to x and y, and to use this expression in the implicit and Lagrange multiplier methods. (See Section 5-8.)

$$\frac{dU}{dx} = \frac{\partial U}{\partial x} + \frac{\partial U}{\partial y} \cdot \frac{dy}{dx}, \qquad a + b\frac{dy}{dx} = 0,$$

so that

$$\frac{dU}{dx} = \frac{\partial f}{\partial x} - \frac{a}{b} \cdot \frac{\partial f}{\partial y}.$$

This is also a function of x and y and can be differentiated in the manner just described:

$$\frac{d^2U}{dx^2} = \frac{\partial}{\partial x}\left(\frac{\partial f}{\partial x} - \frac{a}{b} \cdot \frac{\partial f}{\partial y}\right) + \frac{\partial}{\partial y}\left(\frac{\partial f}{\partial x} - \frac{a}{b} \cdot \frac{\partial f}{\partial y}\right) \cdot \left(\frac{-a}{b}\right),$$

$$\frac{d^2U}{dx^2} = \frac{\partial^2 f}{\partial x^2} - 2\frac{a}{b} \cdot \frac{\partial^2 f}{\partial x\,\partial y} + \frac{a^2}{b^2} \cdot \frac{\partial^2 f}{\partial y^2}. \tag{6-2}$$

If the Lagrange multiplier method is used,

$$L(x, y) = f(x, y) - \lambda(ax + by - k).$$

It is readily verified that

$$\frac{\partial^2 L}{\partial x^2} = \frac{\partial^2 f}{\partial x^2}, \qquad \frac{\partial^2 L}{\partial x\,\partial y} = \frac{\partial^2 f}{\partial x\,\partial y}, \qquad \frac{\partial^2 L}{\partial y^2} = \frac{\partial^2 f}{\partial y^2},$$

$$\frac{d^2U}{dx^2} = \frac{\partial^2 L}{\partial x^2} - 2\frac{a}{b} \cdot \frac{\partial^2 L}{\partial x\,\partial y} + \frac{a^2}{b^2} \cdot \frac{\partial^2 L}{\partial y^2}. \tag{6-3}$$

EXAMPLE 6-21. Determine the values of x and y that maximize the utility index

$$U = -2x^2 + 5xy - y^2, \qquad \text{subject to } x + 3y = 8.$$

First solution (Explicit method). It is desirable to eliminate x rather than y:

$$U = -2(8 - 3y)^2 + 5y(8 - 3y) - y^2$$

$$= -128 + 136y - 34y^2;$$

$$\frac{dU}{dy} = 136 - 68y, \qquad \frac{d^2U}{dy^2} = -68.$$

The critical value of y is 2, the corresponding value of x is 2, and the critical point $(2, 2)$ maximizes U.

Geometric interpretation. The indifference diagram (Fig. 6–14) is a family of hyperbolas all having the same oblique asymptotes. These asymptotes are obtained by solving

$$y^2 - 5xy + 2x^2 = 0$$

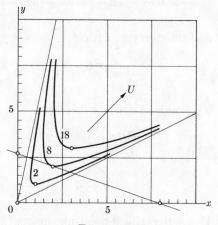

(found by setting $U = 0$) for the ratio of y to x:

$$y = \left(\frac{5 \pm \sqrt{25 - 8}}{2}\right) x,$$

or

$$y = 4.5x \quad \text{and} \quad y = 0.5x$$

(approximately).

For $U = 8$, the hyperbola is tangent to the line $x + 3y = 8$ at $(2, 2)$. As U increases from zero, the hyperbola moves away from the origin. This may be verified by

FIGURE 6–14

finding the intersections of the line $y = x$ with the hyperbolas. The indifference curves for $U = 0, 2, 8,$ and 18 are shown in Fig. 6–14.

Second solution (Implicit method).

$$\frac{dU}{dx} = -4x + 5y + 5x\frac{dy}{dx} - 2y\frac{dy}{dx},$$

$$1 + 3\frac{dy}{dx} = 0,$$

$$\text{or} \quad \frac{dy}{dx} = -\frac{1}{3},$$

$$\frac{dU}{dx} = -4x + 5y - \frac{1}{3}(5x - 2y) = \frac{-17}{3}(x - y),$$

$$\frac{d^2U}{dx^2} = -\frac{17}{3}\left(1 + \frac{1}{3}\right) = -\frac{68}{9}.$$

The conditions for a critical point are $x - y = 0$ and $x + 3y = 8$. Hence the critical point is at $(2, 2)$. Since $d^2U/dx^2 < 0$, U is a maximum.

Third solution (Lagrange multiplier method).

$$L(x, y) = -2x^2 + 5xy - y^2 - \lambda(x + 3y - 8).$$

The necessary conditions are

$$\frac{\partial L}{\partial x} = -4x + 5y - \lambda = 0, \qquad \frac{\partial L}{\partial y} = 5x - 2y - 3\lambda = 0;$$

$$\lambda = -4x + 5y = \frac{1}{3}(5x - 2y), \qquad \text{or} \quad x = y;$$

and this together with $x + 3y = 8$ yields the critical point $(2, 2)$.

$$\frac{\partial^2 L}{\partial x^2} \equiv \frac{\partial^2 U}{\partial x^2} = -4, \qquad \frac{\partial^2 L}{\partial x\,\partial y} = 5, \qquad \frac{\partial^2 L}{\partial y^2} = -2.$$

The value of $d^2 U/dx^2$ is (Eq. 6–3)

$$\frac{d^2 U}{dx^2} = L_{xx} - \frac{2}{3} L_{xy} + \frac{1}{9} L_{yy}$$

$$= -4 - \frac{10}{3} - \frac{2}{9} = -\frac{68}{9} \qquad \text{(as before)}.$$

Hence the critical point maximizes the utility index. The same conclusion could be reached without using $d^2 U/dx^2$ by noting that the value of U at $(2, 2)$ is 8, and at the points where the budget line cuts the axes, U is negative and hence less than 8.

EXAMPLE 6–22. Determine the values of x and y that maximize the utility index

$$U = 108 - [(x - 6)^2 + 2(y - 6)^2],$$

if the budget equation is $3x + 4y = 25$.

The utility index function was written in the above form to emphasize geometric considerations. The indifference curves are ellipses with the center $(6, 6)$, and this point corresponds to $U = 108$. The given equation can be written

$$\frac{(x - 6)^2}{108 - U} + \frac{(y - 6)^2}{(108 - U)/2} = 1,$$

from which the lengths of the semi-axes may be read for any given U. That part of each ellipse where the slope is negative and the curve is convex toward the origin is shown in the diagram (Fig. 6–15).

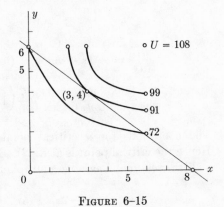

FIGURE 6–15

$$U = 108 - (x - 6)^2 - 2(y - 6)^2, \qquad 3x + 4y = 25,$$

$$\frac{dU}{dx} = -2(x - 6) - 4(y - 6)\frac{dy}{dx}, \qquad \text{where} \quad \frac{dy}{dx} = -\frac{3}{4}.$$

This result reduces to

$$\frac{dU}{dx} = -2x + 3y - 6, \qquad \text{so that} \quad \frac{d^2U}{dx^2} = -2 + 3\left(-\frac{3}{4}\right) < 0.$$

The critical point is found by solving the simultaneous equations

$$-2x + 3y = 6, \qquad 3x + 4y = 25.$$

The result is $x = 3$, $y = 4$, and the corresponding value of U is $U_{\max} = 91$. The corresponding ellipse is tangent to the line $3x + 4y = 25$ at $(3, 4)$ as shown in Fig. 6–15.

EXAMPLE 6–23. Determine the values of x and y that maximize the utility index $U = x^{1/3}y^{2/3}$, if the prices of the two commodities are 1 and 4, respectively, and the expendable income is 12.

The budget equation is $x + 4y = 12$. The values of x and y that maximize U also maximize $Z \equiv U^3$, and the problem becomes that of maximizing $Z = xy^2$ subject to the condition $x + 4y = 12$. It is simpler to eliminate x than y:

$$Z = (12 - 4y)y^2 = 12y^2 - 4y^3,$$

$$\frac{dZ}{dy} = 24y - 12y^2, \qquad \frac{d^2Z}{dy^2} = 24 - 24y.$$

The critical values of y are 0 and 2. If $y = 0$, $Z'' > 0$, and $Z = 0$ corresponds to a minimum Z. If $y = 2$, $Z'' < 0$, $x = 4$, and $Z = 16$; hence $x = 4$, $y = 2$ maximize U under the given condition. These results may be verified geometrically by drawing the indifference map for the Z-function and the line of constraint. (The details are left as an exercise.)

Instead of the utility index U or Z, we could use a new utility index W, defined as $\ln Z$. The values of x and y are found by the implicit method.

$$W = \ln Z = \ln x + 2\ln y, \qquad x + 4y = 12,$$

$$\frac{dW}{dx} = \frac{1}{x} + \frac{2}{y}\cdot\frac{dy}{dx}, \qquad \text{where} \quad 1 + 4\frac{dy}{dx} = 0, \qquad \text{or} \quad \frac{dy}{dx} = -\frac{1}{4}.$$

From

$$\frac{1}{x} + \frac{2}{y}\left(-\frac{1}{4}\right) = 0, \quad \text{or} \quad x = 2y \quad \text{and} \quad x + 4y = 12,$$

the critical point is found to be $x = 4$, $y = 2$.

$$\frac{d^2W}{dx^2} = \frac{d}{dx}\left(\frac{1}{x} - \frac{1}{2y}\right) = -\frac{1}{x^2} + \frac{1}{2y^2}\left(-\frac{1}{4}\right) < 0$$

at the critical point. This point maximizes W and hence U.

EXERCISE GROUP 6–5*

1. If the utility index function is $U = 4xy - y^2$ and the budget equation is $2x + y = 6$, determine the values of x and y that maximize U. Verify the results geometrically.

2. If the utility index function is $U = 4xy - y^2$ and the budget equation is $2x + 5y = 11$, determine the values of x and y that maximize U. Verify the results geometrically.

3. If the utility index function is $U = 8 + 7xy - 3x^2 - 2y^2$ and the budget equation is $x + 3y = 8$, determine the values of x and y that maximize U. Verify the result geometrically.

4. If the utility index function is $U = 27 + 6xy - 2x^2 - y^2$ and the budget equation is $x + y = 9$, determine the values of x and y that maximize U. Solve the problem algebraically in two ways.

5. If the utility index function is $U = 3xy - x^2 - 2y^2$ and the budget equation is $x + y = 12$, determine the values of x and y that maximize U. Solve the problem algebraically in two ways.

6. If the utility index function is $U = 4xy - x^2 - 3y^2$ and the budget equation is $2x + 3y = 45$, determine the values of x and y that maximize U. Use implicit differentiation to find dU/dx and d^2U/dx^2.

7. If the utility index function is $U = 24x + 32y - x^2 - y^2$ and the budget equation is $x + 2y = 9$, determine the values of x and y that maximize U. Draw the indifference map and verify your result.

8. If the utility index function is $U = 24x + 48y - x^2 - y^2$ and the budget equation is $x + 3y = 14$, determine the values of x and y that maximize U. Solve the problem in two ways.

9. If the utility index function is $U = 16x + 26y - x^2 - y^2$ and the budget equation is $3x + 4y = 26$, determine the values of x and y that maximize U. Use implicit differentiation. Justify your conclusions.

10. If the utility index function is $U = 48 - (x - 5)^2 - 3(y - 4)^2$ and the budget equation is $x + 3y = 9$, find the values of x and y that maximize U. Draw several of the indifference curves (ellipses), including the one that is tangent to the budget line.

---

* See footnote for Exercise Group 6–4.

11. If the utility index function is $U = 10 - (x - 4)^2 - 2(y - 4)^2$ and the budget equation is $x + y = 5$, find the values of x and y that maximize U. Solve the problem in several ways. Draw the indifference map showing the ellipses corresponding to $U = 1, 4, 6$, and 10.

12. If the utility index function is

$$U = 80 - 2(x - 4)^2 - 2(x - 4)(y - 4) - (y - 4)^2$$

and the budget equation is $3x + 2y = 10$, determine the values of x and y that maximize U. (a) Solve the problem using the given form of U and implicit differentiation. (b) Simplify the form of U by a translation of axes to the center $(4, 4)$ and change the budget equation accordingly. Solve the problem in this form.

13. If the utility index function is

$$U = 29 - 2(x - 2)^2 - 2(x - 2)(y - 3) - (y - 3)^2$$
$$= -2x^2 - 2xy - y^2 + 14x + 10y$$

and the budget equation is $3x + 2y = 7$, determine the values of x and y that maximize U and find the maximum value of U. Verify your result by drawing the budget line and the ellipse corresponding to $U = U_{max}$. (A translation of axes may help in drawing the ellipse.)

14. Determine the values of x and y that will maximize the utility index $U = x^{1/3}y^{2/3}$ subject to the budget equation $x + y = 6$. Solve the problem by introducing the auxiliary utility index functions (a) $Z = U^3$, and (b) $W = \ln Z$.

15. Determine the values of x and y that maximize the utility index $U = xy^{1/3}$ subject to the budget equation $3x + y = 16$. Introduce the auxiliary utility index functions (a) $Z = U^3$, and (b) $W = \ln Z$.

16. Determine the values of x and y that maximize the utility index

$$U = (x + 2)^{2/3}(y + 1)^{1/3}$$

subject to the budget equation $2x + y = 7$. Let $Z = U^3$. In a diagram show the indifference curve corresponding to Z_{max} and the budget line.

CHAPTER 7

INTRODUCTION TO CURVE FITTING

7–1 Curves through given points. As a final application of analytic geometry and the calculus, the problem of fitting a plane curve to given data is considered. The discussion is brief and no attempt is made to go deeply into the subject of statistics, a subject very important in economics and business.

The number of points required to determine a curve which passes precisely through the given points is the number of essential constants in the equation of the curve. Thus, for example, if only two points are given, then a straight line $y = mx + b$, the special parabolas $y = ax^2 + c$ and $y = \sqrt{a - bx}$, the general power curve $y = ax^n$, and the exponential curve $y = Ae^{kx}$ could all be made to pass through the two points. The substitution of the given data in the selected equation gives two equations in two unknowns, which, in general, determine the essential constants. If three points are given, then a parabola of the form $y = ax^2 + bx + c$, an equilateral hyperbola of the form $y = [a/(x + b)] - c$, as well as other curves, could be made to pass through the three given points.

EXAMPLE 7–1. Consider the demand law

$$p = \frac{4}{x + 1} - 1 = \frac{3 - x}{x + 1}.$$

The points $(0, 3)$, $(1, 1)$, and $(3, 0)$ lie on this curve, and it is possible to find a parabola of the form $p = ax^2 + bx + c$ through these three points. First, it is necessary to solve the simultaneous equations

$$3 = c, \quad 1 = a + b + c, \quad 0 = 9a + 3b + c.$$

Using the value $c = 3$, we obtain two equations in a and b and then eliminate b:

$$
\begin{array}{r l}
a + b & = -2 \left| \begin{array}{r} -3 \end{array} \right. \\
9a + 3b & = -3 \left| \begin{array}{r} +1 \end{array} \right. \\
\hline
6a & = \quad 3, \quad a = \tfrac{1}{2}, b = -\tfrac{5}{2}.
\end{array}
$$

The equation of the parabola is

$$p = \tfrac{1}{2}x^2 - \tfrac{5}{2}x + 3 = \tfrac{1}{2}(x - 2)(x - 3).$$

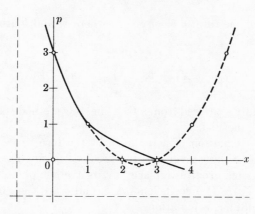

FIGURE 7–1

(Both curves are shown in Fig. 7–1.)   An important concept in curve fitting is that the curve used may be selected arbitrarily from a number of possible curves, with or without theoretical grounds for the selection. Near the given points any such curve might be sufficiently accurate, but away from these points, the results may be in serious error.   In this special example, the parabola cannot be used for a normal demand curve between zero and 3, since the value of p is negative for x between 2 and 3.

7–2 Method of average points.   In general, it is not possible to find a straight line that passes exactly through three or more points, since two points determine a line.   If it is required to find a straight line which approximately fits more than two points, some form of "averaging" must be used.   Several such methods are available.   The method of average points is discussed in this section.   (Another method will be discussed in Section 7–4.)

We first arrange the points in order of increasing x, and divide the set of given points into two nearly equal groups by placing the first half in one group and the other half in a second group.   Each group is replaced by its *average point*, defined as follows: Let X be the arithmetic average of the x-coordinates of the points in the given group, and let Y be the arithmetic average of the y-coordinates of the same points.   Then the point $M(X, Y)$ is the average point of the given group.   For the case in question, there are two average points, $M_1(X_1, Y_1)$ and $M_2(X_2, Y_2)$.   If, for example, there were ten points, arranged in order of increasing x, then M_1 and M_2 are such that

$$X_1 = \frac{x_1 + x_2 + x_3 + x_4 + x_5}{5}, \qquad X_2 = \frac{x_6 + x_7 + x_8 + x_9 + x_{10}}{5},$$

with similar expressions for Y_1 and Y_2.   The two points M_1 and M_2 determine a line of the form $y = mx + b$, where m and b are the solutions of the equations

$$Y_1 = mX_1 + b, \qquad Y_2 = mX_2 + b.$$

If the data is badly scattered from a true line, this method is as satisfactory as any algebraic method.

To obtain the equation of a parabola of the form $y = ax^2 + bx + c$ through more than three given points, three nearly equal groups of points are formed and each group is replaced by its average point, say (X_1, Y_1), (X_2, Y_2), (X_3, Y_3). The coefficients a, b, and c are then determined by solving the simultaneous equations

$$Y_1 = aX_1^2 + bX_1 + c,$$
$$Y_2 = aX_2^2 + bX_2 + c,$$
$$Y_3 = aX_3^2 + bX_3 + c.$$

We eliminate c first, in order to obtain two equations in a and b, and then solve these equations by the method of elimination. Third-order determinants may be used to solve for a, b, and c.

EXAMPLE 7-2. Find a straight line and a parabola which approximately fit the following data:

x	1	2	3	4	5	6	7
y	2	3	4	5	7	9	12

For the line, we place the first four points in the first group. Then the average points are $M_1(5/2, 7/2)$, $M_2(6, 28/3)$. The equations which determine m and b are

$$\frac{7}{2} = \frac{5}{2} m + b, \qquad \text{or} \qquad 7 = 5m + 2b \quad\bigg|\; {-3}$$

$$\frac{28}{3} = 6m + b, \qquad \text{or} \qquad \underline{28 = 18m + 3b} \quad\bigg|\; 2$$

$$35 = 21m$$

The result is $m = 5/3$, $b = -2/3$, and the equation of the line is

$$y = \frac{5}{3} x - \frac{2}{3}.$$

For the parabola, we use the grouping of two, two, and three points. Then we have

$$N_1(3/2,\, 5/2), \qquad N_2(7/2,\, 9/2), \qquad N_3(6,\, 28/3) \doteq M_2.$$

If the coordinates of the above points are substituted into the equation $y = ax^2 + bx + c$, then

$$\frac{5}{2} = \frac{9}{4}a + \frac{3}{2}b + c \quad\big|\;{-1}$$

$$\frac{9}{2} = \frac{49}{4}a + \frac{7}{2}b + c \quad\big|\;{+1}\;\big|\;{-4}$$

$$\frac{28}{3} = 36a + 6b + c \quad\;\big|\qquad\big|\;{+4}$$

$$10a + 2b = 2 \quad\big|\;{-5}$$

$$\underline{95a + 10b = 58/3 \;\big|\;{+1}}$$

$$45a \qquad\;\; = 28/3,$$

$$a = 28/135 \doteq 0.21,$$

$$b = 1 - \frac{28}{27} = -\frac{1}{27} \doteq -0.04,$$

$$c = \frac{5}{2} - \frac{9}{4}\cdot\frac{28}{135} + \frac{3}{2}\cdot\frac{1}{27} = \frac{94}{45}$$

$$\doteq 2.09.$$

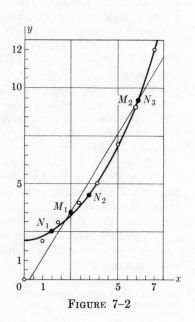

FIGURE 7–2

The equation of the parabola is

$$y = \frac{28}{135}x^2 - \frac{1}{27}x + \frac{94}{45},$$

or

$$y \doteq 0.21x^2 - 0.04x + 2.09.$$

The given data, the straight line, and the parabola are shown in Fig. 7–2.

EXERCISE GROUP 7–1

1. Find equations of the form

(a) $y = mx + b$, (b) $y = ax^2 + c$, (c) $y = \sqrt{a - bx}$

that pass through the two points $(2, 5)$, $(4, 3)$. Show all three curves for $x \geqq 0$ and $y \geqq 0$ in the same diagram.

2. Find equations of the form

(a) $y = mx + b$, (b) $y = ax^2 + c$, (c) $y = \sqrt{a - bx}$

that pass through the points (1, 6), (10, 3). Show all three curves for $x \geqq 0$ and $y \geqq 0$ in the same diagram.

3. (a) Find the equation of the form $y = \sqrt{a + bx}$ that passes through the points (4, 5), (10, 7). Where does this curve cut the Y-axis? (b) Find the equation of the parabola $y = ax^2 + bx + c$ which passes through the three points mentioned in part (a). Draw both parabolas in the same diagram, showing parts where they agree closely and parts where they differ widely.

4. (a) Find the equation of the parabola $y = ax^2 + bx + c$ that passes through the three points (0, 1), (2, 2), (4, 5). (b) Find the equation of the parabola $x = Ay^2 + By + C$ that passes through the three points given in part (a). Draw the appropriate diagram.

5. Proceed as in problem 4 for the points (1, 2), (2, 3), (3, 6).

6. Determine the demand curve $(x + a)(p + b) = c$ that passes through the three points (0, 3), (1, 1), (3, 0). (*Hint:* From the three equations that determine a, b, and c, eliminate c first.)

7. Verify that the three points (0, 4), (1, 1), (2, 0) lie on the hyperbola $y = (4 - 2x)/(x + 1)$. Find the equation of the parabola $y = ax^2 + bx + c$ that passes through these same three points. Show the hyperbola and parabola in the same diagram.

8. Verify that the three points (0, 9), (1, 4), (3, 0) lie on the parabola $y = (x - 3)^2$. Find the hyperbola of the form $(x + b)(y + c) = a$ which passes through these three points. Show the parabola and hyperbola in the same diagram.

9. Use the method of average points to find the equations of the line and parabola that approximately fit the following data.

x	0	1	2	3	4	5
y	1	1	2	4	6	7

Draw the appropriate diagram.

10. Use the method of average points to find the equations of the line and parabola that approximately fit the following data.

x	0	1	2	3	4	5	6	7	8
y	0	1	1	2	3	5	6	8	10

Draw the appropriate diagram.

7–3 Method of least squares. If a set of n numbers $(x_1, x_2, \ldots, x_n)$ is given, it is often desirable to replace the set by a single number through the use of some type of average or estimate. One of the ways to accomplish this is by the method of *least squares*. Let the desired average be $\bar{x}$

and form the differences or *deviations from the average*,

$$x_1 - \overline{x},\ x_2 - \overline{x}, \ldots, x_n - \overline{x}.$$

Some of these deviations are positive and some negative provided x is selected between the largest and smallest values of the given x's. The squares of these differences will be positive. Let S be the sum of the squares of the differences:

$$
\begin{aligned}
S &= (\overline{x} - x_1)^2 + (\overline{x} - x_2)^2 + \cdots + (\overline{x} - x_n)^2 \\
&= n\overline{x}^2 - 2(x_1 + x_2 + \cdots + x_n)\overline{x} + x_1^2 + x_2^2 + \cdots + x_n^2 \\
&= n\overline{x}^2 - (2\textstyle\sum x_i)\overline{x} + \sum x_i^2,
\end{aligned}
$$

where $\sum x_i$ is the sum of the given x's, $\sum x_i^2$ is the sum of the squares of the given x's, and $\overline{x}$ is a variable whose value is to be determined; it is determined so that S has the smallest possible value.

$$\frac{dS}{d\overline{x}} = 2n\overline{x} - 2\textstyle\sum x_i = 0, \qquad \frac{d^2S}{dx^2} = 2n > 0.$$

Therefore

$$\overline{x} = \frac{\sum x_i}{n}.$$

Hence the *arithmetic average* of the numbers makes S a minimum, or $\overline{x}$ *is the best fit to the data in the sense of least squares.*

Suppose the given data is $x_1, x_2, \ldots, x_n$, $(x_i \neq 0)$. Define X as $\log x$ and consider the numbers $X_1, X_2, \ldots, X_n$. Suppose that G is the best fit to the X's in the sense of least squares and g is defined by $G = \log g$. Then

$$
\begin{aligned}
\log g = G &= \frac{X_1 + X_2 + \cdots + X_n}{n} \\
&= \frac{\log x_1 + \log x_2 + \cdots + \log x_n}{n} \\
&= \frac{1}{n} \log (x_1 x_2 \cdots x_n) = \log (x_1 x_2 \cdots x_n)^{1/n}.
\end{aligned}
$$

Then

$$g = (x_1 x_2 \cdots x_n)^{1/n},$$

and hence g is the geometric mean of the given data. It is also a good fit to the data, and in some physical problems this may be preferred to the arithmetic mean. Nevertheless, $\sum (\overline{x} - x_i)^2$, a measure of the sum of the squares of the deviations, is smaller than $\sum (g - x_i)^2$.

EXAMPLE 7–3. For the set of numbers given in the first column of the table below, compare the arithmetic and geometric means. Also compare the sums of the squares of the deviations in the two cases.

A table of squares (see Table II of Appendix) is used in the computation and the results are put in tabular form:

	x	$X = \log x$	$x - \bar{x}$	$(x - \bar{x})^2$	$x - g$	$(x - g)^2$
	2.0	0.3010	−0.56	0.3136	−0.535	0.2862
	2.4	0.3802	−0.16	0.0256	−0.135	0.0182
	2.6	0.4150	+0.04	0.0016	+0.065	0.0042
	2.8	0.4472	+0.24	0.0576	+0.265	0.0702
	3.0	0.4771	+0.44	0.1936	+0.465	0.2162
$\sum$	12.8	2.0205	0.00 (Check)	0.5920		0.5950

$$\bar{x} = \frac{12.8}{5} = 2.56, \qquad G = \frac{2.0205}{5} = 0.4041, \qquad g = 2.535;$$

$$\sum(x_i - \bar{x})^2 = 0.5920 < \sum(x_i - g)^2 = 0.5950.$$

If the given data were measured quantities, the difference would be well within the accuracy of the measurements. It is ordinarily simpler to make the computations with $\bar{x}$ than with g.

7–4 Fitting a line to given data. The method of least squares—*minimizing the sum of the squares of the deviations of the data from an appropriate estimate*—is useful for fitting a set of points in the plane with a curve. Consider first a set of data represented by

$$(x_1, y_1), (x_2, y_2), \ldots, (x_n, y_n)$$

and a straight line of the form $y = mx + b$. For any given x_i, let $\hat{y}_i$ (read: "y circumflex") be the estimate of y obtained from the line; that is, $\hat{y}_i = mx_i + b$. The difference between the given value y_i and $\hat{y}_i$ is called the *y-deviation*. We seek to find m and b so that the sum of the squares of the y-deviations is a minimum. The line so obtained is called the *line of regression of y on x*.

$$S = (b + mx_1 - y_1)^2 + (b + mx_2 - y_2)^2 + \cdots + (b + mx_n - y_n)^2,$$

$$S = \sum(b + mx_i - y_i)^2, \tag{7–1}$$

where the variable parameters are b and m, and all other numbers are constants taken from the given data. The necessary conditions that S

have a minimum are

$$\frac{\partial S}{\partial b} = 0, \qquad \frac{\partial S}{\partial m} = 0,$$

and when these are applied to Eq. (7–1) they become

$$2\sum (b + mx_i - y_i) \cdot 1 = 0,$$
$$2\sum (b + mx_i - y_i) \cdot x_i = 0.$$

These conditions can be written in the following form*:

$$(\sum x)m + nb = \sum y, \tag{7–2}$$
$$(\sum x^2)m + (\sum x)b = \sum xy. \tag{7–3}$$

Since S is always positive and large if either b or m is large, and since conditions (7–2) and (7–3) determine only one set of critical values b and m, this critical point makes S an absolute minimum. (The second derivatives need not be found.)

Consider the equation $y = mx + b$ and the *first moment equation* $xy = mx^2 + bx$ (obtained by multiplying the equation of the line by x). If we substitute the given data in each equation and add, we obtain the equations (7–2 and 7–3) needed to find b and m. The arithmetical computation is best presented in tabular form and the algebraic result may be checked with a geometric diagram. If Eq. (7–2) is divided by n, it becomes

$$m\bar{x} + b = \bar{y}, \tag{7–2a}$$

where $\bar{x} = (\sum x)/n$ and $\bar{y} = (\sum y)/n$. This means that the required line passes through the average point of the given data. This property is useful for checking purposes and leads to a method for simplifying the calculations.

If it is known or assumed that $b = 0$, that is, if an attempt is made to fit given data by a line of the form $y = mx$, the Eq. (7–3) is used in the special form

$$m = \frac{\sum xy}{\sum x^2}. \tag{7–4}$$

We define new numbers x' and y' by

$$x' = x - \bar{x}, \qquad y' = y - \bar{y}.$$

---

* When no misunderstanding can occur, the subscript i is often omitted; thus Σx_i is written Σx, etc.

This is equivalent to a translation of axes to the average point of the system. Since the line of best fit passes through this point, and since this translation of axes does not affect the slope of the line, the equation of the required line is

$$y' = mx', \quad \text{where} \quad m = \frac{\sum x_i' y_i'}{\sum x_i'^2}. \tag{7-4a}$$

EXAMPLE 7–4. (Cf. Example 7–2.) Find the line which is the best fit, in the sense of least squares, to the following data.

x	1	2	3	4	5	6	7
y	2	3	4	5	7	9	12

Since the numbers are small, the calculations are made using Eqs. (7–2) and (7–3). Then, for the purpose of illustration, the problem is resolved by translating the axes and using Eq. (7–4a).

	x	y	x^2	xy	$x' = x - \bar{x}$	$y' = y - \bar{y}$	$x'y'$	x'^2
	1	2	1	2	−3	−4	12	9
	2	3	4	6	−2	−3	6	4
	3	4	9	12	−1	−2	2	1
	4	5	16	20	0	−1	0	0
	5	7	25	35	1	1	1	1
	6	9	36	54	2	3	6	4
	7	12	49	84	3	6	18	9
$\sum$	28	42	140	213	0	0	45	28
	$\bar{x} = 4, \bar{y} = 6.$				(Check)	(Check)		

The moment equations (7–2) and (7–3) and their solution are

$$
\begin{aligned}
28m + 7b &= 42 \mid -4 \\
140m + 28b &= 213 \mid 1 \\
\hline
28m &= 45,
\end{aligned}
\quad \text{or} \quad m = \frac{45}{28},
$$

$$b = 6 - 4m = -\frac{3}{7}.$$

Hence the line of regression of y on x is

$$y = \frac{45}{28} x - \frac{3}{7} \doteq 1.61x - 0.43.$$

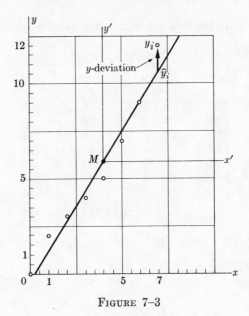

FIGURE 7–3

By the second method, the slope of the line is

$$m = \frac{\sum x'y'}{\sum x'^2} = \frac{45}{28},$$

and the equation of this line is

$$y' = \frac{45}{28} x', \quad \text{or} \quad y - 6 = \frac{45}{28}(x - 4),$$

$$y = \frac{45}{28} x - \frac{3}{7} \quad \text{(as before).}$$

(This result may be compared with that found in Section 7–2 and Fig. 7–2.) The given points, the average point M, the two sets of axes, the line of regression of y on x, and a typical y-deviation (positive if the point is above the line) are shown in Fig. 7–3.

In a practical problem the raw data may involve numbers that are not simple, but which may be made relatively simple data by a change of reference points and a change in the size of units. This is illustrated by the following example.

EXAMPLE 7–5. The first two columns in the table below give average monthly salaries for the stated years. Find the linear trend for this data by the method of least squares.

Let the year be Y, the salary S, and define x and y by

$$x = \frac{Y - 1925}{5}, \qquad y = \frac{S - 100}{5}.$$

Year	Salary	x	y	x^2	xy
1925	\$100	0	0	0	0
1930	120	1	4	1	4
1935	155	2	11	4	22
1940	175	3	15	9	45
1945	210	4	22	16	88
1950	230	5	26	25	130
$\sum$		15	78	55	289

$$
\begin{array}{ll}
15m + \ 6b = \ 78 & -5 \\
55m + 15b = 289 & \ \ 2 \\
\hline
35m \qquad\quad = 188, & \text{or} \quad m = \frac{188}{35} \doteq 5.37,
\end{array}
$$

$$b = 13 - \frac{5}{2} \cdot \frac{188}{35} = -\frac{3}{7} \doteq -0.43.$$

The trend line is

$$y = \frac{188}{35} x - \frac{3}{7} = \frac{1}{35} (188x - 15).$$

In terms of Y and S the above equation becomes

$$\frac{S - 100}{5} = \frac{188}{35} \cdot \frac{Y - 1925}{5} - \frac{3}{7},$$

and

$$S = 5.37(Y - 1925) + 97.9.$$

This result may be verified by observing that $\bar{x} = 5/2$, $\bar{y} = 13$, so that $\bar{Y} - 1925 = 25/2$ and $\bar{S} = 165$, and by showing that the point $(\bar{Y}, \bar{S})$ does satisfy the result obtained.

EXERCISE GROUP 7–2*

1. Consider further the data of Example 7–3. Compare $\sum(x - \bar{x})^2$ with $\sum(x - x_0)^2$, where (a) $x_0 = 2.6$, the middle observation, and (b) $x_0 = 2.5$, the average of the smallest and largest values of x, $(2.5 < \bar{x} < 2.6)$.

---

* The number of problems in this Exercise Group has been kept small because of the time required to make and check all numerical calculations.

2. Compute the arithmetic mean $\bar{x}$ and the geometric mean g for the set of numbers 2, 3, 4, 5, 6, 7. Compare $\sum (x - \bar{x})^2$ with $\sum (x - g)^2$.

3. For the set of numbers 2.1, 4.9, 8.2, 11.7, 14.3, 16.5 (a) compute the arithmetic mean $\bar{x}$ and the geometric mean g, and (b) compare the two sums of the squares of the deviations from the means.

4. (Cf. problem 9, Exercise Group 7–1.) Find the line which is the best fit, in the sense of least squares, to the following data.

x	0	1	2	3	4	5
y	1	1	2	4	6	7

Solve the problem by both of the methods given in Section 7–4. Verify the results geometrically.

5. (Cf. problem 10, Exercise Group 7–1.) Find the line which is the best fit, in the sense of least squares, to the following data.

x	0	1	2	3	4	5	6	7	8
y	0	1	1	2	3	5	6	8	10

Solve the problem by both of the methods given in Section 7–4. Verify the results geometrically.

6. The monthly salaries of a certain group for the stated years is given in tabular form below. Find the linear trend for this data by the method of least squares, and estimate the salary for the years 1945 and 1960 from this trend line.

Y = Year	1920	1925	1930	1940	1950	1955
S = Salary	\$350	375	425	550	750	800

Introduce new variables x and y which involve new reference points and scale units, so that x_i and y_i are relatively simple integers. Verify the answer by showing that $\bar{Y}$ and $\bar{S}$ satisfy the final equation.

7–5 Fitting a parabola to given data. * If the given data does not appear to have a linear trend, a better fit to the data may be found by using the parabola $y = ax^2 + bx + c$ and the method of least squares. For any given x_i let $\hat{y}_i$ be the corresponding estimate $\hat{y}_i = ax_i^2 + bx_i + c$. The y-deviation is

$$y_i - \hat{y}_i = y_i - (c + bx_i + ax_i^2).$$

The sum of the squares of the y-deviations (after the subscript has been dropped) may be written

$$S = \sum (c + bx + ax^2 - y)^2, \tag{7–5}$$

---

* This section and problems 1 through 3 of Exercise Group 7–3 could be omitted without loss of continuity.

which is a positive function of the variable parameters a, b, and c. Necessary and sufficient conditions that S be a minimum are

$$\frac{\partial S}{\partial c} = 0, \qquad \frac{\partial S}{\partial b} = 0, \qquad \frac{\partial S}{\partial a} = 0.$$

When these conditions are applied to Eq. (7–5), they become

$$2\sum(c + bx + ax^2 - y) \cdot 1 = 0,$$
$$2\sum(c + bx + ax^2 - y) \cdot x = 0,$$
$$2\sum(c + bx + ax^2 - y) \cdot x^2 = 0.$$

Hence a, b, and c are the solutions of the moment equations

$$(\sum x^2)a + (\sum x)b + nc = \sum y \qquad \text{(zero moment)}, \qquad (7\text{–}6)$$

$$(\sum x^3)a + (\sum x^2)b + (\sum x)c = \sum xy \qquad \text{(first moment)}, \qquad (7\text{–}7)$$

$$(\sum x^4)a + (\sum x^3)b + (\sum x^2)c = \sum x^2y \qquad \text{(second moment)}. \qquad (7\text{–}8)$$

Consider the equation $y = ax^2 + bx + c$ and those obtained by multiplying this equation by x and x^2, respectively. If we substitute the given data in each equation and add the results, we obtain the equations (7–6, 7–7, 7–8) needed to find a, b and c. If it is known that $c = 0$, or if an attempt is made to fit the data by a parabola of the form $y = ax^2 + bx$, Eqs. (7–7) and (7–8) are sufficient. If it is known that $b = 0$, or if an attempt is made to fit the data by a parabola of the form $y = ax^2 + c$, Eqs. (7–6) and (7–8) are sufficient.

EXAMPLE 7–6. Fit a parabola of the form $y = ax^2 + c$ to the following data, using the method of least squares.

x	0	1	2	3	4
y	1	2	3	5	8

In order to use Eqs. (7–6) and (7–8) it is necessary to compute $\sum x^2$, $\sum x^4$, $\sum y$, and $\sum yx^2$:

	x	y	x^2	x^4	yx^2
	0	1	0	0	0
	1	2	1	1	2
	2	3	4	16	12
	3	5	9	81	45
	4	8	16	256	128
$\sum$	10	19	30	354	187

$$30a + 5c = 19,$$
$$354a + 30c = 187.$$

The solution of the above equations is found to be

$$a = \frac{73}{174} \doteq 0.42, \qquad c = \frac{186}{145} \doteq 1.28,$$

and

$$y = 0.42x^2 + 1.28.$$

7–6 Fitting exponential and power curves. If the given data does not appear to have a linear trend, an exponential curve $y = b \cdot 10^{mx}$ or a power curve $y = bx^m$ may be used. The exponential law $y = b \cdot 10^{mx}$ may be written in the form

$$\log y = \log b + mx,$$

or

$$Y = B + mx, \tag{7-9}$$

where $Y = \log y$ and $B = \log b$. A good fit to the data can often be found by making the sum of the squares of the Y-deviations a minimum. This is not the same as minimizing the y-deviations but it is simpler and gives a good fit when minimizing the y-deviations gives a good fit. The use of Y-deviations instead of y-deviations corresponds to use of the geometric mean instead of the arithmetic mean in the one-dimensional case. Since Eq. (7–9) is linear in the variables x and Y, the methods of Section 7–2 (average points) and Section 7–4 (least squares) can be applied.

EXAMPLE 7–7. Fit an equation of the exponential type to the data of Example 7–6.

x	y	Y	xY	x^2	$\hat{Y}$
0	1	0	0	0	0.034
1	2	0.30	0.30	1	0.256
2	3	0.48	0.96	4	0.478
3	5	0.70	2.10	9	0.700
4	8	0.91	3.64	16	0.922
$\sum$ 10	19	2.39	7.00	30	

The equations

$$(\textstyle\sum x)m + 5B = \sum Y, \qquad (\textstyle\sum x^2)m + (\textstyle\sum x)B = \sum xY$$

become

$$
\begin{array}{r@{}r@{}l}
10m + & 5B & = 2.39 \quad\big|{-2} \\
30m + & 10B & = 7.00 \quad\big|\;\;1 \\
\hline
10m & & = 2.22,
\end{array}
$$

$$m = 0.222, \qquad B = 0.034, \qquad b = 1.08,$$

$$Y = 0.034 + 0.222x, \qquad \text{or} \quad y = 1.08 \cdot 10^{0.222x}.$$

For purposes of comparison the estimated values $\hat{Y}$ obtained from the above equation have been included in the table.

If it is assumed that the data $x = 0$ and $y = 1$ is precise and that the law is of the simpler form $y = 10^{mx}$, then $Y = mx$, where

$$m = \frac{\sum xY}{\sum x^2} = \frac{7}{30}.$$

The law is

$$y = 10^{0.233x}.$$

The power law $y = bx^m$ may be written in the form.

$$\log y = \log b + m \log x,$$

or

$$Y = B + mX, \tag{7-10}$$

where $Y = \log y$, $B = \log b$, and $X = \log x$. Equation (7-10) can be fitted to the given data by the method of least squares, applied in the XY-plane.

EXAMPLE 7-8. Find the parameters for a Pareto law of distribution of incomes from the following data, which approximately represents the distribution of incomes in the United States for the year 1926. Estimate how many millionaires there were in the country at that time.

Income classes	Frequency
$1,000 to 5,000	32,000,000
5,000 to 25,000	1,100,000
25,000 to 250,000	110,000
Over $250,000	4,000

The law is of the form $y = b/x^m$, where y is the number of individuals in the population whose income *exceeds* x. The values of x (in dollars) to be used are 1000, 5000, 25,000, and 250,000. To find the corresponding values of y, the data is changed from the given frequency distribution to the required accumulated distribution of incomes exceeding x:

x	y	$X = \log x$	$Y = \log y$	X^2	XY
$1,000	33,214,000	3.00	7.52	9.00	22.56
5,000	1,214,000	3.70	6.08	13.69	22.50
25,000	114,000	4.40	5.06	19.36	22.26
250,000	4,000	5.40	3.60	29.16	19.44
		$\sum$ 16.50	22.26	71.21	86.76

$$y = \frac{b}{x^m}, \qquad Y = B - mX, \qquad XY = BX - mX^2,$$

$$-16.50m + 4B = 22.26,$$

$$-71.21m + 16.50B = 86.76.$$

The solution of these equations gives $m = 1.61$, $B = 12.19$. Hence

$$Y = 12.19 - 1.61X, \qquad (3 \leqq X \leqq 5.40),$$

$$y = \frac{1.54 \cdot 10^{12}}{x^{1.61}}, \qquad (1000 \leqq x \leqq 250{,}000).$$

If $x = 1{,}000{,}000$, then $X = 6$ and the corresponding value of Y is $12.19 - 9.66 = 2.53$, so that the number of millionaires y is estimated to be 340.

EXERCISE GROUP 7–3*

1. Fit parabolas of the form (a) $y = ax^2 + c$, (b) $y = ax^2 + bx$ to the following data, using the method of least squares.

x	2	4	6	8	10
y	7	12	20	34	50

Draw the appropriate diagram.

2. If the data below is plotted, it appears that it could be approximately fitted by a parabola of the type $y = ax^2$. Which of the moment equations should be used? Explain. Find the corresponding value of a and compare this answer with that which is obtained as follows: Determine the value of a corresponding to each point separately and then find the arithmetic average of these values. Draw the appropriate diagram.

x	1	2	3	4	5
y	4	12	28	50	80

3. Fit a parabola of the form $y = ax^2 + bx + c$ to the following data, using the method of least squares.

x	0	1	2	3	4	5
y	3	2	2	4	6	9

Show the data and the parabola in a diagram.

---

* The number of problems in this Exercise Group has been kept small because of the time required to make and check all the numerical calculations. Even then, and with a selection of problems, two assignments will be required if Section 7–5 and problems 1 through 3 are included.

4. Fit an exponential curve of the type $y = b \cdot 10^{mx}$ to the data of problem 1.

5. Fit exponential curves of the following types to the given data:

(a) $y = b \cdot 10^{mx}$, (b) $y = 4 \cdot 10^{mx}$.

x	0	1	2	3	4	5
y	4	8	12	20	32	50

Draw the corresponding xY-diagrams ($Y = \log y$).

6. Fit a power law of the form $y = ax^m$ to the data of problem 2.

7. (a) Fit a demand law of the form $D = 20/p^k$ to the data given below by applying the method of least squares to the logarithmic form of the demand equation. (It is assumed that if $p = 1$, $D = 20$.) (b) Fit the law $D = A/p^k$ to the same data by the same procedure.

p	2	3	4	5	6
D	7.0	3.9	2.5	1.8	1.4

8. Fit a Pareto distribution law $y = b/x^m$, where y is the number of individuals whose income exceeds x, to the following frequency income data.

Income classes			Frequency
\$2,000	to	5,000	31,200,000
5,000	to	20,000	7,100,000
20,000	to	100,000	660,000
100,000	to	500,000	37,500
Over \$500,000			2,500

Estimate the number of millionaires in the population.

7–7 Linear regression and correlation. Let

$$(x_1, x_2, \ldots, x_n) \quad \text{and} \quad (y_1, y_2, \ldots, y_n)$$

be two given sets of data. The numbers x_i and y_i might arise from an experiment where it is known they are related or from different experiments without any known connection between them. If the sets of number pairs (x_i, y_i) are interpreted as points in the plane, it is then possible to find the line of best fit in the form $y = mx + b$ by minimizing the sum of the squares of the y-deviations. The line so obtained is called the *line of regression of y on x*. When this line is used in estimating or predicting the value of y which corresponds to a given x, it is tacitly assumed that the x's are without error (or deviation) but that all the deviations of the predicted values from the observed values are due to measurements in the y's. The moment equations are

$$(\textstyle\sum x)m + nb = \sum y, \qquad (\textstyle\sum x^2)m + (\textstyle\sum x)b = \sum xy. \qquad (7\text{-}11)$$

If the given data is referred to the average point $(\bar{x}, \bar{y})$ as new origin, so that the line of regression has the simpler form $y' = mx'$, only one moment equation is needed:

$$(\textstyle\sum x'^2)m = \sum x'y'. \qquad (7\text{-}12)$$

If the value of y is assumed known, the value of x can be estimated from the equation

$$x = My + a$$

by minimizing the sum of the squares of the x-deviations, where the typical x-deviation has the form $x_i - (My_i + a)$ and the sum of the squares of these deviations has the form

$$S = \textstyle\sum (a + My_i - x_i)^2.$$

The line so obtained is called the *line of regression of x on y*. The resulting moment equations which determine M and a are

$$(\textstyle\sum y)M + na = \sum x, \qquad (\textstyle\sum y^2)M + (\textstyle\sum y)a = \sum xy. \qquad (7\text{-}13)$$

If the given data is referred to the average point $(\bar{x}, \bar{y})$ as new origin, so that the line of regression has the simpler form $x' = My'$, only one moment equation is needed:

$$(\textstyle\sum y'^2)M = \sum x'y'. \qquad (7\text{-}14)$$

Both lines of regression pass through $(\bar{x}, \bar{y})$ but are usually different lines. The equation for the line of regression of x on y may be solved for y in terms of x,

$$y = \frac{1}{M}x - \frac{a}{M},$$

and compared with $y = mx + b$.

EXAMPLE 7–9. Find the line of regression of x on y for the data given in the first table of Example 7–4.

The given data and the necessary calculations are included in the following table. (Cf. second table under Example 7–4.)

x	y	xy	y^2	$x' = x - \bar{x}$	$y' = y - \bar{y}$	$x'y'$	y'^2
1	2	2	4	−3	−4	12	16
2	3	6	9	−2	−3	6	9
3	4	12	16	−1	−2	2	4
4	5	20	25	0	−1	0	1
5	7	35	49	1	1	1	1
6	9	54	81	2	3	6	9
7	12	84	144	3	6	18	36
Σ 28	42	213	328	0	0	45	76
$\bar{x} = 4, \bar{y} = 6.$				(Check)	(Check)		

Corresponding to Eq. (7–13) we have

$$42M + 7a = 28,$$

$$328M + 42a = 213.$$

Corresponding to Eq. (7–14) we have

$$76M = 45.$$

It is readily verified that both methods lead to the line of regression of x on y:

$$(x - 4) = \frac{45}{76}(y - 6),$$

$$x = \frac{45}{76}y + \frac{34}{76} \doteq 0.59y + 0.45.$$

If the above equation is solved for y, then

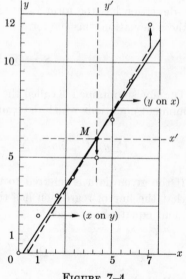

FIGURE 7–4

$$y = \frac{76}{45}x - \frac{34}{45} = 1.69x - 0.76,$$

and this may be compared with the line of regression of y on x found earlier: $y = 1.61x - 0.43$. Both lines are shown in Fig. 7–4; they do not differ greatly.

Coefficient of correlation. If the set of points (x_i, y_i) were exactly on a line, the equations of the two regression lines would be the same. When referred to $(\bar{x}, \bar{y})$ as origin, their equations are $y' = mx'$ and $x' = My'$. These equations are the same if and only if $mM = 1$. If they are not the same, the product mM is used as a measure of the linear relationship between the variables. The *coefficient of correlation* r is defined by

$$r^2 = mM.$$

In Example 7–9 the linear coefficient of correlation is

$$r = \sqrt{\frac{45}{28} \cdot \frac{45}{76}} = \sqrt{1.61 \cdot 0.59} = \sqrt{0.95} = \sqrt{0.97}.$$

In terms of the given data,

$$r^2 = \frac{(\sum x'y')^2}{(\sum x'^2)(\sum y'^2)} = \frac{[\sum(x - \bar{x})(y - \bar{y})]^2}{[\sum(x - \bar{x})^2][\sum(y - \bar{y})^2]}.$$

It is known that r^2 lies between zero and 1, and has the value 1 if perfect linear correlation exists between the variates, that is, if the points all lie on one line. The coefficient r is taken as positive if the lines of regression have positive slopes, and negative if the lines of regression have negative slopes. If $r^2 < 0.7$, the linear relationship between the variates is not often significant, although there may be definite nonlinear relationships between them. (Such matters as these, together with the actual fitting and interpretation of economic data, are treated in a course in statistics.)

EXAMPLE 7–10.   Find the lines of regression and the coefficient of correlation for the data given in the first two columns below.

x	y	x'	y'	x'^2	$x'y'$	y'^2
2	1	−2	−2.2	4	4.4	4.84
3	3	−1	−0.2	1	0.2	0.04
4	2	0	−1.2	0	0.0	1.44
5	6	1	2.8	1	2.8	7.84
6	4	2	0.8	4	1.6	0.64
$\sum$ 20	16	0	0	10	9.0	14.80

$$\bar{x} = 4, \qquad \bar{y} = 3.2, \qquad x' = x - 4, \qquad y' = y - 3.2.$$

The problem is solved by means of Eqs. (7–12) and (7–14). The line of regression of y on x is

$$y - 3.2 = 0.9(x - 4),$$

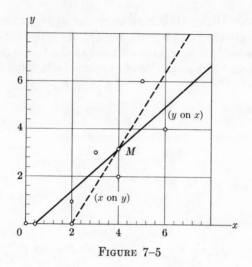

FIGURE 7–5

and the line of regression of x on y is

$$(x - 4) = \frac{9}{14.8} (y - 3.2),$$

$$x = \frac{45}{74} y + \frac{152}{74}, \qquad y = \frac{74}{45} x - \frac{152}{45}.$$

The coefficient of correlation is

$$r = \sqrt{\frac{9}{10} \cdot \frac{45}{74}} = \sqrt{0.55} = 0.74.$$

The lines of regression are shown in Fig. 7–5.

Exercise Group 7–4

1. Verify the results of Example 7–10 by using the moment equations (7–11) and (7–13).

2. Find the lines of regression and the coefficient of correlation for the following data.

x	0	1	2	3	4	5
y	1	1	2	4	6	7

(The line of regression of y on x was found in problem 4, Exercise Group 7–2).

3. Find the line of regression of x on y and the coefficient of correlation for the following data.

x	0	1	2	3	4	5	6	7	8
y	0	1	1	2	3	5	6	8	10

(The line of regression of y on x was found in problem 5, Exercise Group 7-2).

4. Find the lines of regression and the coefficient of correlation for the data given below. Show both lines in a diagram.

x	1	2	3	4	5
y	5	3	3	2	0

5. The data given below was fitted to an exponential curve $y = b \cdot 10^{mx}$ (Example 7-7) by using the logarithmic form of this equation and finding the line of regression of Y on x, where $Y = \log y$. Compare the result with that obtained for the line of regression of x on Y.

x	0	1	2	3	4
y	1	2	3	5	8

6. Fit the data given below with an exponential curve $y = b \cdot 10^{mx}$ by finding the line of regression of x on Y. Compare the result with that obtained in problem 4, Exercise Group 7-3.

x	2	4	6	8	10
y	7	12	20	34	50

7. The data given below may be fitted to a power curve $y = bx^m$ by using the form

$$Y = B + mX, \qquad \text{where} \quad Y = \log y, \ B = \log b, \ X = \log x.$$

Find the line of regression of Y on X and the corresponding power law.

x	7.0	3.9	2.5	1.8	1.4
y	2	3	4	5	6

8. Fit the data given below with a power law by finding the lines of regression of Y on X, and X on Y, where $X = \log x$ and $Y = \log y$.

x	1	2	3	4	5
y	1	2	4	7	11

7–8 Prospect and references. The reader who cares to pursue the subject matter of this book further should acquire a better mathematical background than is required for the study of this text alone. References to standard texts have been made in footnotes. The material of such texts is presented with the prospective student of mathematics, science, or engineering in mind, and the applications are taken from these fields. A knowledge of trigonometry is presupposed. See, for example: Fuller, *Analytic Geometry*, Addison-Wesley, 1954; Daus and Whyburn, *First Year College Mathematics with Applications*, Macmillan, 1949; Thomas, *Calculus and Analytic Geometry*, Addison-Wesley, 1952; and Sherwood and Taylor, *Calculus*, 3rd ed., Prentice-Hall, 1954.

Elementary applications to economics can be found in Schultz, *The Theory and Measurement of Demand*, University of Chicago Press, 1938; Davis, *The Theory of Econometrics*, Principia Press, 1941; and Evans, *Mathematical Introduction to Economics*, McGraw-Hill, 1930.

More advanced applications to economics will require some knowledge of advanced calculus. Standard reference texts include Goursat-Hedrick, *A Course in Mathematical Analysis*, Ginn, 1904 and 1917; Courant, *Differential and Integral Calculus*, 2nd ed., Interscience Press, 1937; Taylor, *Advanced Calculus*, Ginn, 1956; and Apostol, *Mathematical Analysis*, Addison-Wesley, 1957. The required background material is also found in texts written by mathematical economists. Those by Allen, *Mathematical Analysis for Economists*, Macmillan, 1939, and *Mathematical Economics*, St. Martin's Press, 1957, are logical texts to read after the study of the present book. Samuelson, *Foundations of Economic Analysis*, Harvard University Press, 1947, has been referred to on several occasions. Similar material can be found in Bushaw and Clower, *Introduction to Mathematical Economics*, R. D. Irwin, 1957, which contains a more dynamic and realistic approach to the laws of supply and demand than is given in the present book or in some of the texts already noted. Further theory and applications are found in Boulding, *Economic Analysis*, 2nd ed., Harper, 1948; Hicks, *Value and Capital*, 2nd ed., Oxford University Press, 1946; Schneider, *Pricing and Equilibrium*, Macmillan, 1952; Tinberger, *Econometrics*, Blakiston, 1951; and Tintner, *Econometrics*, Wiley, 1952. A preliminary study of statistics is required for some of the above texts.

The very important and rapidly developing field of linear programming has been omitted from this text. For an elementary introduction to the mathematical tools and the economic applications of this subject, the reader may first consult Kemeny, Snell, and Thompson, *Finite Mathematics*, Prentice-Hall, 1957. More advanced ideas and techniques are found in Charnes, Cooper, and Henderson, *Introduction to Linear Programming*, Wiley, 1953; R. Dorfman, *Application of Linear Programming to the Theory of the Firm*, University of California Press, 1951; Dorfman, Samuelson, and Solow, *Linear Programming and Economic Theory*, McGraw-Hill-1958; *Activity Analysis of Production and Allocation* (T. C. Koopmans, Editor) Wiley, 1951; and von Neumann and Morgenstern, *Theory of Games and Economic Behavior*, Princeton University Press, 1944.

The books mentioned here contain extended bibliographies and many references to the current literature. In this respect, Allen's *Mathematical Economics* is specifically cited.

ANSWERS TO PROBLEMS

Exercise Group 1–1

1. (a) 36, (b) 9, (c) two line segments
3. (a) 20, (b) 100, (c) $p = (100 - x)/5$, $(0 \leqq x \leqq 90)$; $p = 2$, $(90 \leqq x \leqq 120)$
6. $x = 8 - (2p/3)$, $p = 12 - (3x/2)$
7. $p = 2(x + 5)/5$
10. (a) Neither, (b) supply, (c) neither, (d) demand

Exercise Group 1–2

1. $(18/7, 34/7)$
3. $(5, 5)$
5. $(24/5, 2)$
7. $(2, 2)$
9. $(1.1, 1.75)$

2. $(8/9, 68/9)$
4. $(15, 6)$
6. $(7.8, 3.6)$
8. $(7.0, 3.8)$
10. $(0.82, 1.01)$

Exercise Group 1–3

1. (a) $11p = 70 - 5x - y$, $y < 70$; $11q = 100 - 4x - 3y$, $x < 25$, (b) $p = 1, q = 2$
2. (a) $9p = 40 - 5x - y, y < 40; 9q = 44 - x - 2y, x < 44$, (b) $x = 4$, $y = 11, p = 1, q = 2$
3. $x = 4, y = 7, p = 6, q = 2$; within restrictions $x < 27, y < 12$
4. $x < 17, y < 11; p = 3, q = 4$
5. $p = 3, x = 4, q = 2, y = 3$; within restrictions $p < 8, q < 4, y < 7$
6. $x = 6.8, p = 3.3, y = 3.5, q = 3.6$; within restrictions $x < 18, y < 13$, $p < 14, q < 17$
7. $x = 3, p = 5, y = 1, q = 3$; within restrictions $y < 3, p < 9, q < 5$
8. $x = 6.5, p = 3.5, y = 3.5, q = 3.5$; within restrictions $y < 8, p < 7$, $q < 4$

Exercise Group 1–4

1. $(8, 4)$
3. $(7, 6)$, $(6.91, 5.77)$
5. $(20, 2)$
7. $(5, 12)$, $(4.9, 12)$
9. $(2.5, 31)$, $(2.37, 31.1)$
11. $(40, 2)$

2. $(30, 25)$
4. $(3, 7)$
6. $(1.9, 29)$, $(1.85, 28.7)$
8. $(2.5, 20)$, $(5/2, 81/4)$
10. $(68, 4)$
12. $(58, 2.8)$, $(58.6, 2.77)$

Exercise Group 1–5

5. $x = 2, y = 2, (0, -2), (-2, 0)$
7. $x = 2, y = 4, (0, 0)$

6. $x = 2, y = -4, (0, -8), (4, 0)$
8. $x = -2, y = 2, (0, -2), (2, 0)$

9. $x = (18 - 3y)/(6 + y)$, $y = (18 - 6x)/(3 + x)$; asymptotes: $x = -3$, $y = -6$; intercepts: (0, 6), (3, 0)

10. $x = (30y - 900)/(y - 40)$, $y = (40x - 900)/(x - 30)$; asymptotes: $x = 30$, $y = 40$; intercepts : (0, 30), (22.5, 0)

EXERCISE GROUP 1–6

1. (6, 5)
2. (6.5, 4.5), (6.49, 4.62)
3. (2, 5)
4. (3.5, 3.5), (3.22, 3.61)
5. (4.2, 7.3)
6. (1.7, 5.5)

7. (a) (0, 2), (2, 3/2), (4, 0); parabola: (1, 15/8), (3, 7/8); hyperbola: (1, 9/5), (3, 1)

8. (a) (0, 4), (2, 3); parabola: (4, 4), (−2, 7); hyperbola: (4, 8/3), (−2, ∞); $y_P = y_H$ yields $x = 0, 0, 2$

9. (b) 15, 10, (c) (10, 5)
10. (b) $x = 34/3$ $y = 17$

EXERCISE GROUP 1–7

1. (a) $p_1 - p = 1/3$, $T = 1/4$, (b) $p - p_2 = 1/3$, $S = 5/12$
2. (a) (2, 6), (b) (20/7, 30/7)
3. $p_1 - p = 1/3$, $T = 1/4$
4. (2.26, 5.48)
5. (a) 3, (b) 3/2
7. (10/7, 20/7), $T = 10/7$
8. (a) (25, 26.25), (b) (34.6, 23.9)
9. (5.67, 5.16)
10. $t = 5.41$, $s = 5.12$

EXERCISE GROUP 1–8

1. $p_1 - p = 4/13$, $q_1 - q = -1/13$
2. From (3, 2) to (3.5, 2.5)
3. $p_1 - p = 2/5$, $q_1 - q = 2/5$
4. $p = 40 - t_1 + t_2$, $q = 62 - \frac{7}{3}t_1 + 2t_2$

EXERCISE GROUP 2–1

1. (a) 1/9, (b) yes
2. (a) 4/11, (b) yes
3. (a) 2/3, (b) 2, (c) 2/5
4. (a) 6, (b) no; $x \to \infty$
5. (a) 0, (b) −3, (c) 7/5, (d) 5/8, (e) 3
6. (a) No, (b) 1/2, (c) 3/4, (d) no
7. (a) $-\Delta x$, (c) 0, $2 - 2x$
8. (a) $2x - 2$, (b) $-2, 0, 4$
9. (a) $-4/(4 + \Delta x)$, (b) $-1/2, -2/3, -1$, (c) $-1, -16/x^2$
10. $-6/x^2$

EXERCISE GROUP 2–2

1. (a) $10x - 10$, (1, 5), (b) $2 - 2x$, (1, 4), (c) $2x - 2$, (1, −4)
2. (a) $3x^2 - 3$, (1, −2), (−1, 2), (b) $3x^2 + 6$, none, (c) $3x^2 - 4x + 1$, (1, −4), (1/3, −104/27)
4. $3x^2 - 6x - 1$
5. $2(x + 1)^2(2x - 1)$
6. (a) −2/3, (b) −50/27
7. (a) $2/(1 - x)^2$, (b) $-5/(4x^2)$, (c) $1/(2x + 4)^2$
8. (a) $-4x/(x^2 + 1)^2$, (b) $(2 - 2x^2)/(x^2 + 1)^2$, (c) $4x/(x^2 + 1)^2$

Exercise Group 2–3

1. $-6x(1 - x^2)^2$ 2. $-6x/(1 + x^2)^4$, 3/8

3. $(12x + 4x^3)/(1 - x^2)^3$

4. (a) $\frac{3}{2}x^{1/2}$, $x \geqq 0$, $y' \to 0$, (b) $2/(3x^{1/3})$, $y \geqq 0$, $y' \to \infty$, (c) $-\frac{1}{2}x^{-3/2}$, $x > 0$, $y \to \infty$, $y' \to \infty$, (d) $1/(3x^{2/3})$, $y' \to \infty$

5. $7.8x^{0.3}$, $2.34/x^{0.7}$ 6. $-8/x^{1.4}$, $11.2/x^{2.4}$

7. $2(x - 1)(2x^2 - x + 1)$ 8. $(1 + x^2)(3x^2 + 4x - 1)/(1 + x)^2$

9. $9(9 + 6x)^{1/2}$, $x \geqq -3/2$ 10. $-1/\sqrt{(8 + 2x)^3}$, $x > -4$

11. $(2 + x)/2\sqrt{(1 + x)^3} > 0$ if $x > -1$

12. ± 1, $\sqrt{2}$

13. $-1/(2y)$, $x < 4$ 14. $\pm 1/2\sqrt{x + 1}$, $x > -1$

Exercise Group 2–4

1. $-y/(2x)$, $3y/(4x^2)$ 2. $-2y/x$, $6y/x^2$

3. $(0, -6, 6)$, $(0, 6, 6)$

4. $(x, y, y', y'') \equiv (1, -2, 9, -12)$, $(2, 2, 0, -6)$, $(3, 0, -3, 0)$, $(4, -2, 0, 6)$

5. ± 2, $\pm 2/\sqrt{5}$ 6. $(12x^2 - 4)/(1 + x^2)^3$

7. $5/(2x^3)$

8. $(2 + 2x^2)/(1 - x^2)^2 > 0$; $4x(x^2 + 3)/(1 - x^2)^3$;
for $-1 < x < 0$, $f''(x) < 0$; $f''(0) = 0$; for $0 < x < 1$, $f''(x) > 0$

9. $-1/(4y^3) = -1/4\sqrt{(4 + x)^3}$ 10. $-\frac{1}{4}(y - 1)^{-3}$

11. $-4/y^3$

12. $y' = 0$ at $(2, 8)$, $(-2, -8)$; $y' = \infty$ at $(4, 4)$, $(-4, -4)$; intercepts $(0, \pm \sqrt{48})$, $(\pm \sqrt{12}, 0)$

Exercise Group 2–5

1.

x	y	y'
-1	0	4
0	3	2
1	4	0
3	0	-4

Concave down

2.

x	y	y'
0	3	-10
1/3	0	-8
3	0	8
5/3	$-16/3$	0

Concave up

3.

x	p	p'
0	4	$-1/8$
7	3	$-1/6$
16	0	∞

Concave down

4.

x	p	p'
0	4	0.25
3	4.65	0.19
5	5	0.17

Concave down

5.

x	p	p'
0	∞	
∞	0	
5	4	$-8/5$
10	1	$-1/5$

Concave up

6.

x	p	p'
0	3	-2
2	1	$-1/2$
6	0	$-1/8$

Concave up

7.

x	y	y'	y''	
0	0	9	-12	
1	4	0	-6	max.
2	2	-3	0	infl.
3	0	0	6	min.

8.

x	y	y'	y''	
0	20	0	-6	max.
1	18	-3	0	infl.
2	16	0	6	min.
-2	0	24	-18	

9.

x	y	y'	y''
0	1	1/4	0
1	9/4	13/4	+
−1	1/4	13/4	−

10.

x	y	y'	y''
0	2	0	+
±2	∞		
±3	−8/5	±1.92	−
±∞	0		

Exercise Group 2–6

1. See problem 7, Exercise Group 2–5.
2. See problem 8, Exercise Group 2–5.

3.

x	y	y'	y''	
0	10	0	−	max.
4/3	8.8	0	+	min.
2/3	9.4	−1.3	0	infl.
−2	−6	20	−	

4.

x	y	y'	y''	
0	0	0	+	min.
±$\sqrt{18}$	324	0	−	max.
±$\sqrt{6}$	180	±120	0	infl.

Absolute max.; relative min.

5.

x	y	y'	y''	
0	0	0	0	infl.
−4	0	−16	+	
−3	−27/4	0	+	min.
−2	−4	4	0	infl.

Absolute min.; no max.

6.

x	y	y'	y''	
0	0	2	0	infl.
1	1	0	−	max.
−1	−1	0	+	min.
±$\sqrt{3}$	±$\sqrt{3}/2$	∓1/4	0	infl.
∞	0			

7.

x	y	y'	y''	
0	0	0	+	min.
±$\sqrt{1/3}$	1/4	±0.65	0	infl.
∞	1			

8. $y'' = -4/y^3$; if $y \neq 0$, $y'' \neq 0$; if $y \doteq 0$, curve on one side of tangent
9. $y'' = 12(x + 2)^{-3} \neq 0$; at $x = -2, y \to \infty$
10. One critical point where y is finite; $x \to \infty$, $y \to a \cdot \infty$; $y'' = 2a \neq 0$

Exercise Group 2–7

2.

x	X	P	p
1	0	0.90	8
4.8	0.68	0	1
2	0.30	0.50	3.2
4	0.60	0.10	1.8
8	0.90	−0.30	0.5

3.

x	X	P	p
1/8	−0.90	1.20	16
1	0	0.60	4
4	0.60	0.20	1.6
8	0.90	0	1

4. (a) $p = 6.533$, (b) $x = 2.411$ 5. (a) 12,500, (b) 8796, (c) \$10,000
6. (X, Y): (2.31, 0), (0.30, 3.22), (0, 3.70), (−0.70, 4.82)

7. (a) 19,500, (b) 43,900, (c) \$4825, (d) line from points (0, 12.3), (7.2, 0)
8. (a) $10^{0.301x}$, $e^{0.693x}$, (b) $10^{-0.699x}$, $e^{-0.307x}$
9. 2.1702, 6.7754, -2.4350 10. 8.76, 0.1142, 64.73, 0.01545

EXERCISE GROUP 2–8

2. (a) 1/4, (b) -4, (c) $(2x - 2)e^{x^2-2x}$, -2 (d) $-4.606x \cdot 10^{-x^2}$, 0
3. (a) $-4e^{-4x}$, (b) $(\ln 0.01)x \cdot 10^{-x^2}$, (c) $-xy/(4 - x^2)$,
(d) $(8 - 3x)/2\sqrt{4 - x}$
4. (a) $-\frac{2}{3}xe^{-x^2}$, (b) $-2xe^{x^2}/(e^{x^2} + 3)^2$
5. $p' = p/4 \neq 0$, $p'' > 0$; points (0, 8), (4, 2.9), (8, 1.1)
6. Minimum at (0, 1), $y'' = y(1 + x^2)$ concave up
7. $(x, y, y', y'') \equiv (0, 0, 3/2, -)$, (9, 3.45, 0.15, $-$)
8. Minimum at (0,0), inflection (± 1, 0.69) with $y' = \pm 1$, (± 3, 2.3)

9.

x	p	p'
0	3	$-1/3$
4.5	0	∞
2.5	2	$-1/2$

10. Circle; (0, 3), $p' = 0$; (3, 0), $p' = \infty$
11. $R' = 3(3 - x)/\sqrt{9 - 2x}$; use $x = 0, 3, 4.5$
12. $R' = (9 - 2x^2)/\sqrt{9 - x^2}$; use $x = 0, \sqrt{9/2}, 3$

EXERCISE GROUP 3–1

1. $-3\frac{1}{3}\%$, $-3/2$, $-3/2$ 2. 10.1%, -2.52, -2.57
3. $-3/2$; see problem 3, Exercise Group 2–7
4. $-1/3$; (1, 27), (3/2, 8), (3, 1); (0, 1.44), (0.18, 0.90), (0.48, 0)
5. $-1/2$, 0   6. ∞, $-5/4$
7. $-(1 + x^2)/(2x^2) = -1/(2 - 2p)$ 8. $-2/x$
9. $p = 7.4e^{-x/8}$ 10. -2

EXERCISE GROUP 3–2

1. Line, equilateral hyperbola, $q' \neq 0$, $q \to 56$
2. (a) $Q = 25,000 + 6000x$, $q = 6000 + 25,000/x$, (b) line, equilateral hyperbola, $q \to 6000$, (c) 63
3. (a) 6, (b) Q parabola, q from $q' = 1 - 4x^{-2}$, $q'' > 0$ and points where $x = 1, 2, 4$
4. Q from (0, 200), (100, 4000), (200, 220), q from (25, 14.5), (100, 10) minimum, (200, 11)
5. (a) $x \geqq 1$, (b) 2, (c) parabola, lowest point (1, 3); hyperbola, lowest point (2, 2)
6. $Q'' = -\frac{1}{4}(x + 8)^{-3/2} < 0$, $q' = -(x + 16)/(2x^2\sqrt{x + 8}) < 0$
7. (a) $q_{min} = 8.56$ at $x = \sqrt[3]{4}$, (b) $Q_1 = x + 8$
8. (a) $Q' = 3(x - 2)^2 + 2 > 0$, (b) $Q_1 = 2x + 32$, (c) 3.8; at $x = 4$, slope $OP = 12$ and $Q' = 14$

9.

x	Q	q	q'
0	4	∞	
4	10.8	e	0
8	29.6	3.7	

10. (a) q monotonically decreases from 12 to 8.54 for $x = 2$, and to 8 when $x \to \infty$.

EXERCISE GROUP 3–3

1. (52. 5, 17.5), $918\frac{3}{4}$
2. (27/4, 9/2), 243/8
4. ($\sqrt{3}$, 18), 31.1
5. (10/3, 400/9), 146
6. (18, 3), 54
7. (2, 1), 2
8. (4, 2.95), 11.80
10. (2, 4), 8

11. $x = 1/3$, $p = 10/3$, $t = 1$, $T_{max} = 1/3$; parallelogram between lines $x = 0$, $x = \frac{1}{3}$ and $p = 2 + x$, $p = 3 + x$

12. $x = 3/2$, $p = 15/2$, $t = 4$, $T_{max} = 6$; $T = \frac{8}{3}(3x - x^2)$

13. $x = \sqrt{3}$, $p = 30$, $t = 24$, $T_{max} = 41.6$

14. $x = 3$, $p = 36$, $t = 24$, $T_{max} = 72$

EXERCISE GROUP 3–4

1. 16
2. 4/3 for $x = 2/3$

3. 263 for $x = 33$; rectangle: width 33, height $p - q$

4. (0.72, 1.38)
5. (1.96, 152)

6. 112/27 for $x = 2/3$; method (a), parallel tangents to parabola and cubic; method (b), area $x(p - q)$

7. $10\sqrt{5} = 22.4$; (a) $\Pi = 15x - x^3$, (b) $R = 20x - x^3$, $Q = 5x$, (c) $p = 15$, $q = 5$, area $\sqrt{5}(p - q)$

8. $8\sqrt{2} = 11.3$; (a) $\Pi = 12x - 2x^3$, (b) $R = 36x - 2x^3$, $Q = 24x$, (c) $p = 32$, $q = 24$, area $\sqrt{2}(p - q)$

9. $p = 2$, $x = 4$, $\Pi_{max} = 1$; when $x = 4$, tangent to $R = x\sqrt{8 - x}$ is parallel to line $Q = 3 + x$.

10. $p = 8/3$, $x = 80/27$, $\Pi_{max} \doteq 5$; near $x = 3$, tangent to $R = x\sqrt{16 - 3x}$ is parallel to line $Q = x$.

11. (a) 4.5, (b) $p = 2.10$, $x = 4.59$, $\Pi_{max} = 5.05$

12. $x = 3.39$, $p = 4$, $\Pi_{max} = 5.18$
13. $x = 3/2$, $p = 81/4$, $\Pi_{max} = 18$

14. $x = 7/3$, $p = 529/9$, $\Pi_{max} = 1372/27 = 50.8$

15. $x = 3.4$, $\Pi_{max} = 7.0$
16. $x = 0.45$, $\Pi_{max} = 0.60$

EXERCISE GROUP 3–5

1. (a) (31/16, 49/4), 15 approximately, (b) $[2 - (t/8), 12 + (t/2)]$, $(16 - t)^2/16$, (c) $t = 8$, $T_{max} = 8$

2. $p_1 - p = 2t/3$, $\Pi_{max} = (4 - t)^2/12$, $T = (4t - t^2)/6$, $T_{max} = 2/3$

3. $x = 33 - (3t/2)$, $T_{max} = 181.5$
4. $p_1 - p = 64 - 49 > 9$

5. (8, 4)
6. (3.12, 2.21)

7. (1.35, 8), $\Pi_{max} = 3.08$
8. (1.95, 11.09), 13.83

9. (a) $(0.565,\ 9.175)$, $p_1 - p = 0.51$, $\Pi_{max} = 2.92$,   (b) $(0.716,\ 8.418)$, $p - p_1 = 0.25$, $\Pi_{max} = 4.84$,   (c) $x_1 = 0.62$, p_1 (tax included) $= 8.90$, $\Delta p = 0.23$, $\Pi_{max} = 3.2$

11. $\Pi_{max} = (2\sqrt{3}/9)(15 - t)^{3/2}$, $T = t\sqrt{(15 - t)/3}$, $t = 10$, $T_{max} = 12.9$

Exercise Group 4–1

1. dy: $(0.2000, 0.0200, 0.0020)$; Δy: $(0.1823, 0.0198, 0.0020)$
2. dy: $(-8/9, -0.444, -0.222, -0.0889)$; Δy: $(-6/9, -0.321, -0.205, -0.0796)$
3. (a) $dy = 0.30$, $\Delta y = 0.31$, (b) $dy = 0.061$, $\Delta y = 0.039$
4. -2, -1.95
5. (a) $(x^3/3) + 3x^2 - 3x + C$, (b) $(x^4/4) + (x^2/2) + \ln x - 1/(2x^2) + C$, (c) $\frac{2}{3}x^{3/2} + 2x^{1/2} + C$, (d) $x - (x^5/5)$
6. (a) $\ln(x + 2) + C$, (b) $\frac{1}{2}\ln(1 + 2x) + C$, $(x > -\frac{1}{2})$, (c) $-\frac{1}{2}e^{-2x} + C$, (d) $2e^{x/2} + C$
7. (a) $x \ln x + C$, (b) $x^2 \ln x + C$, $x^2 \ln x - (x^2/2) + C$
8. (a) $-\frac{2}{3}(8 - x)^{3/2} + C$,   (b) $-\frac{16}{3}(8 - x)^{3/2} + \frac{2}{5}(8 - x)^{5/2} + C$, (c) $-2\sqrt{8 - x} + C$, (d) $-\frac{2}{3}(x + 16)\sqrt{8 - x}$

Exercise Group 4–2

1. $p = 12 - (3x/2)$
2. $p = 12 - x^2$
3. (b) $p = k/x$
4. $p = (6 - x)^2/3$, $(0 \leqq x \leqq 6)$
5. $p = 4 - 6x - (2x^2/3)$
6. 22.1
7. (a) $Q = x^2 + x + 2$, $Q_0 = 2$, (b) $Q = x^2 - x + 4$, $(x \geqq 1/2)$, $Q(0)$ not overhead
8. (a) $Q(x) = x \ln x - x + 4$, (b) $Q(x) = x \ln x - x + 3.614$
10. $R = x\sqrt{3 - x}$; use R and R' for $x = 0, 2, 3$.
11. $R = x\sqrt{18 - 2x}$; use R and R' for $x = 0, 6, 9$.
12. $R = 5.69 - \ln x - (2/x)$; use R, R', R'' for $x = 1, 2, 4$, and R for $x = 1/4$ and 8.

Exercise Group 4–3

1. (a) 36, (b) 36
2. (a) 125/6, (b) 125/6,
4. 9
5. 72
6. 8/3
7. 3.825, 3.831
8. 0.631, 0.632
9. 1.20, 1.19
10. 0.387, 0.386

Exercise Group 4–4

1. 400/3, 36
2. 31.25, 93.76
3. 8/3
4. 36
5. 10.4, 32/3
6. 18, 9/2
7. 78.4, 19.6
8. $425/12 - 304/12 = 121/12$
9. $x_0 = 5/3$, C.S. $= 3.09$
10. $x_0 = \sqrt{12}$, C.S. $= 16\sqrt{3}$

EXERCISE GROUP 5–1

1. (a) Intercepts 4, 3, 2, (b) intercepts −4, 3, 2, (c) intercepts 2, 3, −2

2. Show traces in $x = 0$ and $y = 0$ planes

3. (a) Concave up, $z \geqq 0$, (b) concave down, $z \leqq 25$

4. (a) Concave up, $z \geqq 0$; show elliptic section by $z = 1$ (b) Concave down, $z \leqq 9$; show elliptic section by $z = 0$

5. (a) Center O, $r = 2$, (b) center $(2, 0, 0)$, $r = 2$

6. (a) Traces $z^2 = x^2$, $z^2 = y^2$, circular sections $z = k$, (b) traces $y = \pm 2x$, $z = \pm 3x$, elliptic section $x = 2$

7. Intercepts ± 4, 8, 16; traces $2y = 16 - x^2$, $z = 16 - x^2$, $2y + z = 16$

8. Intercepts 10, $\sqrt{10}$, 10; traces $x = 10 - y^2$, $x + z = 10$, $z = 10 - y^2$

9. $x = 0$, lines $y = 0$ and $2y + z = 8$; $z = 0$, parabola with intercepts $(0, 0, 0)$, $(0, 4, 0)$ and vertex $(8, 2, 0)$; $z = c$, similar parabolas

10. $y = 0$, lines $x = 0$ and $x + z = 8$; $z = 0$, circle, center $(4, 0, 0)$, radius 2; $z = c$, similar circles

EXERCISE GROUP 5–2

1. (a) Parallel lines with intercepts in ratio 4/3, (b) parallel lines with slope −3/2

2. (a) Parallel lines with slope −2, (b) parallel lines with slope 2

3. (a) Circles, center $(0, 0)$, $r = \sqrt{z}$, (b) circles, center $(0, 0)$, $r = \sqrt{25 - z}$

4. (a) Circles, center $(0, 0)$, $r = \sqrt{4 - z^2}$, $(0 \leqq z \leqq 2)$, (b) circles, center $(2, 0)$, $r = \sqrt{4 - z^2}$, $(0 \leqq z \leqq 2)$

5. Parts of congruent parabolas $2y = (16 - z) - x^2$, $z \leqq 16$

6. Circles, center $[(8 - z)/2, 0]$, $r = (8 - z)/2$

7. Equilateral hyperbolas (in first quadrant); $z = 2$, origin alone; as z increases, curve moves away from origin.

8. Equilateral hyperbolas (both branches), including asymptotes $x = 2$, $y = 3$ for $z = 0$

9. Similar concentric ellipses with intercepts $\sqrt{12 - z}$; ellipse for $z = 4$ from points $(0, \pm 4)$, $(\pm 4, 0)$, $(4, 4)$, $(−4, −4)$ $(\pm\sqrt{16/3}, \pm\sqrt{16/3})$

10. Similar concentric ellipses with x-intercept $\sqrt{20 - z}$, y-intercept $\sqrt{10 - (z/2)}$; ellipse for $z = 0$ sketched from intercepts and intersection of curve with $y = x$, $y = -x$, $y = -x/2$

EXERCISE GROUP 5–3

1. Quadrilateral in pq-plane bounded by $p = 0$, $q = 0$, $2p + q = 17$, $p + 2q = 14$

2. Quadrilateral bounded by $p = 0$, $q = 0$, $2p + q = 11$, $p + q = 13$

3. Part of demand plane above quadrilateral bounded by $p = 0$, $q = 0$, $2p - q = 5$, $q - p = 6$

4. Quadrilateral in pqx-space $(6, 0, 0)$, $(0, 0, 18)$, $(0, 3, 24)$, $(24, 27, 0)$

5. Quadrilateral in pqx-space $(1, 0, 0)$, $(0, 0, 2)$, $(0, 2, 4)$, $(3/2, 1, 0)$, quadrilateral in pqy-space $(0, 0, 6)$, $(0, 2, 0)$, $(3/2, 1, 0)$, $(1, 0, 4)$

6. c and d have opposite signs; quadrilateral in pqx-space $(2, 0, 0)$, $(0, 0, 6)$, $(0, 1, 4)$, $(1, 3/2, 0)$, quadrilateral in pqy-space $(2, 0, 4)$, $(0, 0, 2)$, $(0, 1, 0)$, $(1, 3/2, 0)$

7. Lines with variable slope x; parabolas flattening out as y increases

8. (a) As p increases, x decreases and y increases, and as q increases, y decreases and x increases. (b) $p = x^{1/3}y^{2/3}$, $q = x^{2/3}y^{1/3}$

9. (a) As either p or q increases, both x and y decrease. (b) $y = 4x$

10. (a) As either p or q increases, both x and y decrease. (b) $p = 4x/y$, $q = y/x^2$

EXERCISE GROUP 5–4

1. Equilateral hyperbolas; parallel lines, slope -1

2. Generalized hyperbolas; parallel lines, slope -2

3. (a) Equilateral hyperbolas; parallel lines, slope -1; (b) generalized hyperbolas; parallel lines, slope -3

4. (a) Generalized hyperbolas in LC-plane, (b) parallel lines in $\log L \log C$-plane

5. See Fig. 5–13. For $z = 2$, $(u - 1/3)(v - 1/3) = 1/9 = u'v'$, asymptotes $u = 1/3$, $v = 1/3$, point $u' = v' = 1/3$.

6. $(u - 1/3)(v - 2/3) = 2/9 = u'v'$, asymptotes $u = 1/3$, $v = 2/3$, points $u' = 1/3$, $v' = 2/3$, and $u' = 2/3$, $v' = 1/3$

7. See Fig. 5–15. Asymptotes $v = u/2$, $v = 2u$; successive curves correspond to $z = 0, 1, 9, 25$.

8. See Fig. 5–15. Asymptotes $v = u/2$, $v = 3u$; successive curves through $v1, 1)$, $(2, 2)$, $(3, 3)$; other points, corresponding to vertical tangent, where $v = 7u/4$, $(4z/5, 7z/5)$.

EXERCISE GROUP 5–5

1. (a) $-2x + y$, $-2y + x$, -1, -4, (b) $2x + 2y - 2$, $2x + 8y + 4$, 0, 0, (c) $2xe^{x^2+v^2}$, $2ye^{x^2+v^2}$, $2e^-$, 0, (d) $y^2/(x + y)^2$, $x^2/(x + y)^2$, $1/4$, $1/4$, (e) $(y^2 - x^2)/x^2$, $-2y/x$, 3, -4

2. (a) $-2x + 2y$, $2x - 4y$, 2, -8, (b) $2x - 2y + 6$, $-2x + 4y - 8$, 0, 0, (c) $2x/(x^2 + y^2)$, $2y/(x^2 + y^2)$, 2, 0, (d) $2y/(x + 2)^2$, $x/(x + 2)$, $1/4$, $1/2$, (e) $-5 + (y/x^2)$, $-1/x$, -3, -1

4. (a) $-2p/x$, $-q/x$, $-p/y$, $-2q/y$, (b) $-2p/x$, q/x, p/y, $-q/y$, (c) $-2p/x$, q/x, $-2p/y$, $-3q/y$

5. (a) $-1, 1, 2, -1$, (b) $-2, -1, -1, -1$

6. (a) Competitive, $-1.7, 0.8, 0.5, -0.2$, (b) complementary, $-1.5, -0.4, -0.5, -0.4$

7. (a) $1, 1$, (b) $0, 4$ 8. (a) $1, 2$, (b) $1, 1$

EXERCISE GROUP 5–6

1. (a) $-2, 1, -2$, (b) $-4, 5, -4$ 2. (a) $-2, 2, -4$, (b) $-8, 16, -24$

3. (a) $-2y^2/(x + y)^3$, $2xy/(x + y)^3$, $-2x^2/(x + y)^3$, (b) $(4x^2 + 2)z$, $4xyz$, $(4y^2 + 2)z$

4. $-4xy/(x^2 + y^2)^2$; revolve $z = 2\ln x$ about z-axis; circles, center O, $r = e^{z/2}$.

5. $4/(1 + x^2 + y^2)^2$, $-4xy/(1 + x^2 + y^2)^2$; revolve $z = \ln(1 + x^2)$ about z-axis; this curve has minimum at $(0, 0)$, inflection at $(1, 0.69)$; circles, center O, $r = \sqrt{e^z - 1}$.

6. (a) $y' = 0$ at $(1, 2)$, $(-1, -2)$; $y' = \infty$ at $(2, 1)$, $(-2, -1)$; intercepts $\sqrt{3}$, (b) $y' = 0$ at $(\pm 2\sqrt{3}/3, \mp 8\sqrt{3}/3)$; $y' = \infty$ at $(\pm 4\sqrt{3}/3, \mp 4\sqrt{3}/3)$; x-intercepts $\pm\sqrt{2}$, y-intercepts ± 4

7. $y' = 0$ at $(5, 4)$, $(-5, -4)$; $y' = \infty$ at $(4, 5)$, $(-4, -5)$

8. (a) $(8 - 2x - 2)/x$, $-2y/x$, (b) $(10 - 10x - z)/x$, $-1/x$

9. (a) $2x - 2y$, 4, (b) $1 - (x/y)$, $-a^2/y^3$

10. (a) $18 - 6x = 3y$, -6, (b) $-2x + (32/x^3) = -2x + (2y^2/x)$, $-2 - (96/x^4) = -2 - (6y^2/x^2)$

Exercise Group 6–1

1. 16, 0, circular paraboloid
2. (a) 36, 0, (b) 11, elliptical paraboloid
3. (a) $(0, 0)$, $z_{xx} > 0$, $\Delta = 12$, $z_{min} = 28$, (b) $(0, 0)$, $z_{xx} < 0$, $\Delta = 3$, $z_{max} = 48$
4. C.P. $(1, 2)$, $z_{xx} < 0$, $\Delta = 16$, $z_{max} = 68$
5. (a) 13, (b) 8, circles center $(2, 3)$, $r = \sqrt{13 - z}$, $(0 \leqq z \leqq 13)$
6. 400, circles center $(12, 16)$, $r = \sqrt{400 - z}$, $(0 \leqq z \leqq 400)$
7. $\Delta = -1$, $x = y$: minimum at O; $x = -y$: maximum at O
8. C.P. $(0, 0)$, $\Delta = -5$, $x = y$: minimum at O; $x = -y$: maximum at O
9. (a) $(4, 2)$, $\Delta = -1$, (b) $(1, -2)$, $\Delta = -4$
10. (a) $(2, 1)$, $\Delta = 3$, $z_{max} = 3$, (b) $(2, 1)$, $\Delta = -5$, saddle point
11. (a) Absolute minimum, (b) saddle point, (c) absolute minimum
12. Absolute minimum
13. $(0, 0)$, $\Delta = 15$, relative minimum $z = 0$; $(5/2, 5/4)$ $\Delta = -15$, saddle point $z = 125/16$; no absolute maximum or minimum.
14. (a) 16, circles center $(-2, 2)$, $r = \sqrt{16 - z}$, (b) maximum at $(0, 2)$
15. 7 at $(0, 2)$, circles center $(-3, 2)$, $r = \sqrt{16 - z}$
16. (a) $z_{max} = 20$; ellipses, center $(-2, 2)$, expanding as z decreases, $(0 \leqq z \leqq 20)$, (b) on boundary $x = 0$, $y > 0$, $z = 12 - 3(y - 2)^2$, $z_{max} = 12$; on boundary $y = 0$, $x > 0$, $z = 8 - 2(x + 2)^2 < 12$

Exercise Group 6–2

1. $x = 4$, $y = 2$, $p = 24$, $q = 30$, $\Delta = 60$, $\Pi_{max} = 68$; concentric ellipses
2. $x = 4$, $y = 5$, $p = 8$, $q = 10$, $\Delta = 4$, $\Pi_{max} = 41$; concentric circles
3. $x = 3$, $y = 2$, $p = 25$, $q = 24$, $\Delta = 140$, $\Pi_{max} = 90$
4. $x = 3$, $p = 9$, $y = 6$, $q = 9$, $\Delta = 3$, $\Pi_{max} = 63$
5. Saddle point $(3, 2)$, $\Delta = -5$; $\Pi_{max} = 42.25$ for $x = 0$, $y = 6.5$, $p = 12$, $q = 6.5$
7. $x = 3$, $p = 14$, $y = 1$, $q = 8$, $\Delta = 9$, $\Pi_{max} = 37$
8. $x = 3/2$, $y = 7/2$, $p = 7/4$, $q = 3$, $\Delta = 2$, $\Pi_{max} = 41/8$

9. $x = 3, y = 1, p = 13, q = 8, \Delta = 32, \Pi_{max} = 36$

10. $x = 1, y = 2, p = 6, q = 10, \Delta = 24y > 0$ if $y > 0, \Pi_{max} = 8$

11. $x = \sqrt{6}, y = 3/2, p = 28, q = 15/2, \Delta = 72x > 0$ if $x > 0, \Pi_{max} = 24\sqrt{6} - 5/4 = 57.65$

12. $x = \sqrt{5}, y = \sqrt{2}, p = 11, q = 7, \Pi_{xx} < 0$ and $\Delta = 36xy > 0,$ $\Pi_{max} \doteq 28$

13. Four critical points; only $(2, 1)$ satisfy sufficient conditions for maximum, $\Pi_{max} = 25$.

Exercise Group 6–3

1. 22, circles $(u - 3)^2 + (v - 2)^2 = 22 - \Pi$

2. 10, ellipses $4(u - 4)^2 + 2(v - 3)^2 = 10 - \Pi$

3. 16, ellipses $4(u - 2)^2 + 16[v - (5/2)]^2 = 16 - \Pi$

4. 27   5. $39-12\sqrt{2} = 22$

6. $29.1, u = 3, v = 1.65$

7. $u = 2, v = 4, \Pi_{uu} = -10, \Delta = 75/4, \Pi_{max} = 20$

8. $u = 2, v = 1, \Pi_{uu} = -15/2, \Delta = 50, \Pi_{max} = 20$

9. At critical point $(5/2, 1/2), \Delta = -64; \Pi_{max} = 8$ at corner $(4, 2)$

10. At critical point $(1, 1), \Delta = -36; \Pi_{max} = 30$ at corner $(3, 2)$; for points on curves, use $u = 2, u = 3$ and $v = 2$.

11. (a) $\Pi_{max} = 61/3$, (b) $\Pi_{max} = 129/4$

12. C.P. $(u = v = 2/3), \Delta = -324; u = 3, v = 43/12, \Pi_{max} = 34.1$

Exercise Group 6–4

1. 14.2; vertical plane section of paraboloid; concentric circles, radius $\sqrt{16 - z}$, with one tangent to line

2. $z_{min} = 0$; center of circle is on line.

3. $d^2z/dx^2 = 12, z_{min} = 17$; ellipse corresponding to $z = 17$ tangent to line at $(2, 1)$

4. $z_{min} = 5$, point (ellipse) on circle; $z_{max} = 13, z'' = -4$, circle tangent to ellipse at $(2, 0)$

5. $z_{max} = 25, z_{min} = 9$ at end points; circle of constraint tangent to corresponding z-circles

6. $(0, 0); z''$ test fails; $z = 27$, neither maximum nor minimum (inflection); $(3, 9); z'' > 0, z_{min} = 0$.

7. (a) Absolute minimum 17 at $(\pm 2, 1/2)$, (b) same answer as part (a); also relative but not absolute maximum 33 at $(0, 5/2)$

8. (a) 22, (b) 16   9. (a) 22, (b) 29.1

10. (a) 20, (b) 20

Exercise Group 6–5

1. $(2, 2)$; line tangent to hyperbola $x = (12 + y^2)/(4y)$ at $(2, 2)$

2. $(3, 1)$; line tangent to hyperbola $U = 11$ (asymptotes of curve are $y = 0$, $y = 4x$)

3. $(2, 2)$; line tangent to hyperbola $U = 16$ (asymptotes of curve are $y = 3x$, $y = x/2$)

4. $(4, 5)$ 5. $(7, 5)$

6. $(12, 7)$

7. $(5, 2)$; circle center $(12, 16)$, $r = \sqrt{400 - U}$, circle $U = 155$ tangent to line

8. $(5, 3)$; circle center $(12, 24)$, $r = \sqrt{490}$ tangent to line at $(5, 3)$

9. $(2, 5)$; $dU/dx = (-7 - 4x + 3y)/2$, $d^2U/dx^2 = -25/8$

10. Ellipse for $U = 32$ is tangent to line at $(3, 2)$

11. $(2, 3)$; $U = 10$, point ellipse; $U = 4$, ellipse tangent to line at $(2, 3)$; $U = 1$, ellipse cuts line

12. (a) $(2, 2)$, $dU/dx = -x + y$, $d^2U/dx^2 = -5/2$, $U_{max} = 60$

13. $x = 1$, $y = 2$, $U_{max} = 24$; ellipse $2x_1^2 + 2x_1y_1 + y_1^2 = 5$, sketched from intercepts and points where slope is 0 and ∞, is tangent to budget line at $(1, 2)$

14. U maximum for $(2, 4)$ 15. U maximum for $(4, 4)$

16. $(2, 3)$, $Z_{max} = 64$; curve from $(0, 15)$, $(2, 3)$, $(6, 0)$

Exercise Group 7–1

1. (a) $y = -x + 7$, (b) $y = (34 - x^2)/6$, (c) $y = \sqrt{41 - 8x}$; use intercepts to complete curves

2. (a) $y = (-x/3) + (19/3)$, (b) $y = (199 - x^2)/33$, (c) $y = \sqrt{39 - 3x}$; use intercepts to complete curves

3. (a) $y = \sqrt{9 + 4x}$, $(0, 3)$ monotonically increasing,
   (b) $y = (-x^2 + 34x + 180)/60$, maximum y for $x = 17$

4. (a) $y = 1 + (x^2/4)$, (b) $x = (-y^2 + 9y - 8)/3$

5. (a) $y = x^2 - 2x + 3$, (b) $x = (-y^2 + 11y - 12)/6$

6. $(x + 1)(p + 1) = 4$

7. Hyperbola: asymptotes $x = -1$, $y = -2$; parabola: $y = x^2 - 4x + 4$, lowest point $(2, 0)$

8. $(x + 2)(y + 6) = 30$

9. $y = (13/9)x - (1/9)$, $y = (3/16)x^2 + (7/16)x + (47/64)$

10. $y = 1.3x - 1.2$, $y = (x^2 + 3x + 2)/9$

Exercise Group 7–2

1. (a) $0.60 > 0.59$, (b) $0.61 > 0.59$

2. $\bar{x} = 4.5$, $\sum(x - \bar{x})^2 = 17.50$, $g = 4.14$, $\sum(x - g)^2 = 18.46$

3. $\bar{x} = 9.62$, $\sum(x - \bar{x})^2 = 154.4$, $g = 7.84$, $\sum(x - g)^2 = 173.4$

4. $y = (47/35)x + (1/7)$, $y' = (47/35)\,x'$

5. $y = (37/30)x - (28/30)$, $y' = (37/30)\,x'$

6. $S = 13.69(Y - 1920) + 313.5$ through $\bar{Y} = 1936\frac{2}{3}$, $\bar{S} = 541\frac{2}{3}$

Exercise Group 7–3

1. (a) $y = 0.452x^2 + 4.71$, (b) $y = 0.350x^2 + 1.46x$

2. 3.17, 2.39 3. $y = 0.50x^2 - 1.24x + 2.86$

4. $Y = 0.109x + 0.640$, $y = 4.36 \cdot 10.^{0.109x}$

5. (a) $Y = 0.644 + 0.215x$, $y = 4.40 \cdot 10^{0.215x}$, (b) $Y = 0.602 + 0.226x$, $y = 4 \cdot 10^{0.226x}$

6. $Y = 0.576 + 1.85X$, $y = 3.77x^{1.85}$

7. (a) $D = 20/p^{1.49}$, $D = 19.6/p^{1.48}$

8. $y = (2.31 \cdot 10^{13})/x^{1.75}$, 731

EXERCISE GROUP 7–4

2. $y = (47/35)x + (1/7)$, $x = (1/67)(47y + 3)$, $r = 0.97$

3. $y = (37/30)x - (28/30)$, $(x - 4) = (37/48)(y - 4)$, $r = 0.975$

4. $y = -1.1x + 5.9$, $x = (1/6)(-5y + 31)$, $r = -0.96$

5. $x = 5.31Y - 0.54$ or $Y = 0.102 + 0.188x$

6. $x = 9.2Y - 5.87$ or $Y = 0.109x + 0.638$

7. $Y = 0.865 - 0.657X$ or $y = 7.33/x^{0.657}$

8. $Y = 1.49X + 9.9380 - 10$ or $y = 0.867x^{1.49}$ $X = 0.657Y + 0.049$ or $y = 0.843x^{1.52}$

APPENDIX

Table I.   Powers and Roots 223

Table II. Squares 226

Table III. Common Logarithms 230

Table IV. Natural Logarithms 234

Table V.   Exponentials 238

Table I

POWERS AND ROOTS

This table gives directly the square and square root, cube and cube root of the integers from 1 to 100. It is not a useful table for other numbers.

TABLE I

POWERS AND ROOTS

No.	Sq.	Sq. root	Cube	Cube root	No.	Sq.	Sq. root	Cube	Cube root
1	1	1.000	1	1.000	51	2,601	7.141	132,651	3.708
2	4	1.414	8	1.260	52	2,704	7.211	140,608	3.733
3	9	1.732	27	1.442	53	2,809	7.280	148,877	3.756
4	16	2.000	64	1.587	54	2,916	7.348	157,464	3.780
5	25	2.236	125	1.710	55	3,025	7.416	166,375	3.803
6	36	2.449	216	1.817	56	3,136	7.483	175,616	3.826
7	49	2.646	343	1.913	57	3,249	7.550	185,193	3.849
8	64	2.828	512	2.000	58	3,364	7.616	195,112	3.871
9	81	3.000	729	2.080	59	3,481	7.681	205,379	3.893
10	100	3.162	1,000	2.154	60	3,600	7.746	216,000	3.915
11	121	3.317	1,331	2.224	61	3,721	7.810	226,981	3.936
12	144	3.464	1,728	2.289	62	3,844	7.874	238,328	3.958
13	169	3.606	2,197	2.351	63	3,969	7.937	250,047	3.979
14	196	3.742	2,744	2.410	64	4,096	8.000	262,144	4.000
15	225	3.873	3,375	2.466	65	4,225	8.062	274,625	4.021
16	256	4.000	4,096	2.520	66	4,356	8.124	287,496	4.041
17	289	4.123	4,913	2.571	67	4,489	8.185	300,763	4.062
18	324	4.243	5,832	2.621	68	4,624	8.246	314,432	4.082
19	361	4.359	6,859	2.668	69	4,761	8.307	328,509	4.102
20	400	4.472	8,000	2.714	70	4,900	8.367	343,000	4.121
21	441	4.583	9,261	2.759	71	5,041	8.426	357,911	4.141
22	484	4.690	10,648	2.802	72	5,184	8.485	373,248	4.160
23	529	4.796	12,167	2.844	73	5,329	8.544	389,017	4.179
24	576	4.899	13,824	2.884	74	5,476	8.602	405,224	4.198
25	625	5.000	15,625	2.924	75	5,625	8.660	421,875	4.217
26	676	5.099	17,576	2.962	76	5,776	8.718	438,976	4.236
27	729	5.196	19,683	3.000	77	5,929	8.775	456,533	4.254
28	784	5.292	21,952	3.037	78	6,084	8.832	474,552	4.273
29	841	5.385	24,389	3.072	79	6,241	8.888	493,039	4.291
30	900	5.477	27,000	3.107	80	6,400	8.944	512,000	4.309
31	961	5.568	29,791	3.141	81	6,561	9.000	531,441	4.327
32	1,024	5.657	32,768	3.175	82	6,724	9.055	551,368	4.344
33	1,089	5.745	35,937	3.208	83	6,889	9.110	571,787	4.362
34	1,156	5.831	39,304	3.240	84	7,056	9.165	592,704	4.380
35	1,225	5.916	42,875	3.271	85	7,225	9.220	614,125	4.397
36	1,296	6.000	46,656	3.302	86	7,396	9.274	636,056	4.414
37	1,369	6.083	50,653	3.332	87	7,569	9.327	658,503	4.431
38	1,444	6.164	54,872	3.362	88	7,744	9.381	681,472	4.448
39	1,521	6.245	59,319	3.391	89	7,921	9.434	704,969	4.465
40	1,600	6.325	64,000	3.420	90	8,100	9.487	729,000	4.481
41	1,681	6.403	68,921	3.448	91	8,281	9.539	753,571	4.498
42	1,764	6.481	74,088	3.476	92	8,464	9.592	778,688	4.514
43	1,849	6.557	79,507	3.503	93	8,649	9.644	804,357	4.531
44	1,936	6.633	85,184	3.530	94	8,836	9.695	830,584	4.547
45	2,025	6.708	91,125	3.557	95	9,025	9.747	857,375	4.563
46	2,116	6.782	97,336	3.583	96	9,216	9.798	884,736	4.579
47	2,209	6.856	103,823	3.609	97	9,409	9.849	912,673	4.595
48	2,304	6.928	110,592	3.634	98	9,604	9.899	941,192	4.610
49	2,401	7.000	117,649	3.659	99	9,801	9.950	970,299	4.626
50	2,500	7.071	125,000	3.684	100	10,000	10.000	1,000,000	4.642

TABLE II

SQUARES

This table gives directly the squares of numbers from 1.00 to 9.99 to four significant figures, and linear interpolation provides the squares of all four-place numbers from 1.000 to 9.999. For example,

$$(2.374)^2 = 5.617 + 0.4(0.047) = 5.617 + 0.019 = 5.636,$$

since the tabular difference is 0.047, and 0.4(0.047) rounded off to three decimal places is 0.019.

By writing a given number N in *scientific notation* as the product of a number between 1 and 10 multiplied by a power of 10, the square of any four-place number can be found to four significant figures. For example,

$$(23.7)^2 = (2.37 \times 10)^2 = 5.617 \times 100 = 561.7,$$

$$(0.2374)^2 = (2.374/10)^2 = 5.636/100 = 0.05636.$$

This table can also be used to find the square root of any number to four significant figures. If the given number M is between 1 and 100, a direct reading gives $\sqrt{M}$ if M appears exactly as an entry in the table, or a direct reading and linear interpolation if M does not appear exactly as an entry in the table.

$$\sqrt{61} = 7.810$$

does not imply that $(7.810)^2$ is exactly 61, but that it agrees with 61 to four significant figures.

$$\sqrt{62} = 7.87 + 0.01(6/15) = 7.874,$$

since the partial difference (disregarding the decimal point) is 6200 − 6194 = 6, and the tabular difference corresponding to 0.01 is 6209 − 6194 = 15.

If the number M is not between 1 and 100, it is written as such a number multiplied or divided by a positive power of 100, and the above procedure is applied:

$$\sqrt{6200} = \sqrt{62 \times 100} = 7.874 \times 10 = 78.74,$$

$$\sqrt{0.62} = \sqrt{62/100} = 7.874/10 = 0.7874,$$

$$\sqrt{620} = \sqrt{6.20 \times 100} = \sqrt{6.2} \times 10 = 24.90,$$

where $\sqrt{6.2}$ is found by locating the entry 6.200 in the table and directly reading $\sqrt{6.2} = 2.490$. Similarly,

$$\sqrt{0.05636} = \sqrt{5.636/100} = \sqrt{5.636}/10 = 0.2374$$

is found using linear interpolation:

$$\sqrt{5.636} = 2.37 + 0.01(19/47) = 2.374, \quad \text{so that} \quad \sqrt{0.05636} = 0.2374.$$

TABLE II

SQUARES*

To Four Significant Digits
(Square roots may be found by inverse interpolation)

N	.00	.01	.02	.03	.04	.05	.06	.07	.08	.09
1.0	1.000	1.020	1.040	1.061	1.082	1.102	1.124	1.145	1.166	1.188
1.1	1.210	1.232	1.254	1.277	1.300	1.322	1.346	1.369	1.392	1.416
1.2	1.440	1.464	1.488	1.513	1.538	1.562	1.588	1.613	1.638	1.664
1.3	1.690	1.716	1.742	1.769	1.796	1.822	1.850	1.877	1.904	1.932
1.4	1.960	1.988	2.016	2.045	2.074	2.102	2.132	2.161	2.190	2.220
1.5	2.250	2.280	2.310	2.341	2.372	2.402	2.434	2.465	2.496	2.528
1.6	2.560	2.592	2.624	2.657	2.690	2.722	2.756	2.789	2.822	2.856
1.7	2.890	2.924	2.958	2.993	3.028	3.062	3.098	3.133	3.168	3.204
1.8	3.240	3.276	3.312	3.349	3.386	3.422	3.460	3.497	3.534	3.572
1.9	3.610	3.648	3.686	3.725	3.764	3.802	3.842	3.881	3.920	3.960
2.0	4.000	4.040	4.080	4.121	4.162	4.202	4.244	4.285	4.326	4.368
2.1	4.410	4.452	4.494	4.537	4.580	·4.622	4.666	4.709	4.752	4.796
2.2	4.840	4.884	4.928	4.973	5.018	5.062	5.108	5.153	5.198	5.244
2.3	5.290	5.336	5.382	5.429	5.476	5.522	5.570	5.617	5.664	5.712
2.4	5.760	5.808	5.856	5.905	5.954	6.002	6.052	6.101	6.150	6.200
2.5	6.250	6.300	6.350	6.401	6.452	6.502	6.554	6.605	6.656	6.708
2.6	6.760	6.812	6.864	6.917	6.970	7.022	7.076	7.129	7.182	7.236
2.7	7.290	7.344	7.398	7.453	7.508	7.562	7.618	7.673	7.728	7.784
2.8	7.840	7.896	7.952	8.009	8.066	8.122	8.180	8.237	8.294	8.352
2.9	8.410	8.468	8.526	8.585	8.644	8.702	8.762	8.821	8.880	8.940
3.0	9.000	9.060	9.120	9.181	9.242	9.302	9.364	9.425	9.486	9.548
3.1	9.610	9.672	9.734	9.797	9.860	9.922	9.986	10.05	10.11	10.18
3.2	10.24	10.30	10.37	10.43	10.50	10.56	10.63	10.69	10.76	10.82
3.3	10.89	10.96	11.02	11.09	11.16	11.22	11.29	11.36	11.42	11.49
3.4	11.56	11.63	11.70	11.76	11.83	11.90	11.97	12.04	12.11	12.18
3.5	12.25	12.32	12.39	12.46	12.53	12.60	12.67	12.74	12.82	12.89
3.6	12.96	13.03	13.10	13.18	13.25	13.32	13.40	13.47	13.54	13.62
3.7	13.69	13.76	13.84	13.91	13.99	14.06	14.14	14.21	14.29	14.36
3.8	14.44	14.52	14.59	14.67	14.75	14.82	14.90	14.98	15.05	15.13
3.9	15.21	15.29	15.37	15.44	15.52	15.60	15.68	15.76	15.84	15.92
4.0	16.00	16.08	16.16	16.24	16.32	16.40	16.48	16.56	16.65	16.73
4.1	16.81	16.89	16.97	17.06	17.14	17.22	17.31	17.39	17.47	17.56
4.2	17.64	17.72	17.81	17.89	17.98	18.06	18.15	18.23	18.32	18.40
4.3	18.49	18.58	18.66	18.75	18.84	18.92	19.01	19.10	19.18	19.27
4.4	19.36	19.45	19.54	19.62	19.71	19.80	19.89	19.98	20.07	20.16
4.5	20.25	20.34	20.43	20.52	20.61	20.70	20.79	20.88	20.98	21.07
4.6	21.16	21.25	21.34	21.44	21.53	21.62	21.72	21.81	21.90	22.00
4.7	22.09	22.18	22.28	22.37	22.47	22.56	22.66	22.75	22.85	22.94
4.8	23.04	23.14	23.23	23.33	23.43	23.52	23.62	23.72	23.81	23.91
4.9	24.01	24.11	24.21	24.30	24.40	24.50	24.60	24.70	24.80	24.90
5.0	25.00	25.10	25.20	25.30	25.40	25.50	25.60	25.70	25.81	25.91
N	.00	.01	.02	.03	.04	.05	.06	.07	.08	.09

* Reprinted by permission from *Algebra for College Students*, by W. M. Whyburn and P. H. Daus, pp. 260–261. Copyright 1955 by Prentice-Hall, Inc., Englewood Cliffs, N. J.

TABLE II—SQUARES (*continued*)

N	.00	.01	.02	.03	.04	.05	.06	.07	.08	.09
5.0	25.00	25.10	25.20	25.30	25.40	25.50	25.60	25.70	25.81	25.91
5.1	26.01	26.11	26.21	26.32	26.42	26.52	26.63	26.73	26.83	26.94
5.2	27.04	27.14	27.25	27.35	27.46	27.56	27.67	27.77	27.88	27.98
5.3	28.09	28.20	28.30	28.41	28.52	28.62	28.73	28.84	28.94	29.05
5.4	29.16	29.27	29.38	29.48	29.59	29.70	29.81	29.92	30.03	30.14
5.5	30.25	30.36	30.47	30.58	30.69	30.80	30.91	31.02	31.14	31.25
5.6	31.36	31.47	31.58	31.70	31.81	31.92	32.04	32.15	32.26	32.38
5.7	32.49	32.60	32.72	32.83	32.95	33.06	33.18	33.29	33.41	33.52
5.8	33.64	33.76	33.87	33.99	34.11	34.22	34.34	34.46	34.57	34.69
5.9	34.81	34.93	35.05	35.16	35.28	35.40	35.52	35.64	35.76	35.88
6.0	36.00	36.12	36.24	36.36	36.48	36.60	36.72	36.84	36.97	37.09
6.1	37.21	37.33	37.45	37.58	37.70	37.82	37.95	38.07	38.19	38.32
6.2	38.44	38.56	38.69	38.81	38.94	39.06	39.19	39.31	39.44	39.56
6.3	39.69	39.82	39.94	40.07	40.20	40.32	40.45	40.58	40.70	40.83
6.4	40.96	41.09	41.22	41.34	41.47	41.60	41.73	41.86	41.99	42.12
6.5	42.25	42.38	42.51	42.64	42.77	42.90	43.03	43.16	43.30	43.43
6.6	43.56	43.69	43.82	43.96	44.09	44.22	44.36	44.49	44.62	44.76
6.7	44.89	45.02	45.16	45.29	45.43	45.56	45.70	45.83	45.97	46.10
6.8	46.24	46.38	46.51	46.65	46.79	46.92	47.06	47.20	47.33	47.47
6.9	47.61	47.75	47.89	48.02	48.16	48.30	48.44	48.58	48.72	48.86
7.0	49.00	49.14	49.28	49.42	49.56	49.70	49.84	49.98	50.13	50.27
7.1	50.41	50.55	50.69	50.84	50.98	51.12	51.27	51.41	51.55	51.70
7.2	51.84	51.98	52.13	52.27	52.42	52.56	52.71	52.85	53.00	53.14
7.3	53.29	53.44	53.58	53.73	53.88	54.02	54.17	54.32	54.46	54.61
7.4	54.76	54.91	55.06	55.20	55.35	55.50	55.65	55.80	55.95	56.10
7.5	56.25	56.40	56.55	56.70	56.85	57.00	57.15	57.30	57.46	57.61
7.6	57.76	57.91	58.06	58.22	58.37	58.52	58.68	58.83	58.98	59.14
7.7	59.29	59.44	59.60	59.75	59.91	60.06	60.22	60.37	60.53	60.68
7.8	60.84	61.00	61.15	61.31	61.47	61.62	61.78	61.94	62.09	62.25
7.9	62.41	62.57	62.73	62.88	63.04	63.20	63.36	63.52	63.68	63.84
8.0	64.00	64.16	64.32	64.48	64.64	64.80	64.96	65.12	65.29	65.45
8.1	65.61	65.77	65.93	66.10	66.26	66.42	66.59	66.75	66.91	67.08
8.2	67.24	67.40	67.57	67.73	67.90	68.06	68.23	68.39	68.56	68.72
8.3	68.89	69.06	69.22	69.39	69.56	69.72	69.89	70.06	70.22	70.39
8.4	70.56	70.73	70.90	71.06	71.23	71.40	71.57	71.74	71.91	72.08
8.5	72.25	72.42	72.59	72.76	72.93	73.10	73.27	73.44	73.62	73.79
8.6	73.96	74.13	74.30	74.48	74.65	74.82	75.00	75.17	75.34	75.52
8.7	75.69	75.86	76.04	76.21	76.39	76.56	76.74	76.91	77.09	77.26
8.8	77.44	77.62	77.79	77.97	78.15	78.32	78.50	78.68	78.85	79.03
8.9	79.21	79.39	79.57	79.74	79.92	80.10	80.28	80.46	80.64	80.82
9.0	81.00	81.18	81.36	81.54	81.72	81.90	82.08	82.26	82.45	82.63
9.1	82.81	82.99	83.17	83.36	83.54	83.72	83.91	84.09	84.27	84.46
9.2	84.64	84.82	85.01	85.19	85.38	85.56	85.75	85.93	86.12	86.30
9.3	86.49	86.68	86.86	87.05	87.24	87.42	87.61	87.80	87.98	88.17
9.4	88.36	88.55	88.74	88.92	89.11	89.30	89.49	89.68	89.87	90.06
9.5	90.25	90.44	90.63	90.82	91.01	91.20	91.39	91.58	91.78	91.97
9.6	92.16	92.35	92.54	92.74	92.93	93.12	93.32	93.51	93.70	93.90
9.7	94.09	94.28	94.48	94.67	94.87	95.06	95.26	95.45	95.65	95.84
9.8	96.04	96.24	96.43	96.63	96.83	97.02	97.22	97.42	97.61	97.81
9.9	98.01	98.21	98.41	98.60	98.80	99.00	99.20	99.40	99.60	99.80
N	.00	.01	.02	.03	.04	.05	.06	.07	.08	.09

TABLE III

COMMON LOGARITHMS OF NUMBERS

This table gives the *mantissa* (with the decimal point omitted) of the common logarithm of numbers between 1 and 9.99. The mantissa of a number of four significant digits is found by linear interpolation. The *characteristic* is supplied by rule:

If a number is greater than 1, its characteristic is positive and is one less than the number of digits to the left of the decimal point.

If a number is between 0 and 1, its characteristic is negative and is numerically one greater than the number of zeros between the decimal point and first nonzero digit.

The above characteristic may be written as $k - 10$, where k is 9 minus the number of zeros between the decimal point and first nonzero digit.

If log N is given, these rules are reversed to locate the decimal point, after the sequence of digits is found from the mantissa by reverse reading of the table and linear interpolation.

APPENDIX

Table III

Common Logarithms of Numbers

N	0	1	2	3	4	5	6	7	8	9
0	...	0000	3010	4771	6021	6990	7782	8451	9031	9542
1	0000	0414	0792	1139	1461	1761	2041	2304	2553	2788
2	3010	3222	3424	3617	3802	3979	4150	4314	4472	4624
3	4771	4914	5051	5185	5315	5441	5563	5682	5798	5911
4	6021	6128	6232	6335	6435	6532	6628	6721	6812	6902
5	6990	7076	7160	7243	7324	7404	7482	7559	7634	7709
6	7782	7853	7924	7993	8062	8129	8195	8261	8325	8388
7	8451	8513	8573	8633	8692	8751	8808	8865	8921	8976
8	9031	9085	9138	9191	9243	9294	9345	9395	9445	9494
9	9542	9590	9638	9685	9731	9777	9823	9868	9912	9956
10	0000	0043	0086	0128	0170	0212	0253	0294	0334	0374
11	0414	0453	0492	0531	056ʋ	0607	0645	0682	0719	0755
12	0792	0828	0864	0899	0934	0969	1004	1038	1072	1106
13	1139	1173	1206	1239	1271	1303	1335	1367	1399	1430
14	1461	1492	1523	1553	1584	1614	1644	1673	1703	1732
15	1761	1790	1818	1847	1875	1903	1931	1959	1987	2014
16	2041	2068	2095	2122	2148	2175	2201	2227	2253	2279
17	2304	2330	2355	2380	2405	2430	2455	2480	2504	2529
18	2553	2577	2601	2625	2648	2672	2695	2718	2742	2765
19	2788	2810	2833	2856	2878	2900	2923	2945	2967	2989
20	3010	3032	3054	3075	3096	3118	3139	3160	3181	3201
21	3222	3243	3263	3284	3304	3324	3345	3365	3385	3404
22	3424	3444	3464	3483	3502	3522	3541	3560	3579	3598
23	3617	3636	3655	3674	3692	3711	3729	3747	3766	3784
24	3802	3820	3838	3856	3874	3892	3909	3927	3945	3962
25	3979	3997	4014	4031	4048	4065	4082	4099	4116	4133
26	4150	4166	4183	4200	4216	4232	4249	4265	4281	4298
27	4314	4330	4346	4362	4378	4393	4409	4425	4440	4456
28	4472	4487	4502	4518	4533	4548	4564	4579	4594	4609
29	4624	4639	4654	4669	4683	4698	4713	4728	4742	4757
30	4771	4786	4800	4814	4829	4843	4857	4871	4886	4900
31	4914	4928	4942	4955	4969	4983	4997	5011	5024	5038
32	5051	5065	5079	5092	5105	5119	5132	5145	5159	5172
33	5185	5198	5211	5224	5237	5250	5263	5276	5289	5302
34	5315	5328	5340	5353	5366	5378	5391	5403	5416	5428
35	5441	5453	5465	5478	5490	5502	5514	5527	5539	5551
36	5563	5575	5587	5599	5611	5623	5635	5647	5658	5670
37	5682	5694	5705	5717	5729	5740	5752	5763	5775	5786
38	5798	5809	5821	5832	5843	5855	5866	5877	5888	5899
39	5911	5922	5933	5944	5955	5966	5977	5988	5999	6010
40	6021	6031	6042	6053	6064	6075	6085	6096	6107	6117
41	6128	6138	6149	6160	6170	6180	6191	6201	6212	6222
42	6232	6243	6253	6263	6274	6284	6294	6304	6314	6325
43	6335	6345	6355	6365	6375	6385	6395	6405	6415	6425
44	6435	6444	6454	6464	6474	6484	6493	6503	6513	6522
45	6532	6542	6551	6561	6571	6580	6590	6599	6609	6618
46	6628	6637	6646	6656	6665	6675	6684	6693	6702	6712
47	6721	6730	6739	6749	6758	6767	6776	6785	6794	6803
48	6812	6821	6830	6839	6848	6857	6866	6875	6884	6893
49	6902	6911	6920	6928	6937	6946	6955	6964	6972	6981
50	6990	6998	7007	7016	7024	7033	7042	7050	7059	7067
N	0	1	2	3	4	5	6	7	8	9

TABLE III—COMMON LOGARITHMS OF NUMBERS (*continued*)

N	0	1	2	3	4	5	6	7	8	9
50	6990	6998	7007	7016	7024	7033	7042	7050	7059	7067
51	7076	7084	7093	7101	7110	7118	7126	7135	7143	7152
52	7160	7168	7177	7185	7193	7202	7210	7218	7226	7235
53	7243	7251	7259	7267	7275	7284	7292	7300	7308	7316
54	7324	7332	7340	7348	7356	7364	7372	7380	7388	7396
55	7404	7412	7419	7427	7435	7443	7451	7459	7466	7474
56	7482	7490	7497	7505	7513	7520	7528	7536	7543	7551
57	7559	7566	7574	7582	7589	7597	7604	7612	7619	7627
58	7634	7642	7649	7657	7664	7672	7679	7686	7694	7701
59	7709	7716	7723	7731	7738	7745	7752	7760	7767	7774
60	7782	7789	7796	7803	7810	7818	7825	7832	7839	7846
61	7853	7860	7868	7875	7882	7889	7896	7903	7910	7917
62	7924	7931	7938	7945	7952	7959	7966	7973	7980	7987
63	7993	8000	8007	8014	8021	8028	8035	8041	8048	8055
64	8062	8069	8075	8082	8089	8096	8102	8109	8116	8122
65	8129	8136	8142	8149	8156	8162	8169	8176	8182	8189
66	8195	8202	8209	8215	8222	8228	8235	8241	8248	8254
67	8261	8267	8274	8280	8287	8293	8299	8306	8312	8319
68	8325	8331	8338	8344	8351	8357	8363	8370	8376	8382
69	8388	8395	8401	8407	8414	8420	8426	8432	8439	8445
70	8451	8457	8463	8470	8476	8482	8488	8494	8500	8506
71	8513	8519	8525	8531	8537	8543	8549	8555	8561	8567
72	8573	8579	8585	8591	8597	8603	8609	8615	8621	8627
73	8633	8639	8645	8651	8657	8663	8669	8675	8681	8686
74	8692	8698	8704	8710	8716	8722	8727	8733	8739	8745
75	8751	8756	8762	8768	8774	8779	8785	8791	8797	8802
76	8808	8814	8820	8825	8831	8837	8842	8848	8854	8859
77	8865	8871	8876	8882	8887	8893	8899	8904	8910	8915
78	8921	8927	8932	8938	8943	8949	8954	8960	8965	8971
79	8976	8982	8987	8993	8998	9004	9009	9015	9020	9025
80	9031	9036	9042	9047	9053	9058	9063	9069	9074	9079
81	9085	9090	9096	9101	9106	9112	9117	9122	9128	9133
82	9138	9143	9149	9154	9159	9165	9170	9175	9180	9186
83	9191	9196	9201	9206	9212	9217	9222	9227	9232	9238
84	9243	9248	9253	9258	9263	9269	9274	9279	9284	9289
85	9294	9299	9304	9309	9315	9320	9325	9330	9335	9340
86	9345	9350	9355	9360	9365	9370	9375	9380	9385	9390
87	9395	9400	9405	9410	9415	9420	9425	9430	9435	9440
88	9445	9450	9455	9460	9465	9469	9474	9479	9484	9489
89	9494	9499	9504	9509	9513	9518	9523	9528	9533	9538
90	9542	9547	9552	9557	9562	9566	9571	9576	9581	9586
91	9590	9595	9600	9605	9609	9614	9619	9624	9628	9633
92	9638	9643	9647	9652	9657	9661	9666	9671	9675	9680
93	9685	9689	9694	9699	9703	9708	9713	9717	9722	9727
94	9731	9736	9741	9745	9750	9754	9759	9763	9768	9773
95	9777	9782	9786	9791	9795	9800	9805	9809	9814	9818
96	9823	9827	9832	9836	9841	9845	9850	9854	9859	9863
97	9868	9872	9877	9881	9886	9890	9894	9899	9903	9908
98	9912	9917	9921	9926	9930	9934	9939	9943	9948	9952
99	9956	9961	9965	9969	9974	9978	9983	9987	9991	9996
100	0000	0004	0009	0013	0017	0022	0026	0030	0035	0039
N	0	1	2	3	4	5	6	7	8	9

TABLE IV

NATURAL LOGARITHMS

This table gives the natural logarithms of numbers between 1 and 10. Any number M can be written in scientific notation as $M = N \times 10^k$, where $1 \leq N \leq 10$, and k is a positive or negative integer. Hence

$$\ln M = \ln N + k \ln 10 = \ln N + k(2.3026),$$

and $\ln M$ can be found.

$$\ln 2.43 = 0.8879 \qquad \text{(direct reading)},$$
$$\ln 24.3 = 0.8879 + 2.3026 = 3.1905,$$
$$\ln 0.243 = 0.8879 - 2.3026 = -1.4147 = 8.5853 - 10.$$

If $\ln M$ is given, and is not a decimal fraction between 0 and 2.3026, the operation above is reversed by adding or subtracting an appropriate multiple of 2.3026 until such a decimal fraction is obtained. For example:

If $\ln M = 0.9010$, then $M = 2.462$ (direct reading and interpolation).

If $\ln M = 3.9010$, then $\ln M/10 = 3.9010 - 2.3026 = 1.5984$,

$$M/10 = 4.945, \qquad \text{and } M = 49.45.$$

If $\ln M = -3.9010$, then $\ln 100M = -3.9010 + 2(2.3026)$
$$= 0.7042,$$
$$100M = 2.022, \qquad \text{and } M = 0.02022.$$

TABLE IV

NATURAL LOGARITHMS*

	.00	.01	.02	.03	.04	.05	.06	.07	.08	.09
1.0	0.0000	0.0100	0.0198	0.0296	0.0392	0.0488	0.0583	0.0677	0.0770	0.0862
1.1	.0953	.1044	.1133	.1222	.1310	.1398	.1484	.1570	.1655	.1740
1.2	.1823	.1906	.1989	.2070	.2151	.2231	.2311	.2390	.2469	.2546
1.3	.2624	.2700	.2776	.2852	.2927	.3001	.3075	.3148	.3221	.3293
1.4	.3365	.3436	.3507	.3577	.3646	.3716	.3784	.3853	.3920	.3988
1.5	.4055	.4121	.4187	.4253	.4318	.4383	.4447	.4511	.4574	.4637
1.6	.4700	.4762	.4824	.4886	.4947	.5008	.5068	.5128	.5188	.5247
1.7	.5306	.5365	.5423	.5481	.5539	.5596	.5653	.5710	.5766	.5822
1.8	.5878	.5933	.5988	.6043	.6098	.6152	.6206	.6259	.6313	.6366
1.9	.6419	.6471	.6523	.6575	.6627	.6678	.6729	.6780	.6831	.6881
2.0	.6931	.6981	.7031	.7080	.7129	.7178	.7227	.7275	.7324	.7372
2.1	.7419	.7467	.7514	.7561	.7608	.7655	.7701	.7747	.7793	.7839
2.2	.7885	.7930	.7975	.8020	.8065	.8109	.8154	.8198	.8242	.8286
2.3	.8329	.8372	.8416	.8459	.8502	.8544	.8587	.8629	.8671	.8713
2.4	.8755	.8796	.8838	.8879	.8920	.8961	.9002	.9042	.9083	.9123
2.5	.9163	.9203	.9243	.9282	.9322	.9361	.9400	.9439	.9478	.9517
2.6	.9555	.9594	0.9632	0.9670	0.9708	0.9746	0.9783	0.9821	0.9858	0.9895
2.7	0.9933	0.9969	1.0006	1.0043	1.0080	1.0116	1.0152	1.0188	1.0225	1.0260
2.8	1.0296	1.0332	.0367	.0403	.0438	.0473	.0508	.0543	.0578	.0613
2.9	.0647	.0682	.0716	.0750	.0784	.0818	.0852	1.0886	.0919	.0953
3.0	.0986	.1019	.1053	.1086	.1119	.1151	.1184	.1217	.1249	.1282
3.1	.1314	.1346	.1378	.1410	.1442	.1474	.1506	.1537	.1569	.1600
3.2	.1632	.1663	.1694	.1725	.1756	.1787	.1817	.1848	.1878	.1909
3.3	.1939	.1969	.2000	.2030	.2060	.2090	.2119	.2149	.2179	.2208
3.4	.2238	.2267	.2296	.2326	.2355	.2384	.2413	.2442	.2470	.2499
3.5	.2528	.2556	.2585	.2613	.2641	.2669	.2698	.2726	.2754	.2782
3.6	.2809	.2837	.2865	.2892	.2920	.2947	.2975	.3002	.3029	.3056
3.7	.3083	3110	.3137	.3164	.3191	.3218	.3244	.3271	.3297	.3324
3.8	.3350	.3376	.3403	.3429	.3455	.3481	.3507	.3533	.3558	.3584
3.9	.3610	.3635	.3661	.3686	.3712	.3737	.3762	.3788	.3813	.3838
4.0	.3863	.3888	.3913	.3938	.3962	.3987	.4012	.4036	.4061	.4085
4.1	.4110	.4134	.4159	.4183	.4207	.4231	.4255	.4279	.4303	.4327
4.2	.4351	.4375	.4398	.4422	.4446	.4469	.4493	.4516	.4540	.4563
4.3	.4586	.4609	.4633	.4656	.4679	.4702	.4725	.4748	.4770	.4793
4.4	.4816	.4839	.4861	.4884	.4907	.4929	.4951	.4974	.4996	.5019
4.5	.5041	.5063	.5085	.5107	.5129	.5151	.5173	.5195	.5217	.5239
4.6	.5261	.5282	.5304	.5326	.5347	.5369	.5390	.5412	.5433	.5454
4.7	.5476	.5497	.5518	.5539	.5560	.5581	.5602	.5623	.5644	.5665
4.8	.5686	.5707	.5728	.5748	.5769	.5790	.5810	.5831	.5851	.5872
4.9	.5892	.5913	.5933	.5953	.5974	.5994	.6014	.6034	.6054	.6074
5.0	.6094	.6114	.6134	.6154	.6174	.6194	.6214	.6233	.6253	.6273
5.1	.6292	.6312	.6332	.6351	.6371	.6390	.6409	.6429	.6448	.6467
5.2	.6487	.6506	.6525	.6544	.6563	.6582	.6601	.6620	.6639	.6658
5.3	.6677	.6696	.6715	.6734	.6752	.6771	.6790	.6808	.6827	.6845
5.4	1.6864	1.6882	1.6901	1.6919	1.6938	1.6956	1.6974	1.6993	1.7011	1.7029

* Reprinted by permission from *Calculus*, 3rd. Ed., by G. E. F. Sherwood and A. E. Taylor, pp. 564–565. Copyright 1953 by Prentice-Hall, Inc., Englewood Cliffs, N. J.

Table IV—Natural Logarithms (*continued*)

	.00	.01	.02	.03	.04	.05	.06	.07	.08	.09
5.5	1.7047	1.7066	1.7084	1.7102	1.7120	1.7138	1.7156	1.7174	1.7192	1.7210
5.6	.7228	.7246	.7263	.7281	.7299	.7317	.7334	.7352	.7370	.7387
5.7	.7405	.7422	.7440	.7457	.7475	.7492	.7509	.7527	.7544	.7561
5.8	.7579	.7596	.7613	.7630	.7647	.7664	.7681	.7699	.7716	.7733
5.9	.7750	.7766	.7783	.7800	.7817	.7843	.7851	.7867	.7884	.7901
6.0	.7918	.7934	.7951	.7967	.7984	.8001	.8017	.8034	.8050	.8066
6.1	.8083	.8099	.8116	.8132	.8148	.8165	.8181	.8197	.8213	.8229
6.2	.8245	.8262	.8278	.8294	.8310	.8326	.8342	.8358	.8374	.8390
6.3	.8405	.8421	.8437	.8453	.8469	8485	.8500	.8516	.8532	.8547
6.4	.8563	.8579	.8594	.8610	.8625	.8641	.8656	.8672	.8687	.8703
6.5	.8718	.8733	.8749	.8764	.8779	.8795	.8810	.8825	.8840	.8856
6.6	.8871	.8886	.8901	.8916	.8931	.8946	.8961	.8976	.8991	.9006
6.7	.9021	.9036	.9051	.9066	.9081	.9095	.9110	.9125	.9140	.9155
6.8	.9169	.9184	.9199	.9213	.9228	.9242	.9257	.9272	.9286	.9301
6.9	.9315	.9330	.9344	.9359	.9373	.9387	.9402	.9416	.9430	.9445
7.0	.9459	.9473	.9488	.9502	.9516	.9530	.9544	.9559	.9573	.9587
7.1	.9601	.9615	.9629	.9643	.9657	.9671	.9685	.9699	.9713	.9727
7.2	.9741	.9755	.9769	.9782	.9796	.9810	.9824	.9838	.9851	1.9865
7.3	1.9879	1.9892	1.9906	1.9920	1.9933	1.9947	1.9961	1.9974	1.9988	2.0001
7.4	2.0015	2.0028	2.0042	2.0055	2.0069	2.0082	2.0096	2.0109	2.0122	.0136
7.5	.0149	.0162	.0176	.0189	.0202	.0215	.0229	.0242	.0255	.0268
7.6	.0281	.0295	.0308	.0321	.0334	.0347	.0360	.0373	.0386	.0399
7.7	.0412	.0425	.0438	.0451	.0464	.0477	.0490	.0503	.0516	.0528
7.8	.0541	.0554	.0567	.0580	.0592	.0605	.0618	.0631	.0643	.0656
7.9	.0669	.0681	.0694	.0707	.0719	.0732	.0744	.0757	.0769	.0782
8.0	.0794	.0807	.0819	.0832	.0844	.0857	.0869	.0882	.0894	.0906
8.1	.0919	.0931	.0943	.0956	.0968	.0980	.0992	.1005	.1017	.1029
8.2	.1041	.1054	.1066	.1078	.1090	.1102	.1114	.1126	.1138	.1150
8.3	.1163	.1175	.1187	.1199	.1211	.1223	.1235	.1247	.1258	.1270
8.4	.1282	.1294	.1306	.1318	.1330	.1342	.1353	.1365	.1377	.1389
8.5	.1401	.1412	.1424	.1436	.1448	.1459	.1471	.1483	.1494	.1506
8.6	.1518	.1529	.1541	.1552	.1564	.1576	.1587	.1599	.1610	.1622
8.7	.1633	.1645	.1656	.1668	.1679	.1691	.1702	.1713	.1725	.1736
8.8	.1748	.1759	.1770	.1782	.1793	.1804	.1815	.1827	.1838	.1849
8.9	.1861	.1872	.1883	.1894	.1905	.1917	.1928	.1939	.1950	.1961
9.0	.1972	.1983	.1994	.2006	.2017	.2028	.2039	.2050	.2061	.2072
9.1	.2083	.2094	.2105	.2116	.2127	.2138	.2148	.2159	.2170	.2181
9.2	.2192	.2203	.2214	.2225	.2235	.2246	.2257	.2268	.2279	.2289
9.3	.2300	.2311	.2322	.2332	.2343	.2354	.2364	.2375	.2386	.2396
9.4	.2407	.2418	.2428	.2439	.2450	.2460	.2471	.2481	.2492	.2502
9.5	.2513	.2523	.2534	.2544	.2555	.2565	.2576	.2586	.2597	.2607
9.6	.2618	.2628	.2638	.2649	.2659	.2670	.2680	.2690	.2701	.2711
9.7	.2721	.2732	.2742	.2752	.2762	.2773	.2783	.2793	.2803	.2814
9.8	.2824	.2834	.2844	.2854	.2865	.2875	.2885	.2895	.2905	.2915
9.9	2.2925	2.2935	2.2946	2.2956	2.2966	2.2976	2.2986	2.2996	2.3006	2.3016
10.0	2.3026									

Table V

Exponential Functions

This table gives a brief tabulation of positive and negative powers of e, useful for curve plotting after the result is rounded off. Because of the brevity of the table, interpolation is not too reliable.

TABLE V

EXPONENTIAL FUNCTIONS

x	e^x	e^{-x}	x	e^x	e^{-x}
.00	1.0000	1.0000	2.5	12.182	.0821
.05	1.0513	.9512	2.6	13.464	.0743
.10	1.1052	.9048	2.7	14.880	.0672
.15	1.1618	.8607	2.8	16.445	.0608
.20	1.2214	.8187	2.9	18.174	.0550
.25	1.2840	.7788	3.0	20.086	.0498
.30	1.3499	.7408	3.1	22.198	.0450
.35	1.4191	.7047	3.2	24.533	.0408
.40	1.4918	.6703	3.3	27.113	.0369
.45	1.5683	.6376	3.4	29.964	.0334
.50	1.6487	.6065	3.5	33.115	.0302
.55	1.7333	.5769	3.6	36.598	.0273
.60	1.8221	.5488	3.7	40.447	.0247
.65	1.9155	.5220	3.8	44.701	.0224
.70	2.0138	.4966	3.9	49.402	.0202
.75	2.1170	.4724	4.0	54.598	.0183
.80	2.2255	.4493	4.1	60.340	.0166
.85	2.3396	.4274	4.2	66.686	.0150
.90	2.4596	.4066	4.3	73.700	.0136
.95	2.5857	.3867	4.4	81.451	.0123
1.0	2.7183	.3679	4.5	90.017	.0111
1.1	3.0042	.3329	4.6	99.484	.0101
1.2	3.3201	.3012	4.7	109.95	.0091
1.3	3.6693	.2725	4.8	121.51	.0082
1.4	4.0552	.2466	4.9	134.29	.0074
1.5	4.4817	.2231	5	148.41	.0067
1.6	4.9530	.2019	6	403.43	.0025
1.7	5.4739	.1827	7	1096.6	.0009
1.8	6.0496	.1653	8	2981.0	.0003
1.9	6.6859	.1496	9	8103.1	.0001
2.0	7.3891	.1353	10	22026.	.0000
2.1	8.1662	.1225			
2.2	9.0250	.1108			
2.3	9.9742	.1003			
2.4	11.023	.0907			

INDEX

INDEX

Area, by approximation, 116
  as consumers' and producers' surplus, 118
  as a definite integral, 114
Arithmetic average, 179, 183, 191
Asymptote, horizontal, 19 ff., 81, 128, 135
  oblique, 136, 173
  vertical, 19 ff., 81, 128, 135
Average, arithmetic, 179, 183, 191
  cost, 83–86
  geometric, 183, 191
  point, 179, 185, 195
Axioms, of addition, 35, 36
  of continuity, 36
  least upper bound, 36
  of linear measure, 35
  of multiplication, 35, 36
  of order, 1, 35, 36

Base, 67, 68, 71
  change of, 71
Binomial theorem, 47
Bi-unique, 3
Bound, greatest lower, 36
  least upper, 36
  upper, 36
Bounded set, 36
Budget equation, 170 ff.

Chain rule of differentiation, 50, 74
Change of base, 71
Characteristic, 229
Common logarithms, 71, 229
Competition, 2, 4, 7, 159
Competitive goods, 130–132, 139, 140
Complementary goods, 130–132, 139
Completing the square, 12, 148
Composite function, differentiation of, 53
Concavity, 24, 61

Constant elasticity of demand, 82
Constant of integration, 107
Constant product curves, 134
Constraint, maximum and minimum under, 164
Consumers' surplus, 118
Continuity, 1, 36 ff., 84
Continuous at a point, 38
Continuous functions, 40, 42 ff.
Continuous in an interval, 38
Continuous variable, 36
Contour map, 127
Correlation coefficient, 196
Cost, average, 83–86
  marginal, 84
  total, 83
Cost functions, cubic, 86
  exponential, 86
  linear, 84
  logarithmic, 86
  normal, 84
  quadratic, 85
Critical points, 64, 149
Cubic cost function, 86
Curve fitting, 178 ff.
Curve tracing, 59 ff.
Curvilinear sections of surface, 155

Definite integral, 113, 114
Delta process, 43, 44, 138
Delta x, 40
Demand, elasticity of, 79, 140
Demand and supply, for several variables, 8
Demand curves, 2, 118
  exponential, 75
  generalized hyperbola, 69
Demand functions, 2, 154
Demand laws, hyperbolic, 21, 178
  linear, 5
  parabolic, 12

241

Demand surfaces, 130
  linear, 131
Demand and supply curves, 2, 3
Derivative, 41
Derivative of, a composite function, 53
  a constant, 47
  a constant times a function, 48
  a difference, 45
  a function of a function, 53
  a product, 45
  a quotient, 46
  a sum, 44
  exponential function, 73, 74
  higher order, 57, 142
  logarithmic function, 73, 74
  x^n, 47, 48, 51, 52
Determinant, 150
Deviation from the average, 183
Difference quotient, 40, 143
Differential of x and of y, 106
Differentiation (*see also* Derivative)
  chain rule of, 50 ff., 74
  implicit, 56, 143
  partial, 124
Divisibility, ultimate, 1

Economic stability, 155
Edgeworth's paradox, 33
Effect of taxation on monopoly, 101
Elasticity of demand, 79, 82
  partial, 140
Ellipse, 128, 129
Equilateral hyperbola, 19 ff., 128, 133,
  135, 178
Equilevel curve, 127
Equilibrium, 7 ff., 120, 121
  after taxation, 92, 101
Explicit method for extrema, three
    variables, 164
  two variables, 164
  under constraint, 172
  utility index, 173
Exponential cost function, 86
Exponential curve, 68, 178
Exponential functions, 67
  derivative of, 73
Exponential table, 237

Exponents, 67
Extrema (*see* Maximum and
  Minimum)

Factors of production, 134, 159
Fitting, an exponential curve, 191
  a line, 184
  a parabola, 189, 190
  a power curve, 191
Free commodity, 3, 5
Function of a function, differentiation
  of, 53
Functions, of one variable, 2 ff., 40 ff.
  of two variables, 124 ff.

Gaps, 35, 36
Generalized hyperbola, 82, 134
Geometric mean, 183, 191
Government tax revenue, 27
Graphical analysis, 1 ff.

Hotelling's example, 33
Hyperbola, equilateral, 19 ff., 128, 133,
  135, 178
  generalized, 82, 134
Hyperbolic laws, 19–25

Implicit differentiation, 56, 58, 143–
  145, 164
Implicit method for extrema, three
    variables, 168
  two variables, 164
  utility index, 173
Increment of y, 40 ff., 106
Indefinite integral, 107
Indifference curve, 127
Indifference map, 127
Infinite decimals, 36
Infinite divisibility for cost function,
  84
Infinity, 39
Inflection, point of, 61, 65
Input, 134, 159
Integral, definite, 113
  indefinite, 107, 114
Integration, 106–123
  formulas of, 107

as inverse of differentiation, 107
  by substitution, 108
Intercept form of a line, 5
Intercepts, 6, 12 ff.
Inverse, of differentiation, 107
  functions, 2, 4, 68
    derivative of, 52
  proportion, 19

Joint cost, 139, 154

Lagrange multiplier method, 166, 168,
      173
Laws of, differentiation, 44
  demand and supply, 5
  economics, 1
  exponents, 67
  limits, 39
  logarithms, 68
    change of base of, 71
Least squares, 182 ff.
Least upper bound, 36, 38
Limit, 35, 37
  and axiom of continuity, 38
Limit of, dependent variable, 38
  independent variable, 38
  product, 39
  quotient, 39
  sequence, 38
  sum, 39
Line, 5 ff.
Line of regression, of x on y, 195
  of y on x, 186, 194
Linear cost function, 84
Linear demand function, 7, 131, 139
Linear equations, 5
  in several variables, 8–11
Linear laws of demand and supply,
      5, 6
Linear measure, 3, 5
Logarithmic cost function, 86
Logarithmic differentiation, 76
Logarithmic function, derivative of,
      73
Logarithms, 68
  common, 71, 229
  natural, 71, 233

Mantissa, 229
Marginal cost, 83, 112, 139, 166
Marginal cost and supply function,
      122
Marginal demand, 84
  partial, 138
Marginal productivity, 139
Marginal revenue, 89, 90, 93, 110
Marginal utility of money, 166
Market equilibrium, 7 ff., 120
  effect of taxation on, 26–29, 92, 101
  hyperbolic laws, 21–23
  linear laws, 7, 8
    several variables, 9
  quadratic laws, 16
  two commodities, 31
Maximum and minimum, absolute, 63,
      148
  explicit method, 164
  functions of two variables, 148, 149
  geometric interpretation, 166
  implicit method, 164, 168
  Lagrange method, 166
  necessary conditions, 63, 149
  relative, 63, 148
  sufficient conditions, 63, 150
  under constraint, 164
Maximum profit, 95
  geometric interpretation of, 96
  stable and unstable, 159
  under monopoly, 95, 96, 122, 154
Maximum revenue, 90
  from taxation, 92
Maximum utility index subject to
      budget equation, 172
Measurable, 1, 35, 170
Method of least squares, 184
Minimum (see Maximum)
  average cost, 87
Moment equations, 185, 190, 195
Monopolist, 95
Monopoly, effect of taxation on, 101
  and the production of two commodi-
      ties, 154
  profit under, 95
Monotonically decreasing, 3, 41
Monotonically increasing, 4

Natural logarithm, 71, 233
Neighborhood, 38
Normal cost function, 84
Normal demand laws, 2, 9, 33
Normal production curve, 24
Normal supply laws, 4, 9, 33
Number e, 73

Ordered magnitudes, 170
Output, 134, 159
Overhead, 84, 85

Parabola, 12, 178, 180
Parabolic laws, 12–15
Pareto's law, 69, 192
Partial derivatives, 137
  of second and higher order, 142
Partial differentiation, 124
Partial elasticity of demand, 140
Partial marginal demand, 138
Points of inflection, 61, 65
Power curve, 178
Powers and roots, 221
Preference, 170
Price, highest, 3, 5, 13
Probability curve, 76
Probability integral, 116
Producers' surplus, 119
Production curve, 24
Production functions, 134
Production with two inputs, 159
Profit under monopoly, 95
Pure competition, 2, 4, 7, 159

Quadratic cost functions, 85
Quadratic demand functions, 13,
  16
Quadratic supply functions, 14, 16

Rate of change, of slope, 61
  of y, 59
Real number system, 35
Rectangular coordinates, 124
Revenue, 77, 89–92, 154

curve, 77
from taxation, 27

Saddle point, 150
Sales tax, 101
Scientific notation, 233
Secant, slope of, 41, 106
Second derivative, 57, 142
Sequence, 37
Significant, 9, 33
Slope, 5, 138
  of curve, 41
  increasing or decreasing, 61
  of line, 5
  positive or negative, 59
  of secant, 41, 106
  of tangent, 41, 106
Squares, 224
Square root, 224
Subsidy, 27, 101
Supply curve, 1–9, 26, 119
  as a line, 5
  as a parabola, 14, 15
Supply function, 3
  logarithmic, 75
Supply law, 1–9
  linear, 5
  normal, 4
Surface, 154
  section of, 155

Tangent, slope of, 41, 106
Tax, additive, 26, 92
  sales, 29
Taxation, total revenue from, 101
  for two commodities, 31
Translation of axes, 19, 186

Utility, 170
  index, 170–172

x-deviation, 195

y-deviation, 184, 187, 189, 191